THE POLITICAL ECONOMY OF POSTWAR
RECONSTRUCTION

The Political Economy of Postwar Reconstruction

PETER BURNHAM
Lecturer in Sociology
University of Warwick

St. Martin's Press   New York

First published in the United States of America in 1989

Printed in Hong Kong

ISBN 0–312–03075–4

Library of Congress Cataloging-in-Publication Data
Burnham, Peter, 1959–
    The political economy of postwar reconstruction/Peter Burnham.
        p.   cm.
    Bibliography: p.
    Includes index.
    ISBN 0–312–03075–4: $40.00 (est.)
    1. Great Britain—Economic policy—1945– 2. Reconstruction (1939–1951)—
Great Britain. 3. Economic assistance, American—Great Britain. 4. United
States—Foreign economic relations—Great Britain. 5. Great Britain—Foreign
economic relations—United States.   I. Title.
HC256.5.B87   1990
338.941—dc19
                                                                88–36595
                                                                    CIP

Contents

Preface   vii

List of Abbreviations   xiv

**1 The International State System and Theories of
Postwar Reconstruction**   1

    I   Introduction   1

    II   Hegemony and the international state system   2

    III Hegemony and British postwar reconstruction   5

    IV An alternative view of postwar reconstruction   8

2 Towards the Washington Negotiations   14

    I   The economic basis of Britain's request for aid   16

    II   The political rationale for Anglo-American
collaboration   29

3 The Washington Loan Agreement   43

    I   The negotiation of the loan   43

    II   Assessing the Agreement   48

    III Neo-bilateralism and the loan   54

4 The Marshall Offensive   71

    I   The 1947 Crisis   73

    II   American and British attitudes to Marshall   80

    III The Administrative Apparatus   87

    IV Assessing the impact of the Marshall Plan   96

5 The Revision in State Strategy   116

    I   A new Sterling crisis   117

    II   Devaluation and multilateralism   122

    III A revision in state strategy   135

6 The Impact of Rearmament   150

    I   Expanded British accumulation and American
        policy   152

    II   Economic growth and rearmament   161

7 Conclusion   177

    I   State, Capital and the 'General Interest'   180

    II   Inter-imperialist rivalry and global circuits of
        accumulation   183

Appendix: The Changing Structure of Monetary Account
               Areas in 1947   189

Notes   191

Bibliography   211

Index   225

Preface

At every action, no matter by whom performed, make it a practice to ask yourself, 'What is the object in doing this?' But begin with yourself; put this question to yourself first of all.

Marcus Aurelius, *Meditations*[1]

The relevance of a book on postwar reconstruction to contemporary politics is not immediately apparent. However the crisis which social democratic forms of political organisation now face have their roots in the political compromise of the postwar era. The present study is an analysis of the political and economic determinants of international capital reconstruction specifically focused on Anglo-American struggles over the direction of British economic policy. The objective therefore is not to provide a self-contained analysis of Britain under Attlee.[2] However the conclusions of the study are relevant to current political debate. Consider for instance Tony Benn's views of the postwar administrations. Benn suggests that 'if a Labour government was elected that did just what the 1945 government did, it would be so revolutionary that it would take your breath away'.[3] One of the main conclusions of this study is that socialists in Britain must reassess the Attlee years by balancing the governments' achievements in social policy with a realistic appraisal of Attlee's objective to refashion British imperialism and restore international capitalist relations. It is simply untrue to suggest that postwar Labour Britain was 'blown off its socialist course' or 'forced to capitulate' on economic policy because of American pressure. The following account stresses Britain's active and successful resistance to such pressure and the unquestioned acceptance in Labour's Cabinet of the necessity to restore international capitalist viability to the British economy.

The study also throws light on one of the most fundamental and important questions in serious political discourse – how far can the capitalist state reform the economy? It will be suggested that the role of the capitalist state is essentially negative, removing barriers to accumulation. These obstacles to capital accumulation do not, however, directly confront the state but appear as fiscal, financial and monetary crises. If the state is to overcome these barriers it must develop a strategy that will enable capital to expand successfully accumulation without replacing the rule of the market. The primary

vii

barrier to the state developing a successful accumulation strategy in 1945 lay not in the resistance of the working class or even in the limited availability of labour power, but turned more specifically on reconstructing international trade and payments networks to progressively expand the extent of the market without draining sterling reserves. The persistently unsatisfactory nature of the trade-off between Labourist public expenditure increases and balance of payments crises will continue to plague social democratic governments who remain ultimately committed to maintaining the rule of the market.

POLITICAL ECONOMY AND THE 'STATE'

The conceptual framework which informs this study is guided by the principle that the compartmentalisation of social science into distinct academic disciplines is a major barrier to understanding. An approach based on Marx's critique of classical political economy requires a study of how politics influences the economy and vice versa whilst recognising that historically the separation of the polity and the economy is specifically bound-up with the rise of capitalism as a distinct set of social relations. On the most basic level Marxian political economy undercuts the dominant view that economics, politics, sociology and history have distinct subject boundaries by recognising that economic laws are not natural but socially determined.[4] It is, for instance, only by restricting economics to a study of individual rational choice – abstracting, therefore, from its social and historical foundations and context – that a space is created for an equally alienated and fragmented analysis of individual social action which may then be called sociology. A brief review of the central characteristics of the Weberian and Marxian approaches to the state will elucidate these remarks.

Methodologically Weber's political sociology reflects his general concern to establish sociology as a science concerned with the interpretative understanding of social action linked to a causal explanation of its course and consequences.[5] Without attempting in this space a comprehensive review of this methodology, it can be pointed out that Weber's concern with social action leads into a study of understanding individual meanings and motives, and the development of a typology of motivational characteristics. The

Weberian approach is thus committed to accepting both the structural
variability and the historical specificity of data. An approach centred
on disclosing the meanings and intentions held by isolated individuals
gives a somewhat fragmentary appearance to Weber's writings – an
appearance it has been suggested[6] that belies the unity in Weber's
corpus – which rests upon the overall theme of the importance of the
'inner logic' of ideas as world views that guide the flow of interests.
This overall methodological stance has an important consequence for
Weber's understanding of the notions of class and the state.

Weber's schema classifies actions not only with regard to their
typical value orientations but also according to the types of means
and ends to which they are directed. Variables which therefore
comprise a social order, such as the economy, the polity and 'civil
society', are given no overall structure in Weber's assessment,
but rather each has a 'real autonomy' which precludes any over-
determining element. Political actions, therefore, although they may
have economic implications, are deemed as not directly oriented to
economic gain and as such must be analysed independently of
economic factors since their orientation is to a distinctive form of
action. This position is often championed by neo-Weberians as
offering a methodology which has no preconceived image of society
or its patternings and thus replaces theoreticism within sociology by
pure empirical assessment. However the true consequence of Weber's
position is that an analysis concerned simply with the construction of
a typology of motivation characteristics is only able to study the *given*
institutions and organisations of society resting on the abstraction of
the social individual from within the historical social relations within
which he/she is constituted. Such a move severely restricts sociology
to a pluralist empiricism lacking in explanatory power since the mere
elaboration of a typology of hypothetical social action can explain
neither the systematic connections between values, social relations
and institutions nor ironically provide an adequate interpretation of
the historical specificity of the capitalist process of production and
its consequences.[7] The validity of this criticism is aptly illustrated by
a brief look at Weber's notions of class and state as they developed
from his methodological framework.

Weber's preoccupation with the autonomy of the economy from
the polity, and the latter from 'civil society', finds expression in his
statement that political action is directed to the achievement of
political power for its own sake. Types of action and corresponding
organisations must be analysed independently of one another. Thus

'one can define the modern state sociologically only in terms of the specific means peculiar to it, as to every political association, namely the use of physical force'.[8] Emphasising three aspects of the modern state – its territoriality, its monopoly of the means of physical violence and its legitimacy – Weber offers an account of the relations between accumulation and the state in purely political terms.

At one remove, his analysis of class mimics that of the state inasmuch as classes for Weber consist of individuals pursuing a common economic interest and they constitute in themselves only one limited aspect of the distribution and struggle for power, with 'status groups' and political parties at least as significant.[9] The notion of class is thus linked to the concept of 'class situation' which 'is ultimately market situation'.[10] Since class derives from a common economic situation it can be classified either with regard to the differentiation of property holdings (property class) or to non-property resources such as occupational skill (acquisition or commercial class). Social class is thus constructed to comprise a number of groupings whose class situation is similar and within which individual and generational mobility is easy. This finally reveals an overall classification into working class, petit bourgeoisie, propertyless intelligentsia and specialists, and classes based on property or educational resources. The class structure is thus composed of a plurality of social groups which are based on 'readily possible and typically observable' characteristics.

In the same way as the state is seen as autonomous and characterised by empirical factors (territorially based legitimate use of force), class is a notion only appropriate to empirically observable economic ends and takes as its starting point the relations of distribution as determined by an uncritically examined notion of the market. The creation of 'the market' as a historically determined institution resting upon prior relations of production is overlooked in the Weberian assessment.

It is clear that Weber's pluralist conception of society provides the basis for much state theorising. Not only Mann but many 'post-Marxist'[11] accounts put forward a conception of state and class which is essentially Weberian but claims to offer some combination of notions deriving both from Weber and Marx. However the Weberian and Marxian positions are incompatible.

Methodologically Marx rejects a starting point based on the abstract individual: 'my standpoint from which the development of the economic formation of society is viewed . . . can less than any other make the individual responsible for relations whose creature he remains . . . however much he may subjectively raise himself above them'.[12] Individuals are dealt with only as personifications of economic categories, of particular class relations and interests, and as Marx noted in relation to the critics of Ricardo: 'what other people reproach him [Ricardo] for i.e., that he is unconcerned with "human beings" and concentrates exclusively on the development of the productive forces when considering capitalist production, is precisely his significant contribution'.[13]

This approach does not introduce a positive anti-humanism as some critics suggest.[14] Rather, it is adopted because it corresponds to the alienated character of capitalist social relations (including that of the capitalist state) in which social relations between people take the form of relations between things. The social form of the capitalist relations of production invalidates an approach which simply begins from the individual. To assume that social relations between individuals are expressed as a goal which appears to exist for its own sake, is to neglect the underlying processes which gave rise to those relations.[15]

Marx's use-value/exchange-value distinction (and its corresponding concrete/abstract labour distinction) makes it clear that the relations of production are not simply relations concerning the purchase and sale of labour power on which you could construct classes in a Weberian fashion, but are the relations constituted by the valorisation process, that is, relations of a total process of social reproduction governed by the law of value. The extraction of surplus value, and the class relations on which this is premissed, have a foundation in production, and classes, therefore, are not simply aggregates of individuals determined in the Weberian sense by relations of exchange. Since the valorisation of capital appears as the starting and the finishing point, as the motive and purpose of production – 'capital's historic mission and justification'[16] – it is in the development of the contradiction between value and use-value that the relations of distribution, circulation and consumption are subsumed under the relations of production. These latter relations are therefore not distinct from society but rather 'the relations of production in their totality constitute what are called the social relations, society, and specifically, a society at a definite stage of historical development'.[17]

In marked contrast to the Weberian pluralist assessment, which takes certain variables as given and studies each in an independent fashion (the independence of class and state for instance), Marx approaches the social formation as an interacting set of processes historically specified and inserted in such a way that all relations are subsumed under the capital relation as the basis of the valorisation process. The notion of class is therefore analytically prior to the distribution process, forming the basis of the production process on which accumulation is constituted, whilst the apparent separation of the state from the economy cannot be taken at face value but is rather seen as a form taken by the relations of production – a form in which the state is actually directly incorporated into capitalist reproduction. The Marxian position on class and the state is aptly summarised in *Capital*, volume 3, with the assessment:

> the specific economic form in which unpaid surplus labour is pumped out of the direct producers determines the relationship of rulers and ruled, as it grows directly out of production itself and in turn reacts upon it as a determinant. But on it is based the entire formation of the economic community growing out of the productive relations themselves, and therewith its specific political form likewise. It is always the direct relationship of the owners of the conditions of production to the direct producers . . . which holds the innermost secret, the hidden foundation of the entire social structure . . . and hence the specific form of the state in each case.[18]

Marx theorised the development of the liberal form of the state in terms of the contradiction of interests between particular capitals and capital-in-general. The relentless nature of capitalist accumulation implies that unless the authority of the market is imposed on particular capitals, they will seek to overcome the barrier of the market by suppressing competition, and ultimately by the use of force. For Marx, out of this very contradiction between the interest of the individual and that of the community, the latter takes an independent form as the state, divorced from the real interests of individual and community. 'Just because individuals seek *only* their particular interest, which for them does not coincide with their communal interest . . . the latter will be imposed on them as an interest "alien" to them, and "independent" of them, as in its turn a particular, peculiar, "general" interest'.[19] The state therefore embodies the power of capital-in-general (against the power of the working class and the direct demands of particular capitals), whilst the abstract nature of state power enables the state to represent itself both ideologically and politically as the embodiment of the general interest.

Marxian political economy illustrated here through a review of Marx's understanding of class and the state (as a totality in which class forms the basis of surplus value extraction and thus of accumulation, and in which the state as a form of the social relations of production acts to regulate the latter primarily in terms of law, property and money) is an alternative framework to the dominant Weberian approach which is built upon maintaining boundaries between disciplines defined in terms of typologies of action.

Finally, by way of introduction, I should point out that the term 'state' is used throughout this book not only to refer to the policy-making executive of elected government (the Cabinet) but also to encompass the work of permanent institutions in the Civil Service (the Treasury, the Foreign Office). As I shall later make clear, the primary task of British postwar economic policy was to restructure the international payments system in order to sustain trade under conditions of world production and trade imbalance. The complex nature of this restructuring meant that economic policy was left largely in the hands of civil servants and 'expert' advisers. A focus on the state, therefore, rather than simply the government is justified since economic policy was the prerogative of state officials (particularly in the Treasury), and politicians played a subordinate role in deciding the fundamental strategies open to Britain in this period.

This study is a modified version of my PhD thesis submitted to the Department of Sociology in the University of Warwick in May 1987. I wish to thank Tony Elger and Andrew Gamble for comments on the earlier thesis. My greatest debt, however, is to Simon Clarke whose sharp observations improved the text and are a constant source of encouragement.

List of Abbreviations

BIS   Bank for International Settlements
CAB   Cabinet Papers
CBI   Confederation of British Industry
CEEC Committee for European Economic Co-operation
CFEP Commission on Foreign Economic Policy
ECA   Economic Co-operation Administration
EPU   European Payments Union
ERP   European Recovery Programme
FBI   Federation of British Industry
FO   Foreign Office
FRUS Foreign Relations of the United States
GDP   Gross Domestic Product
GNP   Gross National Product
HC   House of Commons
IDC   Imperial Defence College
IMF   International Monetary Fund
MFN   Most Favoured Nation clause
MRC   Modern Records Centre
NSC   National Security Council
OECD Organisation for Economic Co-operation and Development
OEEC Organisation for European Economic Co-operation
PRO   Public Records Office
T   Treasury Papers

1 The International State System and Theories of Postwar Reconstruction

I INTRODUCTION

> The market therefore must be continually extended, so that its relationships and the conditions governing them assume ever more the form of a natural law independent of the producers and become ever more uncontrollable
>
> (Marx, 1894)[1]

The development of the capitalist mode of production is synonymous with the development of international trade and the creation of a world market. The constant expansion of this market is a prerequisite for maintaining high profit levels and ultimately for the maintenance of the capitalist order itself. A world economy driven by the creed 'Accumulate, accumulate! This is Moses and the prophets'[2] implies a logic of ceaseless production for production's sake. Nevertheless, increases in both the production and the realisation of profit continue to depend on removing arbitrary geographical barriers to the expansion of capital.

Increased international mobility of capital has not led to the transcendence of the nation-state system. Whilst exploitation conditions are standardised nationally, sovereign states, via the exchange rate mechanism, are interlocked internationally into a hierarchy of price systems.[3] The complex set of relations which constitute the present international state system have developed, if in a somewhat uneven fashion, alongside the growing process of the internationalisation of capital. But the state system is still primarily one of politically constructed nation-states which provide both the domestic political underpinning for the mobility of capital and offer rudimentary institutional schemes aimed at securing international property rights as a basis for the continued expansion of capital.[4]

The central theme of this book is that whilst the majority of neo-Marxist writers have neglected to focus attention on this contradiction

1

between national state sovereignty and the global process of the socialisation of the productive forces, international relations theorists, with their overwhelmingly realist emphasis on institutions, formal diplomacy and zero-sum power games, have failed adequately to examine the nature of the international state system.

As a positive contribution to developing work in this area this study concentrates on understanding relations between nation-states in the international order via a close historical analysis of the international pressures brought to bear on the British state's strategy for postwar economic reconstruction. It will be argued that the restoration of the postwar capitalist order took place in a context of inter-imperialist rivalry where competing nation-states vied for the most advantageous position in the global system of production and exchange.

However, restoring the international circuits of capital did not act against the nation-state. A changing global context of accumulation strategies need not imply a narrowing down of opportunities for the nation-state. On the contrary, postwar reconstruction furthered the extension of statehood and consolidated national state power as competing states restored domestic profitability through a process of collaboration and conflict within the international system.[5] This interpretation cuts across the neo-realist view of international state relations and in particular exposes the weakness of seeing the postwar order in terms of a theory of hegemonic stability.

II   HEGEMONY   AND   THE   INTERNATIONAL   STATE SYSTEM

The set of hypotheses which make up hegemonic stability theory is not a coherent or homogenous body of ideas. The proponents of the theory vary in assessing how a hegemon is to be recognised, how hegemons use their power and which historical episodes qualify as examples of hegemonic leadership.[6] But despite particular shifts in emphasis the central propositions of the theory are well developed.

Challenging Friedman and Schwarz's study of the causes of interwar American crisis, Kindleberger began popularising this approach by arguing, in somewhat functionalist terms, that the international economy requires a single leader – a hegemon – to act as a 'benevolent despot' to maintain international stability, 'for the world economy to be stabilised, there has to be a stabiliser, one stabiliser'

(Kindleberger, 1973, p. 305). Lack of leadership, according to Kindle-berger, renders the economic system dangerously unstable. The 1929 world depression became so severe, therefore, because of the absence of a nation willing and able to act as a stabilising hegemon. Kindleberger thus concludes 'the international economic and mone-tary system needs leadership. . . . Britain performed this role in the century to 1913; the United States in the period after the Second World War to, say, the Interest Equalisation Tax in 1963' (ibid., p. 28). Whilst Kindleberger focuses on the conditions necessary for the endurance (and thereby also the breakdown) of the existing system, Gilpin and Krasner's interest in the emergence of stability leads them to extend the initial theory and argue that hegemony is a prerequisite to the formation of liberal international regimes.[7] Thus Krasner, for instance, only qualifies this link between hegemonic power and open international trading systems by attempting to take account of past state decisions on domestic social structures as well as on international economic structures (Krasner, 1976, p. 318). Whilst the open nature of liberal trading systems is thereby accounted for in terms of the stability brought to bear by a hegemonic power in ascendency in the nineteenth century (British state domination) and between 1945 and 1960 (American hegemony), historical anomalies to this correlation are explained by Krasner in terms of 'societal groups preventing hegemonic nations from making policy amendments in line with state interests' (ibid., p. 318).

Hegemonic stability theory therefore puts forward two central propositions. First, it asserts that a hegemonic power both creates a stable international economic order and pursues policies which lead to collectively desirable outcomes for *all* states in the international system. To paraphrase Kindleberger, the world economic system is unstable unless one nation acts to create stability. When either an ageing or a potential new hegemonic leader fails to take up its international responsibilities and parochially turns to protect its perceived private interest, 'the world public interest goes down the drain, and with it the private interests of all' (Kindleberger, 1973, p. 292). Secondly, therefore, since the existence of a hegemon is necessary for the existence of order, hegemonic decline leads to global disorder.[8] Hence interpretations of the current crisis in the international economy relate hegemonic decline to the collapse of international regimes.

As a form of explanation this approach is not restricted to international relations theorists. Often utilising what Keohane refers to as a 'crude basic force model' (Keohane 1984, p. 34) of hegemonic power which asserts an automatic predictive link between dominance, power and leadership, many Marxist writers understand the current economic disorder in terms of a crisis of hegemony.[9] Altvater's recent study of the crisis of the world financial system, for instance, adopts this classic decline of American hegemony stance.[10] Unless the hegemon can sustain a global economic system in which all participating countries can benefit, he argues, 'the global system is endangered, as is the hegemon itself' (Altvater, 1987, p. 47). Following the predictable recanting of the cycle of *pax hegemonica* which instances Britain in the nineteenth century and America after 1945 as supreme hegemonic powers, Altvater concludes that since 1970 institutions have lost legitimacy and the world has awoken from the American dream. The novelty and the seriousness of the present crisis, however, is that in contrast to the decline of British hegemony there is currently no power – like the United States fifty or so years ago – that is a serious contender for the role of hegemon.

Moreover, the popularity of this orthodox hegemonic interpretation is likely to be accelerated amongst radicals as the work of the French 'regulation school' theorists becomes more widely read. The regulationists – who offer the potential of some distinct conceptual advances over neo-classical institutionalism and the more ambiguous versions of 'late capitalist' development theory – unfortunately adopt the simplistic divide between British and American hegemony as a way of distinguishing international cohesion and crisis in the transition from extensive to intensive regimes of accumulation.[11]

Whilst it is useful to distinguish between the types of claim advanced by the basic force hegemonic writers, the more sophisticated 'qualified hegemony' position of Keohane, Hirsch and Doyle, and the Gramscian hegemony view of Cox and Gill,[12] the weaker versions of the approach often end with little more than the tautology that hegemony is sufficient for co-operation.[13] Furthermore, even the most stringent critics of the *decline* of American hegemony thesis continue to accept a view of international relations as determined by hegemonic power. Witness, for instance, the work of Russett and more prominently Susan Strange who sharply point up the shortcomings of understanding the present crisis as one of declining hegemony and yet conclude on the terrain of the conventional approach that 'America will enjoy the power to act as a hegemon for some time to come' (Strange, 1987, p. 571).[14]

III HEGEMONY AND BRITISH POSTWAR RECONSTRUCTION

Recently the theory of hegemonic stability has come under scrutiny. The major critics of the approach have been concerned with its adequacy as a theory of economic behaviour, as a theory of collective action and as a theory of economic decline.[15] The major premise of the whole approach, however, that American hegemony was established after 1945 and that the USA therefore forced its model of development on postwar Europe, has gone largely unexamined.[16] With doubt already cast on the validity of seeing nineteenth-century Britain as an exemplar of a stabilising hegemon,[17] the usefulness of the whole framework would seem to rest upon the accuracy of viewing the postwar order as one resulting from the imposition of American dominance.

The present study therefore sets out to analyse this claim by focusing in detail on Anglo-American economic and political bargaining between 1945 and 1951. A primary objective is to bring out *Britain's* perspective on postwar reconstruction to complement the recent studies by Hogan, Milward and Wexler[18] who, by concentrating primarily on American documentary sources (and in Milward's case an impressive array of Western European material), have implicitly questioned the imposition of American dominance thesis.

The claim that Britain capitulated to American dominance in 1945, thereby transferring the mantle of international hegemon to the United States, is a view widely accepted across the political spectrum. The 'capitulation thesis', as I shall call it, forms the cornerstone for liberal and neo-Marxist writers alike. It is nevertheless little more than an enduring myth. But in the field of international relations where theory and policy are intertwined such myths can be 'extremely powerful, persistent, and dangerous'.[19]

The capitulation thesis isolates five decisive moments in the process of postwar reconstruction when American hegemony was firmly established over the British state and economy. These moments occurred in the course of the 1945 Washington loan agreement, the convertibility crisis of 1947, the Marshall Aid offensive, sterling devaluation in 1949, and the programme of Korean rearmament in 1950. A sophisticated example of the capitulation account is found in Brett's various writings which neatly illustrate the imposition of American hegemony argument.[20]

The guiding thread of Brett's work is that in the postwar era 'the relative automony of the state was decisively moderated not so much by the power of the domestic bourgeoisie as by that of its foreign counterpart in the United States'.[21] Increasing subordination to the United States 'pushed the government away from planning towards traditional capitalistic mechanisms' whereby complete British integration into the 'American dominated liberal capitalist alliance' laid the seeds for subsequent economic decline. This interpretation, assumed by Radice to be 'beyond dispute',[22] begins from a particular reading of the state's involvement in the Washington loan negotiations from which further acts of subordination flow.

The British state, it is claimed, could either have adopted a 'bilateralist or an Atlanticist' policy orientation in 1945.[23] The former would have meant detailed domestic planning and the development of an autonomous economic strategy, whilst the latter looked to increased American borrowing and the adoption of rapid trade liberalisation policies. Rather unpatriotically, Brett assumes, Keynes (acting on behalf of the UK in the Washington talks) was 'unable to resist a series of dreary capitulations' to the American negotiators. The American extraction of 'fundamental concessions in exchange for very limited promises of financial assistance' – by which is meant the state's obligations on convertibility and non-discrimination signed to secure the $3.75 billion loan – signalled a 'sometimes slavish and faintly ludicrous' British support for US policy and the abandonment of 'a more autonomous and self-sufficient line'.[24] With regard to the loan agreement, Brett leaves no room for doubt: 'capitulation to American hegemony had been rapid and complete'.[25]

This orthodox account is further supported by Gott's brief review of British policy.[26] Drawing solely on Foreign Office documents – to the total neglect of Treasury and Economic Staff memoranda – he concludes that the loan marked 'the moment when Britain became, if not a colony, then a client state of the Americans'.[27] In an American orbit of power Britain took its junior partner position with hardly a protesting voice.

The British state's subsequent international economic strategy is defined in the context of the loan agreement as a series of acts which turned 'Britain into a willing American client' gradually creating conditions which were to guarantee 'a decline into economic and political mediocrity'.[28] The balance of payments crisis of 1947 is therefore seen as the result of the 'enforced attempt' to introduce convertibility in July of that year, and it is claimed that without this attempt 'the huge sterling losses' would have been avoided. Moreover,

British negotiation with America over the European Recovery Programme (the Marshall Plan), begun in late 1947 and concluded in the summer of 1948, is interpreted as 'involving more concessions on both foreign and domestic economic policy'. The Marshall Plan, it is claimed, 'legally bound the Attlee government' to greater liberalisation through participation in the Organisation for European Economic Co-operation (OEEC), discouraging an independent British planned trade programme and increasing the close ties of America and Europe. For Brett the terms of Marshall clearly indicated that British financial policy was now open to dictation from the US government.[29]

Even Van der Pijl's sophisticated and extremely useful analysis of capitalist class formation in the North Atlantic area concludes that through the Marshall offensive 'the Pax Americana was imposed on the economic ruins of the defunct Pax Britannica in Europe'.[30] The Marshall Plan allowed the liberal internationalist bourgeoisie in Europe, with a background in either the colonial or Eastern European circuit of money capital, to restructure their interests in a wider Pax Americana, with the Marshall offensive leading to a 'concrete transformation of the European class structure along the lines of the US model'.[31]

Thus by 1949 the development of an autonomous internal or external economic policy was untenable – 'the pass had already been sold'.[32] Devaluation in September 1949 is seen as grossly excessive and positively injurious to British interests whilst the rearmament programme carried out under Gaitskell represented 'the end product of the processes of subordination to the global strategy of the United States which Bevin and Attlee had established as the keystone of British policy'.[33] In an overall context whereby the Labour government 'felt swayed by the need to back up the Americans at almost all costs',[34] the Washington loan episode had initiated British economic decline. The liberalisation measures implicit in this agreement had been extended in the Marshall Plan and culminated in Cripps's excessive devaluation. Korean rearmament intensified the economic slide causing the 'heart of British manufacturing industry and engineering to be virtually pulled out of operation'.[35] In short, this view sees postwar reconstruction as a process directed by the hegemonic American administrations who 'forced their model of development on the rest of the world'.[36]

IV AN ALTERNATIVE VIEW OF POSTWAR RECONSTRUCTION

The capitulation thesis and hegemonic stability theory are, to paraphrase Truman, 'two halves of the same walnut'.[37] By focusing on the immediate postwar years this study in effect challenges the hegemony approach in its heartland. As an analysis of political and economic history the topic has a limited importance. The primary significance of this exploration lies in its assessment of the nature of postwar capitalist reconstruction and the implications which can be drawn concerning relations between nation-states.

The account which follows, therefore, provides an empirical critique of the capitulation thesis and a theoretical critique of hegemonic stability theory. The alternative account of postwar reconstruction which emerges from an analysis of the primary sources shows the inability of the United States to impose its rule and the precarious nature of capitalist reintegration in the postwar era. This reintegration cannot be theorised as the result of the imposition of a nation-state's dominance in the international order. Neither can it be reduced to the assumed interests of a global capitalist class. Rather, it was the outcome of an uneven process whereby nation-states working within domestic political constraints pursued individual accumulation strategies in the context of re-establishing conditions for global accumulation.

The key episodes of intergovernmental negotiation which characterise the restoration of postwar capitalism clearly illustrate the contradictory relations of collaboration and conflict which exist between nation-states. Constructing an efficient mechanism for international exchange was a prerequisite for all nations in 1945. However, whilst the expansion of American accumulation primarily depended on the financial reintegration of Western Europe, the British state perceived its fundamental interests to lie primarily with the Sterling Area nations.

Britain's ambivalent stance towards Western Europe and the United States placed her in a unique position in the inter-state system. On the one hand, the British state was the supreme advocate of Western European resistance to the hegemonic aims of the United States. But this attitude of collaboration co-existed with one of conflict towards Western Europe which found its expression in Britain's withdrawal from vigorous intra-European trade in 1949, in favour of reviving Commonwealth trading links. For its part, the

United States clearly wished to impose itself as the super-imperialist state. Much of its policy was therefore designed to subordinate Britain and prevent the British state establishing a privileged position in Western Europe. These American objectives were continually frustrated in the postwar period and had been largely abandoned by 1950.

Whilst Britain's long-term objective was to re-establish sterling as a world currency, this aim should not be seen as simply serving US wishes or realising the interests of the City of London against 'national interests'. It was based on a material necessity, to overcome the primary barrier to accumulation which was the inappropriate structure of production and trade experienced in the dollar gap. Britain therefore used dollar aid to restructure trade, stimulate production and reduce the dollar gap to gain some degree of independence from the United States.

On the domestic front, the Labour government rejected a radical socialist solution to the economic problems facing Britain in 1945. This should come as no surprise to anyone familiar with the history and policy of the Labour Party from 1900 to the present day.[38] Attlee's dismissive attitude to radical socialism is well revealed in his remarks to a delegation visiting Moscow in 1954 when he commented to the British Ambassador: 'Have you read any of this Marxist stuff? . . . I've read none of it, you know.'[39]

Thus, to realise Labour's programme of domestic reconstruction the state required rapid accumulation which could only be achieved if Britain could reconstruct an adequate international payments system to facilitate trade and secure regular imports of essential commodities and raw materials.

Although the United States held a virtual monopoly of essential raw materials in 1945 and had unrivalled production facilities, Britain had a significant bargaining position based on the strength of sterling as a world currency and the City of London as the world's premier financial centre. These factors (together with Britain's relative political and economic strength *vis-à-vis* the other nations of Western Europe – at least until 1947) meant that to achieve its foreign economic policy aims the United States had no alternative but to work through Britain, realising that the UK held the key to the US penetration of Europe. The postwar years were thus characterised by a series of complex negotiations in which the British Treasury succeeded in thwarting the more strident US aspirations. The first such negotiation was the Washington loan agreement.

With traditional trade routes inoperative in war-damaged Western Europe, Britain had no alternative but to seek dollar aid. Alternative policies to seeking US aid could not overcome the problem that bringing more deficit nations into the Sterling Area would not assist the UK to overcome its own deficit. Keynes therefore negotiated a $3750 million loan from the United States and accepted a series of obligations which were designed to force the UK into a subordinate position within a US-dominated multilateral economic system. It is on this basis that the 'capitulation thesis' begins its account of British subordination. But an analysis of primary sources which traces the fate of these obligations (sterling convertibility, non-discrimination in trade and tariff reduction), shows that from the outset Britain did not take the obligations seriously. The British state needed dollars to implement its reconstruction programme. Economic strategy had a dual orientation which consisted of neo-bilateral trade and payments arrangements and American dollar aid. Candidly the Treasury took the view, 'we have broken our agreements left and right . . . (the only remaining question is) . . . how far we can dress it up to look as if we were inside it'.[40] The capitulation thesis cannot draw support from the episode of the Washington loan agreement.

By 1947 the British state was facing a severe economic crisis. The origins of this crisis, however, did not lie with the convertibility obligation or in industrial stagnation. The crisis was one of foreign currency reserves which had dwindled because of the expansionist programme pursued by the government. Whilst Britain sought new dollar aid to meet this crisis (and to continue domestic reconstruction), the United States sought a new strategy to achieve its foreign economic policy aims following the failure of the Washington loan agreement to secure these ends.

The Marshall Plan arose to meet this American objective, yet in its final form it simply fed Britain more dollars without achieving the European integration which was its political rationale. The evidence for this conclusion is drawn from a study of the administration of Marshall aid (via its agencies, the CEEC and the OEEC), the negotiation of the Economic Co-operation Agreement and the industrial and trade restructuring which the United States attempted in association with Marshall. The Marshall Plan sought to integrate Britain within a regional multilateral clearing system creating a single Western European market with the necessary political and economic stability to exist within a US-dominated world multilateral system. British resistance at every stage of this plan transformed the notion of integration into one of non-committal co-ordination which was coaxed into displaying sufficient signs of co-operation to enable dollar aid to flow. As with the Washington loan capitulation account, the Marshall Plan capitulation thesis is an inaccurate assessment of postwar economic restructuring.

The outbreak of a new sterling crisis in 1949 was followed by devaluation and a revision in the British state's economic policy. The fact that, in contrast to 1947, Britain was almost alone in experiencing a severe balance of payments crisis in 1949 indicates the precarious nature of Britain's trading structure at this time.

Whilst the major nations of Western Europe engaged in vigorous intra-European trade, Britain concentrated on renewing its traditional trading links with the Commonwealth. The limited and inflexible capacity of Sterling Area nations to increase or even sustain exports to the United States plus sterling's role as a world reserve currency meant that economic fluctuations in the United States set up unique pressures on British reserves. The decision to resolve the sterling crisis by devaluation indicated that the Treasury's primary objective would be the achievement of a pattern of world trade in which dollar and non-dollar nations operated together within a single multilateral system. The United States welcomed this declaration and attempted a new route to their objectives via a policy of harmonising trade and payments arrangements in the European Payments Union (EPU).

The US Treasury and the State Department were, however, divided on the extent to which the EPU would further American aims, and this indecision allowed Britain to defuse its more radical implications. A dramatic upturn in British economic fortune following devaluation (although not in any way causally related to this measure), plus European dissatisfaction with Britain's continued resistance to multi-lateralising trade, had the effect that the UK proposed to enter the EPU if the United States would grant particular concessions relating to the privileged position of sterling.

By the end of Cripp's chancellorship Britain had moved away from the neo-bilateral dual accumulation strategy and had established an economic policy based on the twin pillars of regional multilateral payments in Europe, while consolidating traditional trading arrange-ments with the Sterling Area. Britain had resisted this last postwar assertion of American hegemony and the EPU could no longer be interpreted as the first step towards Western European political and economic integration.

The inability of the United States to impose its foreign economic policy in Western Europe accentuated the domestic political crisis facing the State Department in 1950. America's apparently passive response to Soviet expansionism in Eastern Europe, France's return to Indochina and the withdrawal of Chiang Kai-shek from mainland China led to attacks on Marshall and charges of incompetence being lodged by McCarthy against Acheson.[41] In this early Cold War climate of hysteria and intimidation Congress faced the prospect that, with Marshall Aid tapering off, the United States would suffer a falling export surplus and experience domestic economic stagnation. Massive US and European rearmament in the wake of the Korean hostilities not only emphasised the importance of the United States in the defence of liberal capitalism but also provided a solution to this imminent American economic crisis. Contrary, however, to the capitulation account, the British decision to rearm was not an example of the UK bowing to American pressure, but was a decision taken by the government to show the United States that Britain had attained independent economic status in Western Europe and would not be treated as 'just another necessitous European nation'.[42] Whereas rearmament interrupted British economic growth in the check it caused to exports, many sectors of productive capital (in particular the motor trade and civil construction industries) greatly benefited from the programme via subsidised construction of new plant and buildings. Rearmament came at a time when a number of economic difficulties arose to slow economic growth. Its selective impact was temporary and relatively easily reversed.

The postwar years did not see the imposition of US hegemony over the direction of British or European economic reconstruction. By the end of 1951 the United States was no nearer its ambition of creating a US-dominated world multilateral system than it had been in 1945. The British state, by contrast, had overcome the primary barriers to accumulation which had constrained the economy in 1945, and despite sterling crises had established a payments system which facilitated high rates of growth. The argument of this book suggests that the very success of Britain's resistance to American pressure may have proved her later undoing. As a consequence of withdrawal from Europe the UK continued its traditional geographical distribution of exports and was largely excluded from the expanding intra-Western Europen trade markets where high levels of demand for manufactured goods boosted productivity and stimulated exports. But this argument introduces a long-term perspective which is clearly absent in capitalist economic policy-making. European integration (and compliance with the US wish for early sterling convertibility) and the scrapping of Commonwealth relationships were inconceivable for the postwar state since it would have entailed a radical restructuring of production and trade and the abandonment of the privileged world role for sterling. Having gained hard-won advances in economic growth since 1945 the Treasury was justifiably resistant to risking future economic performance for the benefit of dubious American political objectives. The following decade saw a generalised European economic boom which cannot be theorised as a consequence of an American hegemon imposing international economic co-operation, nor can it accurately be seen as the smooth working of the 'Bretton Woods system'. The boom was the result of individual nations pursuing specific accumulation policies in an unevenly reconstructed Western European trade and payments system characterised by inter-imperialist rivalry. Once the British strategy had been formulated it had its own developmental logic which, if only by default, produced a period of sustained capitalist prosperity.

The following chapters elaborate this alternative assessment of postwar reconstruction and the conclusion begins the difficult task of constructing a non-reductionist framework for the analysis of inter-state relations.

2 Towards the Washington Negotiations

The immediate economic constraints facing postwar Britain derived from the legacy of the war which had seriously disrupted international production and thrown into chaos international trade and payments systems. On political as well as economic grounds the Attlee government had rejected a radical socialist approach to these problems. The principles adopted by the wartime coalition government of regulating the production and circulation of use-values on the basis of collective need were progressively dismantled by the Attlee administration as exhortations to production were directed towards the reconstruction of British imperialism and the concomitant subordination of the working class. The realisation of the Labour government's programme of domestic reconstruction, which gave high rhetorical priority to the maintenance of full employment and the expansion of welfare, depended on the state overseeing rapid economic growth. But to achieve increased economic performance Britain needed to reconstruct an international payments system which would facilitate international trade and secure the regular import of essential commodities and raw materials.

The primary barrier to rapid accumulation in 1945 was therefore the uneven development of world capitalism which had produced a serious disequilibrium in production and trade between the Eastern and Western hemispheres. The British state's postwar economic strategy turned on finding a solution to its balance of payments problems which were a manifestation of this disequilibrium. To expand the economy successfully the state had to meet its existing balance of payments deficit in addition to finding extra dollars to pay for increased imports of essential materials that were abundant only in the Western hemisphere. The need to maximise accumulation was thus translated into the need to accumulate world currency. In 1945 the state therefore sought a solution to this problem by constructing an international payments system which would allow maximum commodity trade in inconvertible sterling whilst minimising the outflow of dollars needed for essential American purchases.

The postwar structure of world production and trade left Western

Europe heavily dependent on the economic resources of the United States. Yet despite British weakness and the strong economic position of America, Britain had a substantial bargaining position resting on two factors. First, New York could not take over London's role as the primary international financial centre. The domestic political regulations which enmeshed New York, and the material economic organisation of its banking system and money markets, prevented New York from becoming the world's financial centre. The United States therefore relied upon rebuilding the strength of sterling as a world currency to sustain the financial role of London. Secondly, Britain was, at least until 1947, in a much stronger political and economic position than the rest of Western Europe. The success of American foreign economic policy in the early postwar years therefore rested upon successful negotiation with Britain, given the latter's importance (or more accurately its perceived importance by the Americans) in world trade and European political affairs.

The postwar British Treasury concentrated on exploiting these strengths to subvert the American objectives of world domination, and to coax the United States into accepting a US/UK partnership to the mutual interest of each party. Britain thus resisted American attempts to restructure accumulation which were based on the notion of a subordinated Britain integrated within an American dominated multilateral system. Whilst the most pressing task of British economic policy was to restructure the international payments system to sustain trade in conditions of world production and trade imbalance, the British state's long-term objective was to re-establish sterling as a world currency but at a pace which would not be damaging to the developing economy and which would allow the state at some point in the future to secure an Atlantic partnership multilateralism. The complexities involved in following such a fine line of economic strategy meant that economic policy was left largely in the hands of civil servants and 'expert advisers'. Tracing the development of postwar economic strategy, therefore, means tracing the thought and action of state officials, associated principally with the Treasury. Cabinet ministers had no direct expertise of these involved issues. Politicians therefore played little part in deciding the fundamental strategies open to Britain in this period.

This chapter clarifies the issues involved in the run-up to the American loan agreement. It reviews Britain's economic position in 1945, and focuses on the economic and political rationale for seeking temporary financial assistance from the United States. It also considers the aims of American foreign economic policy following the surrender of Japan, and points to the constraints on the internationalisation of American capital. The loan agreement, signed between the governments of the United Kingdom and the United States on 6 December 1945[1] is the benchmark from which crucial decisions regarding the development of the postwar economic world were formulated. The negotiations had important consequences for all forms of capital within the total circuit of international accumulation. The agreement therefore directly affected international money capital via its strictures on convertibility, the postwar role of sterling and the position of London as the major financial and banking centre. Similarly its impact on commodity capital was experienced via a clause on discrimination affecting the structure of trade within Western Europe, between Britain and the Sterling Area, and between the latter and the United States. Lastly the agreement was seen by many as a prelude to restructuring productive capital via the utilisation of new capital equipment, new regimes of accumulation and the necessity of directing industry towards export production. This chapter sets the context for an assessment of these themes as an introduction to Chapter 3 which places the loan agreement within a broader discussion of trade and payments arrangements under Dalton's Chancellorship.

I THE ECONOMIC BASIS OF BRITAIN'S REQUEST FOR AID

Legacy of the War

In May 1945 Keynes circulated to the War Cabinet a memorandum 'Overseas Financial Policy in Stage III',[2] concerned with the optimal path for British accumulation.[3] The announcement by Truman on 21 August 1945 that following the surrender of Japan all contracts for lend-lease were cancelled, forced the government to seriously consider Keynes's options and decide upon the best path for economic reconstruction. In contrast to the position of the United States, which by the close of the war had rapidly expanded its industrial plant and doubled in real terms its national output, the depleted UK economy faced two major problems.

The first arose out of the deficit in the external balance of payments that was forecast to develop during the first three or so years when the necessary adjustments could be made – principally a restriction on imports and a 75 per cent increase in exports over the 1938 figure – to restore financial equilibrium. The second problem concerned the indebtedness of the UK to overseas nations arising from the massive proportions of the sterling balances and other accumulated liabilities since 1939.

Almost 25 per cent of prewar national wealth – estimated at £30 000 million, in September 1939[4] – had been destroyed by 1945. Shipping tonnage was now less than three-quarters of its prewar figure. Massive physical destruction of property (estimated at £1450 million) and serious impairment of industrial capital accompanied considerable domestic disinvestment (£885 million). Large scale external disin-vestment (£4198 million) intensified the serious deterioration in the external position as a result of the realisation of external capital assets (£1118 million), an increase in external liabilities (£2879 million), and a decrease in gold and dollar reserves (£152 million).

The extensive liquidation of foreign securities, repatriation of loans by overseas debtors and increased interest payments to holders of sterling debts caused by the UK's heavy war expenditure overseas had the result that the net income from overseas investment in 1945 was less than half the 1938 figure. The UK export trade had been deliberately abandoned during hostilities so that manpower, production and materials could be fully mobilised. The index of the volume of exports which stood at 100 in 1938 had fallen to 30 by 1944 with the value of commercial exports falling from £471 million in 1938 to a figure of £258 million by 1944.[5] Exports of coal, metal and engineering goods had virtually ceased. Cotton piece goods were only 27 per cent the prewar figure, and it was only with goods such as whisky and pottery, where demand could be met from prewar stocks, that exports neared the 50 per cent mark.[6]

The increase in the volume of exports needed to finance a 1938 scale of imports was agreed on the spur of the moment in a midnight conversation between Keynes and Austin Robinson to be 75 per cent.[7] Yet senior Treasury officials were aware that it would not be sufficient to restore 1938 as 25 years earlier they had attempted misguidedly to reconstruct 1913.[8] 1938 had seen a balance of payments deficit equivalent to 8 per cent of British imports and unemployment ran at an annual figure of 1 870 000.

The increase in overseas indebtedness – the second major problem resulting from the enormous cash expenditure on the maintenance and supply of UK forces overseas – had risen from a figure of £760 million in 1938 to £3355 million by June 1945 and continued to rise even at the end of hostilities.[9] When sales of foreign investments and a small amount of gold and dollars were also added to the sterling liabilities accumulated during the war, the net change on capital account between 1939 and 1945 amounted to £4700 million.[10]

The problem of the size of the sterling balances was exacerbated by the fact that the character and distribution of the debts precluded any common approach to their solution. Differences in Britain's political relations with creditor nations posed problems, specifically with two of the largest creditors, India and Egypt. Many of the debts were the result of local military expenditure incurred by the UK (Egypt is an example) whilst others were the result of trading operations (Argentina, for instance). Moreover, whilst a large number of the debts were held by the central bank or currency authority of the creditor nation, others were widely spread amongst commercial banks and private individuals. The character of the debts thus posed specific economic problems for the Attlee administration and meant that the UK could not take seriously the US suggestion that they should be viewed as a homogeneous entity and simply written off.

The UK ended the war with the largest external debt in history and with a level of reserves which had fallen to £3 million in April 1941, recovering to £450 million by June 1945 only because of the payment for US forces in the Sterling Area.[11]

To meet the cumulative deficit on external balance of payments which was estimated at £1250 million over three years and to release part of the accumulated sterling balances – a necessary move to assist the depleted economies of the largest creditor nations, India and Egypt – the government realised that it must receive some form of external credit to avoid, in Dalton's view, 'our people [being] . . . driven . . . deeper into the dark valley of austerity . . . facing . . . greater hardships and privations than even during the war'.[12]

This complicated postwar situation provided the economic rationale for the British state to seek temporary financial help from the only nation which could meet the urgent need for money to buy supplies for consumption and the regeneration of domestic and exporting industries on the world market. Yet to develop a more precise understanding of Britain's international economic position at the close of hostilities we need to go beyond bald statistical presentation and portray the underlying movements in the international circuits of capital accumulation that had taken place by 1945. First, I shall turn to the circulation of commodity capital and analyse how recent changes in international trade affected the British balance of payments up until 1945.

The Trade Structure in 1945

The first point to stress is that historically the UK had been the largest commodity market in the world. In 1938 Britain absorbed one-fifth of the exports of the rest of the world, with 37 nations directing one-tenth or less of their exports to Britain, 57 one-fifth or less, and four directing three-fifths of their exports to the UK.[13] Conversely, in 1938 52 per cent of UK exports went to countries other than the United States for which the UK was the chief market, whilst 4 per cent went to the US, 21 per cent to countries for which the US was the chief market, and 23 per cent to nations which found their chief market neither in the US nor the UK. The fact that even in 1938 the UK imported 17 per cent of US exports whilst the US absorbed only 4.4 per cent of UK exports was to prove an ill omen for the pattern of postwar British commodity trade. As regards the main constituents of the British import/export accounts, the principal imported commodities prewar were food and raw materials with 'luxury' manufactured goods the mainstay of the British export programme. Thus, on annual average between 1934 and 1938 the UK imported 88 per cent of grain flour, 93 per cent of fats, 82 per cent of sugar and over 74 per cent of fruit.[14] In all, well over half the UK's food supplies were imported. With regard to prewar intra-European trade in foodstuffs two movements are discernible. First, bread grains and cereals moved from Poland, Hungary and south-east Europe to the UK, Germany and Austria – with intra-European trade providing 20 per cent of Europe's total grain imports in 1935.[15] Secondly, with grain excepted, the flow of the rest of European foodstuffs was chiefly directed to the UK which in 1938 drew 22 per cent of her total food imports from Europe.

The UK economy was equally dependent on the importation of vast quantities of raw materials. Thus with coal an exception, the UK imported its entire cotton supplies, nine-tenths of its wool, a third of its iron ore, 90 per cent of its timber and all of its natural rubber supplies.[16] In 1938 the UK had an import surplus with every European country except Greece and Turkey, with British trade in textiles, machinery and manufactured goods, together with important invisible receipts, providing a trade and payments balance.

Between 1938 and 1945 significant changes occurred in this pattern

transforming the relative equilibrium in international trading positions. Intra-European trade in foodstuffs and raw materials fell
sharply below prewar levels, with Eastern European nations no
longer able to export grain and several even becoming importers.[17]
The massive decline of trade within Europe (which constituted in
1938 30 per cent of world trade but by 1946 only 17 per cent of the
world total) was exacerbated by the collapse of Germany which
resulted in approximately $1000 million worth of trade being lost in
both directions in Europe.[18] This decline of European exports
corresponded to a significant expansion of US exports evidenced in
the fact that in 1938 Europe's exports to overseas nations were three
times the total of US exports, but by the end of 1946 the US total
was slightly larger than the exports of all the European nations
combined.

During the later war years close links developed between the
economies of the United States, Canada and the UK. Under lend-
lease the US and Canada not only provided 40 per cent of the UK's
munitions requirements, they also provided a quarter of Britain's
total food supply and a significant proportion of raw materials (in
1944, 30 per cent of all US aid to Britain was non-munitions).[19]

The growth of the United States in international trade between
1938 and 1945 must also be seen in the context of the movements
towards the relative self-sufficiency of the American continent with
regard to imports. This tendency on the part of the US was exemplified
in the attempt to make itself independent of raw material imports
from outside the Western hemisphere. The creation in the early 1940s
of the tin smelter on the Texas seaboard and the propagation of the
synthetic rubber plantation industry are examples of this development.[20] By 1947 the US had achieved a balance of trade surplus of
$9975 million and an overall balance of payments figure in excess of
$8700.[21] With respect to commodity trade this was a position reached
not only as a consequence of the close-knit economic system of the
Customs Union of the United States – allowing trade preferences to
nations such as Puerto Rico, a major sugar supplier – but also from
high US import tariffs and export industry subsidies and programmes
such as the agricultural support price and acreage allotment programme.

When it is also realised that the principal commodities in the British
export trade to the US in 1946 consisted of such items as pottery,
whisky, linoleum, knitted goods and books,[22] and not a single one of
these leading commodities was among the twenty most valuable

categories of US imports, it becomes clear that the UK faced
the prospect of substantial visible trade deficits with the Western
hemisphere. Indeed, at the beginning of Attlee's term of office the
US occupied only sixth position in the league charting Britain's
geographical distribution of exports, that is to say, someway behind
the value and volume of British exports to India, South Africa,
Denmark, Australia and Eire.[23]

Throughout the 1930s Britain had financed much smaller trade
deficits through a high level of invisible earnings. These earnings had
chiefly derived from interest on foreign (often US) investments,
activities of British companies operating outside Europe, from the
services of merchant fleets (as carriers of cargo which the Board of
Trade estimated earned approximately £100 million per annum[24])
and from foreign tourism in Europe, insurance premiums, commis-
sions and other miscellanea arising out of foreign travel and trade.
Allied to these invisible earnings, Britain had previously reduced
trade deficits with the US by earning dollars in third markets such as
the Far East, India and Malaya. Both of these avenues had been
severely curtailed by 1945. With regard to invisible earnings, whereas
in 1938 net invisible income for Europe from non-European sources
amounted to $2.16 billion – an amount equalling Europe's deficit on
trade account[25] – by the end of 1946 Europe had a net deficit on
invisible account of $0.6 billion, $0.4 billion of which was directly
with the United States. The loss of invisible incomes corresponded
to many dollar-earning third markets being closed to British exports
since the underdeveloped nations faced similar reconstruction tasks
to those in Europe and were drawn to the United States as the
dominant supplier for food, raw materials and capital goods rather
than accept restricted trade patterns with the UK.

This short analysis of the underlying changes experienced in the
international commodity markets up until 1945 has pointed to the
tremendous obstacles facing the renewal of capital accumulation in
Britain at the end of the war. It has specifically highlighted the rise
of the United States and the conditions of international trade
disequilibrium which were implicit in the unbalancing of commodity
trade between the Western and Eastern hemispheres. This disequilibrium was not confined to the international circulation of commodity
capital but was mirrored in the spheres of productive and money
capital to present the British state with fundamental economic
problems, the first step towards the resolution of which lay with the
participants in the Washington loan negotiations. Only by analysing

developments in these other aspects of capital accumulation can we arrive at a more complete assessment of the international position of British capital on the eve of Labour's parliamentary victory.

International Production in 1945

It is, of course, no surprise that a maldistribution in the world's demand and supply for internationally traded commodities corresponded to an underlying imbalance in the structure of world production. At the height of the industrial revolution (1840–60) the UK led not only in the volume of world manufacturing production but also in the volume of external trade. However, by 1938 the UK accounted for only 9 per cent of the world total for manufacturing production – as against 31 per cent in 1870 – falling somewhat behind Germany (10.7 per cent), Russia (18.5 per cent) and the United States (32.3 per cent).[26] To understand this position of relative imbalance in world production which existed in the mid-1940s we need to identify the underlying conditions which gave rise to the dominance of the US in the interwar period and isolate the comparable factors which were absent from productive capital in the UK.

The productive dominance of the US over Western Europe had its origins in the decade after 1909 when the American iron and steel industry ceded its position as the fastest growing industry to the transportation machinery, oil and chemical industries – in short, the industries associated with the Rockefeller nexus.[27] The nascent automobile industry headed by Ford in the transportation machinery category was crucial for the developing productive output of the US. In Europe a comparable breakthrough of the automobile industry and the associated restructuring of capital did not occur. The Fordist socialisation of the productive forces under mass production conditions in the US, particularly in the interwar period, not only affected automobile production but was also significant for class relations in general. The Fordist productive strategy was significant in three principal areas.[28]

First, it introduced the assembly line and mass production techniques, replacing the skilled worker characteristic of Taylorism with the semi-skilled operative. Furthermore Fordism carried with it the recognition that wages are not just a cost but also an outlet for capitalist production. It thereby anticipated Keynesian demand-side economic policy by approaching the standardisation of the automobile as an example of the intimate relationship between mass production and mass consumption. Finally, Ford extended industrial management beyond the workplace to the sphere of the constitution and reproduction of labour power – intervening in the determination of household budgets, family practices and the propagation of 'puritanical' ethics – in an attempt to homogenise the workforce and produce a well-adjusted psycho-physical equilibrium preventing the psychological collapse of the worker exhausted by the new productive techniques.[29]

The Fordist strategy therefore broke the resistance of the skilled workforce, tapping the large reservoir of cheap unskilled labour and dramatically raising the rate of exploitation. In this way articulating rising living standards and a flexible format of labour relations the American automobile industry engendered a dynamic automotive-industrial complex involving the growing oil, rubber and glass industries whilst pioneering new marketing and maintenance practices, stimulating suburbanisation, the development of road networks and the management of mass consumerism. Through the revolutionary nature of its practices and the rationalisation of the class structure which it promoted, Fordism rapidly became in the interwar years the dominant mode of US capital accumulation with its influence spreading well beyond the automobile industry.

The material conditions enabling such a transformation of production relations are traceable to developments like that of the continuous wide-strip steel mills, which were pioneered in the USA in the interwar period as the natural corollary to the growth in demand for all types of flat steel products.[30] The first of these mills was laid down in the US in 1924 where the growth in demand for flat products was initially apparent in the motor industry but whereupon the vast output of consistently good quality cheap steel from the continuous strip mills gave rise to the search for new outlets, and the twin processes of production and consumption growth became cumulative. The importance of the continuous wide-strip steel mills and the cold rolling of flat products for US capital accumulation was evident in all major manufacturing industries from motor vehicles, shipbuilding and container industries (food canning industries) to capital goods manufacturing (railways, electrical power, general mechanical engineering, office equipment, construction industries) and the production of vast quantities of standardised consumer durables from washing machines, refrigerators and cookers to a multiplicity of domestic appliances. In all these sectors of productive capital the constrast with Western Europe is striking. By the 1930s the United States had a well established continuous wide-strip steel mill industry with total production of thin sheet steel increasing 277 per cent between 1929 and 1948. Total production throughout the entire nations of Western Europe increased by only 34 per cent over the same period, with the UK possessing only one, partially complete, continuous strip mill by 1940.[31]

The imbalance in the structure of world production which existed at the cessation of hostilities thus reflected not only the short-term effects of the UK's war-mobilised industrial situation but had much more complex origins to do with the regimes of accumulation pursued respectively in Western Europe and the United States. On the one hand the UK and Western Europe had been locked into a predominantly extensive regime of capital accumulation.[32] Growth in output encountered recurrent obstacles and increases in capital stock did not alter existing production techniques thereby resulting in low productivity growth. The United States, even in the interwar years, had entered upon a predominantly intensive regime of accumulation. Advances in the technical and social organisation of work (increases in the rate of relative surplus value extraction and the development of a social norm of consumption together with the efficient organisation of investment) had ensured rapid productivity growth. Under the conditions of extensive capital accumulation growth in output and technical change occurred in a faltering fashion only in Department I (the production goods industries) with Department II (consumption goods industries) remaining largely unchanged. By contrast the phase of intensive accumulation achieved a balanced and significant expansion of both departments and a sustained generalised increase in productivity understood not only in a narrow technical sense but in an international context integrating industrial, commercial and financial interests involving a restructuring of class relations.

An abundance of capital and superior production techniques coupled with a large internal market provided the US with an enormous advantage in most fields of industrial production. The strength of US productive capital, allied to underlying movements in the international commodity markets, created a postwar situation of serious international trade and production disequilibrium between the Western and Eastern hemispheres. British exports to the Western continent thus faced apparently insuperable problems at a time when Attlee had pledged to increase exports 75 per cent above the prewar figure.

Having outlined transatlantic developments in the production and circulation of commodities as they affected British accumulation up until 1945, it is now possible to analyse the underlying movements in the international spheres of money capital up until the cessation of hostilities – an aspect which is vital to this study, given the importance attached in the Washington agreement to the use and role of sterling.

The Position of Sterling in 1945

It will become clear from the course of this account that whereas Britain in the late nineteenth and early twentieth centuries had promoted sterling as the key international currency with the City of London the major commercial and financial centre, this was principally because Britain's domestic economy depended for its growth on increased levels of world trade based on colossal exports of capital by the UK between 1870 and 1914. From 1918 onwards, however, the decline in Britain's percentage of the world total of manufacturing production (corresponding to the rise of the US percentage) indicated that the material foundations of sterling as the top international currency were crumbling. Yet the United States – with an increased material capacity to support the dollar as the key international currency – was reluctant to assume the role Britain had successfully played up until this point principally because (regardless of institutional obstacles which will be detailed later and which could have been surmounted) the US domestic economy was far less dependent than that of Britain on movements within the world economy. This reticence on the part of the United States was equally evident in the postwar period, as seen initially in the obligations of the Washington loan agreement which attempted to resurrect sterling and underwrite its role as the top currency.

The emergence of sterling as an international currency occurred as international trade patterns in the mid-nineteenth century became increasingly focused on Britain.[33] The economic weight of the UK in world commerce, the economic advantages of a politically far-flung Empire pursuing a policy of free trade, the efficiency of United Kingdom international service industries such as shipping and in-surance, and the increasing flow of capital exports all extended the international use of sterling both within the Empire and beyond. Sterling's ability to finance approximately 60 per cent of world trade between 1860 and 1913 and in the same period to take up £4000 million of long-term securities from overseas[34] was achieved through a rapid internationalisation of the London capital and money markets and an expansion in the rate of growth of banks established in London for operation abroad, particularly in nations providing primary products. Thus the total number of overseas and foreign banks in London grew continuously from a figure of ten in 1842 to over 120 by the 1890s.[35] The extension of British banks into the domestic banking structure of many foreign nations was concomitantly very high. For example, by 1914 British banks controlled approximately a third of the deposits of the Brazilian banking system and over a quarter of those lodged in Argentina and Chile.[36]

By the eve of the First World War the City of London and the sterling system had developed into a complex and highly institutionalised structure for facilitating international financial transactions. The ability to attract short-term funds from the European gold standard countries through the interest rate mechanism (raising the rate of interest in the money markets when the Bank of England's gold reserves came under pressure) enabled Britain to sustain an overall surplus in the balance of payments between 1850 and 1913.[37] A consequence of the international sterling system was thus the extreme dependence of British capitalism on the state of the world economy. The successful continuation of international investment by the UK and growth in world markets depended on rising levels of international trade, the ability of the UK to continue exporting long-term capital, and the proclivity of overseas territories to absorb British goods and services.

The 1914 World War effectively halted the flow of credit from London and whilst most countries continued to define their currencies as equal to certain quantities of gold they acted to halt international gold shipments and close down free gold markets. The war shattered the basis of an already unstable gold standard order which continued to exist only in the sense that currencies were nominally based on gold.[38] From this period onwards it is clear that the British economy was no longer in a position to provide the material foundations upon which the international financial role of sterling had been built.

With the liquidation of approximately $3 billion worth of European (predominantly British) investments in the United States, as well as American loans made by J.P. Morgan and the Federal Reserve Bank of New York (totalling $300 million) to Britain in the aftermath of the First World War, the control panel of the Atlantic circuit of money capital effectively shifted from London to New York, turning the United States from the world's leading debtor to the world's leading creditor nation.[39] The accumulation of vast debts, the curtailment of overseas investments, the termination of colossal long-term capital export and the loss of invisible earnings meant that the British economy could not support sterling as an international currency, particularly in the face of the strong and freely available dollar – the most obvious candidate to replace sterling. Although representatives of American international money capital such as Morgan and Thomas Lamont sought to make New York the geographical centre of world banking and finance (and although both the economic base and Britain's ability politically to guarantee the sterling system had all but been destroyed) the old British institutional structure and its class base remained.

In addition to prevailing nationalist sentiment in the US, three major obstacles prevented New York financial markets from becoming the world's financial centre. The highly fragmented structure of the banking system, the regulations established under the New Deal which tightly restricted the financial operations of the various deposit institutions, and lack of experience in risk evaluation and managerial autonomy *vis-à-vis* direct shareholders' interests, were features delaying this geographical shift. Britain's dependence on world markets moreover meant that despite (or even because of) its relative economic decline, the international role of sterling was essential to the production and international circulation of commodities.

The interwar period was thus characterised by a close interdependence of US and British money capital, with the UK providing institutional facilities for a restoration of the gold standard and the US effectively underwriting sterling as the key international currency. The dollar's strength was not accompanied by the growth of New York as the major international banking and commercial centre. America's decentralised and thereby inappropriate banking network[40] and a configuration of class interests reflected in Roosevelt's New Deal policies gave prominence to nationalist solutions to America's economic problems which largely precluded internationalist solutions based on notions of New York and the dollar as the pivot of a new international monetary order. In conditions of British economic weakness and American inability and unwillingness to assume the international monetary role which Britain had carried out prior to 1914, the 1931 financial crisis ended the gold standard and ushered in a decade of exchange controls. Britain's negotiation of the Ottawa Trade Agreements reinforcing imperial preferences, and the enactment in the US of protectionist bills such as the Smoot–Hawley tariff and the imposition of quantitative restrictions, thus culminated in the emergence of a confused monetary state of loosely defined currency blocs.

The restrictions imposed on the movements of money capital by these blocs is a subject taken up in the following chapter which will discuss the working of the Sterling Area and the mechanism of 'dollar pooling'. It suffices at this stage to understand that an international monetary system composed of increasingly antagonistic blocs – the sterling bloc composed largely of the British Dominions (except Canada), British colonies, Egypt, Denmark, Norway, Sweden, Finland, Estonia, Portugal and Siam; a loose US bloc including Canada; and a European gold bloc[41] – could not serve as a basis for the future expansion of international capital. The chaos of the pre-1945 monetary system led analysts in both the US and the UK to seek the construction of a new postwar international monetary order.

The predominant American notion that a new international system could be constructed without fundamentally changing the old established role of sterling or the centrality of the City of London (provided that the US now play a more responsible stabilising role) emerged as the primary solution in the Washington negotiations. However this solution did not address the issue of the relative weakness of the British economy which had been a principal cause of the international monetary confusion prior to 1945. Nor did it appreciate the new burdens imposed on the UK arising out of wartime debt and damage and the development of a significant maldistribution in the structure of world production and in the world's demand and supply for internationally traded commodities.

This survey of the principal movements in the international circuits of capital accumulation up until 1945 has demonstrated the precarious domestic and international position of the British economy inherited by the Attlee administration. The immediate problems of the forthcoming deficit in the external balance of payments and the massive proportions of the sterling balances formed the British state's primary economic rationale for negotiating an American credit. However, the underlying trade and productive disequilibrium and the state of international monetary chaos were also under deep consideration by both sides and, as will be shown, were the real issues facing the negotiators in their various attempts to restructure British accumulation. Having laid bare the British state's economic rationale for approaching the United States the remainder of this chapter will seek to uncover the political rationale for this collaboration as it existed for both parties in the negotiations.

II THE POLITICAL RATIONALE FOR ANGLO-AMERICAN COLLABORATION

Keynes and British Policy

The British state's position in August 1945 was largely defined in terms of Keynes's memorandum 'Overseas Financial Policy in Stage III', referred to earlier, which had been one of the few in-depth attempts at analysing economic policy in the wake of the defeat of Germany. Before reviewing the contents of this memorandum it is worth considering the intellectual standpoint of Keynes in 1945 since, as Clarke – postwar member of the Overseas Finance Division of the Treasury – recorded on the day of Keynes's death on 22 April 1946, throughout the war and early postwar years Keynes had been the 'brains and the conscience' of the Treasury.[42]

Keynes's strong advocacy of economic multilateralism espoused before, during and after the loan negotiations stands in sharp relief to his interwar views on national self-sufficiency. Arguing the benefits of a greater measure of national self-sufficiency and economic isolation between countries than that which existed before 1914 (when the UK was the industrial, commercial and financial centre of the world economy) Keynes concluded in 1933 that the economic advantages of the international division of labour must seriously be questioned.[43] His critique of maximum international specialisation and the maximum geographical diffusion of capital regardless of its seat of ownership led Keynes to sympathise with those who would minimise rather than maximise economic entanglement between nations. However, this advocacy of gradually bringing the producer and the consumer within the ambit of the same national economic and financial organisation gave way, in the wake of the increasing chaos of international money capital in the late 1930s and early 1940s to a marked turnaround in Keynes's perspective.[44]

Belief in the efficiency and necessity of economic multilateralism increasingly informed Keynes's thought and action from the early 1940s onwards. In contrast to national self-sufficiency wherein bilateral nation-to-nation trade and monetary agreements predominate, multilateralism is the model of a system in which a nation balances its international accounts with a number of different nations.[45] Ideally multilateralism refers to a situation in which nations would be incorporated into one payments system with all currencies freely convertible, thereby enabling surplus earned in trade with one nation to be used to balance deficits with other nations. The notion of currency convertibility is essential to the concept of multilateralism and is worth clarifying. Currency convertibility refers to the ability of anyone to exchange domestic for foreign currency at some agreed rate of exchange on demand. In the case of Britain, for instance, this would mean allowing all countries which have payments agreements with Britain (that is, are in the same payments system as Britain if more than one system co-existed) to use the proceeds of their sales in Britain to buy goods in other countries, or simply exchange sterling assets for foreign goods or assets (a situation contrary to that which existed in the early 1940s when sterling was only convertible within the Sterling Area and exchangeable for other currencies only after British consultation). In addition to currency convertibility, economic multilateralism also implies, on a minimum definition, the reduction of trade barriers and a non-discriminatory application of those that remain. Whilst in practice multilateralism does not require the absolute elimination of trade barriers, any obstacles placed in the way of foreign purchases must theoretically apply in equal measure to all nations. Trade thereby ideally flows in accordance with the market price mechanism encouraging the international division of labour and specialisation according to the principle of comparative advantage.

These principles represent the essence of the multilateralism ostensibly espoused and reaffirmed by all the participants in the loan negotiations. The British state's support for multilateralism as a long-term objective can be traced to Keynes's advocacy of this position, expressed from 1941 onwards, and in particular in his important March 1945 memorandum. In that paper Keynes counterposed three possible paths open to the British state. Arguing that this 'is not a well chosen moment for a declaration of our financial independence of North America',[46] Keynes explored the implications of such independence and drew four conclusions. First such a move would require a continuation of war rationing and controls more stringent than at present for, say, three to five years after the war. Secondly, national planning and direction of foreign trade on the lines of the Russian model would need to be instituted. Thirdly, such policies would result in a serious retardation of colonial development and Far Eastern rehabilitation, and fourthly, in the long run they would lead to a virtual abandonment of all overseas activities whether military or diplomatic. Economic isolationism would engender unacceptable levels of hostility from Canada and the US and lead to serious political and social disruption at home. This 'Austerity' alternative of 'starvation corner' was counterposed to another equally unsatisfactory option, that of 'Temptation'. Although preferable to the former option, the path of Temptation would mean Britain accepting a very large American loan perhaps of $8 billion on US terms with immediate free convertibility of the sterling balances, major reduction in imperial preference, full sterling convertibility and non-discriminatory trading even during the Bretton Woods provisional period. Keynes's main objection to this option lay less in the problems of shouldering the burden of such credit and turned more on the fact that Britain would be surrendering control of economic policy to the dictates of the US State Department.

Rejecting these alternatives Keynes outlined the 'best path both technically, politically and psychologically' under the rubric of 'Justice'. This would involve a contribution of approximately $3 billion from the USA – the 'cost of the war to the USA for a fortnight' – together with a dollar refund to the UK for purchases Britain had made in the US before lend-lease became fully operative, and the scaling down, funding and convertibility of parts of the sterling balances which would enable '*de facto* convertibility' of sterling within a year after the end of the war. It is important to clarify this last feature to distinguish it from what Keynes regarded as the unacceptable notion of convertibility outlined in the path labelled Temptation. In the wake of confusion on this point Keynes later outlined in correspondence with Lord Brand (Treasury representative in Washington 1944–6) that he was using a 'Pickwickian, Bretton Woods sense' of the term which did not mean 'that the Sterling Area countries can take their balances away for any purpose whatever, e.g. to turn them into gold or to set up a dollar reserve of their own in New York'.[47] In essence, under conditions of '*de facto* convertibility' Keynes assumed that 'everything would proceed as at present except that there would be no pressure from us on the rest of the Sterling Area to refrain from any purchase in the US which they considered themselves rich enough to make, and equally no pressure to buy preferentially in the Sterling Area as compared with North America, except in gradual liquidation of their funded sterling debt'.[48] As far as this early memorandum is concerned Keynes defined convertibility under the Justice rubric as relating exclusively to the Sterling Area nations – not to the use of sterling by non-Sterling Area members such as the South American and Western European nations, which was the real bone of contention in the negotiations with the US. In this instance Keynes seemed to be referring to a state of non-discrimination rather than currency convertibility as the latter is normally understood.[49]

By 23 July 1945, after lengthy Treasury meetings, Keynes had clarified his earlier confusion stating that if the US were to offer the financial assistance proposed, Britain would probably have to abandon the idea of a transitional inconvertible period and accept the full Bretton Woods obligations from a fixed date approximately one year after VJ Day.[50] The overall emphasis of Keynes's paper made it clear that 'no fair solution can be reached without the participation of the Americans'.[51] With such participation he estimated Britain would be able to face the economic future without serious anxiety.

In contrast to his interwar theorising, Keynes was now a supreme advocate of the restoration of multilateral world trade. Under Anglo-American auspices encapsulating the healthy rules of mutual advantage and equal treatment, multilateralism was in 'the prime interest of our country', calculated to restore prosperity and prestige and eliminate the hostile tendencies of bilateral barter, discriminatory practice and economic blocs.[52] In short, Keynes regarded his proposals for collaboration with the US as the capstone of the great constructive effort on which he had embarked in the early 1940s to create a worldwide multilateral economic system.[53]

The British state's position was not synonymous with the one advocated by Keynes yet the latter was very influential and the British state drew freely on his ideas, particularly in the official statements endorsing multilateralism which helped secure the American line of credit during the loan negotiations. Yet despite Keynes's dominance at the Treasury and his persuasive influence over Dalton (uneasily aware of the tutor-student relationship established at Cambridge nearly 40 years before[54]), to fully understand the British state's official endorsement of Keynes's Justice option (which *mutatis mutandis* not only formed the basis of Britain's negotiating position but clearly approximated the final agreement) we need to consider the historical precedents favouring the political decision for initial economic collaboration with the United States.

Precedents for Postwar Anglo-American Economic Collaboration

Three such precedents can be discerned occurring within a four year period prior to the loan negotiations. First, the Charter arising out of the Atlantic Conference begun on 9 August 1941 between

Roosevelt and Churchill presented a definition of Anglo-American postwar economic objectives in which collaboration was prominent. For instance, Churchill added a fifth paragraph expressing 'the desire to bring about the fullest collaboration between all nations in the economic field',[55] whilst the infamous fourth clause, although amended, originally proposed to 'promote mutually advantageous economic relations between [the US and the UK]) . . . through the elimination of any discrimination in either the US or the UK against the importation of any product originating in the other country'.[56] It is worth pointing out that the principal amendment to the fourth clause was made at the insistence of Churchill who safeguarded the Ottawa Agreements regarding imperial trade preference by inserting the saving clause 'with due respect for existing obligations'. Despite Welles's later disclaimer that 'it was fully understood . . . that this reservation was inserted solely to take care of . . . merely temporary impediments to the more far-reaching commitment originally envisaged in that article',[57] Churchill had managed to extract from Roosevelt the assurance that Britain was no more committed to the abolition of imperial preference than the American government was committed to the total abolition of their high protective tariffs. We need to be clear on this issue since it remained a source of confusion for many analysts in the subsequent discussions concerning trade discrimination raised by the non-discrimination obligation of the Washington Agreement.

Closely following this advocacy of equal access to trade and international collaboration came the signing of the Mutual Aid Agreement on 23 February 1942. In particular Article Seven, which was signed as the British 'consideration' for the generosity of American lend-lease policies, encouraged further discussion on collaborative postwar trade policy. In essence Article Seven made provision for agreed action by the US and the UK 'directed to the expansion, by appropriate international and domestic measures, of production, employment and the exchange and consumption of goods . . . and . . . to the elimination of all forms of discriminatory treatment in international commerce . . . and to the reduction of tariffs and other trade barriers'.[58] These mutually interdependent obligations, extracted largely as a *quid pro quo* for the provision of lend-lease, were seen by *The Times*[59] as opening up the prospect of the two governments working together 'to promote prosperity for all instead of competing for selfish advantage', evidently reaffirming the favourable political climate for collaborative postwar reconstruction. As with the Atlantic Charter it must be realised that the terms of the draft did not state directly that non-discriminatory trade policies would be adopted but only that 'agreed action' towards this end should be an Anglo-American objective. By linking trade liberalisation to the expansion of employment and drawing a parallel between the reduction of UK trade discrimination and substantial US trade barrier reductions Article Seven became a particularly significant reference point in the subsequent American loan discussions.

The final development worth pointing to in this context was the compromise of the Keynes and White plans (two blue-prints of a mechanism for international monetary co-operation) presented in April 1944 as the Joint Statement by Experts on the Establishment of an International Monetary Fund, the key provisions of which were embodied in the Articles of Agreement of the International Monetary Fund adopted at Bretton Woods in July 1944. This financial develop-ment was linked to proposals for an International Bank for Reconstruction and Development, whose plan had been published in November 1943, whilst in early 1945 Board of Trade representatives from London and Washington began a series of commercial policy negotiations culminating in the publication of the 'Proposals for Consideration by an International Conference on Trade and Employ-ment'.[60] These negotiations reflected a significant measure of agree-ment between the US and the UK on issues initially raised in the Mutual Aid Agreements, such as linking the reduction of trade barriers to the maintenance of full employment, and provided an important framework for both the Washington Agreement and the subsequent Havana International Trade Charter. Although there are many difficulties in assessing the true value of the Bretton Woods agreements there is little doubt that these political manoeuvrings created a postwar environment conducive to a collaborative solution to Britain's immediate postwar economic problems.

The British state's political rationale for seeking American assist-ance in the early postwar transitional period was thus clearly defined. Whilst it is inaccurate to assume that the state's position was synonymous with the views of Keynes who, dominating the Treasury, wished for a restructuring of British capital along Atlanticist multi-lateral lines, there were many historical precedents favouring Anglo-American economic collaboration. Indeed, prior to the disclosure of the obligations involved in the Washington Agreement, which sparked off a wave of resistance to collaborative multilateralism, it is difficult to find any important representative of the British state (with the notable exception of R. Clarke in the Treasury) or the economy without at least a theoretical commitment to multilateralism. Thus, whilst it may not be surprising that *The Banker* saw only one road open to mercantile Britain 'to fully co-operate with the United States', and Charles Lidbury – President of the Institute of Bankers and Chief General Manager of Westminster Bank – with few provisos acclaimed the benefits of 'genuine multilateralism' on the American scale,[61] it is interesting to note that Clive Baillieu – postwar President of the Federation of British Industries – agreed that a 'multilateral world economic system will be as much in Britain's interest as in that of any Dominion',[62] once Britain had adjusted to the change in status from a creditor to a debtor nation. Official Labour Party policy carried a similar conviction. Both Dalton and Cripps announced in Cabinet meetings that the Labour Party was committed to making a sincere attempt to secure co-operation with other countries towards a multilateral system of world trade.[63] Similarly Attlee looked towards mutually 'advantageous solutions' conducted on 'multilateral non-discriminate bases' for the establishment of a world trading and monetary system.[64] But it is important to be clear on this point. Whilst the belief in the value of multilateralism appeared universal this is not to argue that the British state capitulated to American hegemony, as for instance argued by Brett.[65]

Keynes's position may indeed have been that British capital should be restructured along multilateralist (largely American) lines. Yet the historical precedents cited above and the general theoretical support for multilateralism expressed not a capitulation to American hegemony but simply a view that, given an environment conducive to Anglo-American economic collaboration, the *first step* towards negotiating a solution of Britain's economic problems lay in joint US/UK Washington discussions. In fact, the *de jure* multilateral commitments on the part of the British state belied an application of *de facto* neo-bilateral alternatives, as I shall later demonstrate, a contradiction the British state was adept at concealing behind the argument that the Sterling Area was in any case the world's largest multilateral system.

British policy prior to the negotiations amounted to little more than the belief that multilateralism was ultimately beneficial to the UK provided Britain was not asked to 'multilateralise unilaterally' before the end of the Bretton Woods transitional phase. To understand how the American participants in the loan negotiations attempted to force Britain into such a position and realign the UK accumulation strategy in accordance with the wishes of the US State Department, it is necessary to end this review of the road towards the Washington Agreements with an analysis of US foreign economic policy objectives as they stood in the winter of 1945.

US Foreign Economic Policy in 1945

It is easy to assume that, following the implementation of Fordist accumulation strategies after 1914 which had given US capital an incomparable competitive position in the world economy, a direct line can be drawn in US foreign economic policy from Wilsonian internationalism to Truman's assertions of Atlantic universalism. Such a view conceals the important foreign policy conflict experienced particularly, though not exclusively, under the Roosevelt Administration. In the latter's term of office this conflict was significant enough to manifest itself in terms of a struggle between the Treasury and State Departments. Whilst the State Department, staffed by Cordell Hull, Dean Acheson and William Clayton, advocated the notion of a massive US export surplus to stimulate the domestic economy in the context of world multilateralism, the Treasury led by Henry Morgenthau and Harry Dexter White favoured not only an extension of the domestic policies of the New Deal but also an international application of New Deal policies in the context of a world system of national capitalisms pursuing full employment and the creation of international institutions funnelling capital into underdeveloped areas to promote international monetary stability.[66] The eventual defeat of the Treasury view was partially a result of the disorganisation of the American working classes who stood to gain significantly from the Treasury programme but whose lack of support allowed Truman to gain power upon Roosevelt's death in April 1945. Subsequent Treasury reshuffles with Morgenthau replaced by Fred Vinson – a conservative Southern Democrat with State Department views on international economics – further diminished White's influence. Yet the momentary dominance of the Treasury in the early 1940s left its mark in the provisions of the Bretton Woods agreements. Unless recognition is given to the configuration of interests represented by the Treasury at this point in US policy development, it is difficult to understand how the idea of the international monetary system devised at Bretton Woods was formulated, since its articles clashed strongly with certain aspects of US State Department policy which regained ascendency in the period prior to the loan negotiations.

The articles of agreement signed at Bretton Woods derived from White's earlier notions of an International Stabilisation Fund and International Bank. Following various compromises (involving consultation with Keynes and others) negotiations were signed for the creation of the International Monetary Fund and International Bank both intended to facilitate the expansion of international trade and contribute to the promotion and maintenance of high levels of employment and real income. The 44 nations party to the agreement would be allowed to maintain restrictions on current transactions for a five-year postwar transition period after which extensions to the continuing use of restrictions would be granted after consultation.[67] (The Fund, however, had no real powers to guarantee that any nation would lift restrictions after the five-year period even if consultation had not been entered into at this stage.) In addition to measures designed to provide stable and orderly exchange rates (currency maintenance at a constant exchange rate relative to other members' currencies; avoidance of competitive exchange rate depreciation; exchange rate changes of over 10 per cent only after consultation) the Fund would have resources of $8.8 billion in gold and national currencies on which nations could draw to correct maladjustments in their balance of payments. Nations running chronic surpluses could moreover have their currencies declared scarce and be subject to trade discrimination by other member countries. It is certainly the case that technical problems dogged many of the proposals. For instance, the 'scarce currency clause' proposed that a currency could only become scarce after countries had exercised their full drawing rights under the Fund and used their 'quotas' to purchase the currency in question from the Fund in exchange for their own currencies. However, limitations on the extent and speed of withdrawal plus increasingly high rates of interest levelled on nations frequently using their drawing rights and the ability of the Fund to borrow more of the currency in question, resulted in the emaciation of the clause with dollars, for instance, remaining in good supply within the Fund whilst being extremely scarce in reality in the immediate postwar years.[68] Nevertheless, the key point to note is that the Bretton Woods agreements bear the mark of the US Treasury Department under Roosevelt and were viewed with growing dissatisfaction by members of the State Department.

In this sense it is inaccurate to portray the 'Bretton Woods system' as providing American capital with the optimal structure for the integration of the international circuits of capital. Although the agreements in theory made exchange stabilisation possible, slowly broadening into a basis for currency convertibility and a multilateral trade and payments system, in the State Department view (which dominated US foreign economic policy from April 1945 onwards) the articles allowing such a long delay in removing controls would be disastrous for the creation of US style multilateralism, a central tenet of which was to maintain a long-running US export surplus.

In its return to dominance in US foreign economic policy-making the State Department enshrined the former aims of US internationalist policy based on two fundamentals. First, maximum production in the US, and secondly, maximum trade throughout the world, together with advocacy of the Most Favoured Nation Clause under which no state can give a preference of any kind to a near neighbour or kindred state without conceding the same advantage to all other states. As Kipping, the postwar Director General of the Federation of British Industries, perceived, the US in taking this attitude were doing no more than advocating a principle which the British applied with great tenacity in the nineteenth century.[69] A US-style multilateralist world economy would eliminate political interference whilst upholding the laws of the market, allowing trade and capital to flow freely across national boundaries creating the markets and the investment opportunities necessary for a massive international expansion of US capital ensuring a large export surplus and increasing US bank and industrial growth. This overall objective, aiming first at the integration of Western European circuits of capital, and secondly at the integration of the former into a US dominated world economic structure (excluding, of course, the Soviet Union and the East European nations) had specific policy implications for the United Kingdom.

Focusing on Britain as the lynchpin of its strategy (perhaps foolishly, given the importance of France and Germany to the reconstruction of Western Europe), the US State Department besieged the UK on two fronts. First, realising that the conditional form of the Most Favoured Nation Clause was a rather ineffective practical basis for the policy of non-discrimination in trade, the State Department sought a much more extensive and rigid application of non-discrimination. Specifically they sought the elimination of the British Imperial Preference system formalised at Ottawa in 1932 and the abolition of the so-called discriminatory aspects of the Sterling Area dollar pooling mechanism. The workings of both these systems will be detailed in the following chapter which will also consider the validity of the US objections lodged against the systems. It suffices at present simply to point out the significance of this issue for US foreign economic policy prior to the Washington Agreements.

Contrary to the solutions proposed at Bretton Woods, the revised US economic policy aimed at the immediate abolition of exchange controls. In correspondence with the British Treasury, William Clayton, Assistant Secretary of State for Economic Affairs, stated in June 1945, 'we believe that exchange controls on current transactions however necessary in wartime are restrictive of free competition on the basis of commercial values and therefore restrictive of free enterprise . . . we want them ended as soon as practicable. The State Department is supporting measures which will aid in ending this unhappy situation'.[70]

The second front taken by the Americans aiming to end this 'unhappy situation' focused on lifting the major obstacle to increased world trade (as they saw it), the inconvertibility of sterling and the wartime eclipse of London as the world's major financial centre. Not only did sterling have access to an institutional structure through which international transactions could flow but US policy makers were acutely aware of the dollar shortage which would occur in the immediate postwar world and realised that trade within Europe and between Europe and the Sterling Area could only proceed multilaterally in the short term if sterling was made convertible.[71] The alternative was intra-European trade based on a system of bilateral agreements. The restricted nature of bilateral trading would adversely effect the freest possible flow of factors promoting efficiency and integration and as such constitute a serious obstacle to America's global strategy. The importance of sterling was all the greater given the continuing reluctance of New York bankers and the institutional inappropriateness of its banking system to promote the dollar and New York as the major world financial centre. Yet here again the Bretton Woods agreement on a lengthy five-year transitional phase threatened to scupper America's global integrative strategy.

To understand the development of US economic policy in the wake of these difficulties it is important to be aware that the State Department circumvented the obstacles to their plans inherent in the Bretton Woods agreements by recasting their international monetary policy in the light of the so-called Key Currency proposals. Nevertheless it is inaccurate to claim – as does Block[72] – that the Americans simply forgot that Bretton Woods had ever occurred and instead pursued wholeheartedly the Key Currency proposals. Rather, the Key Currency proposals substantially informed US policy throughout the Washington Agreement and Marshall Aid phase, whilst particular aspects of Bretton Woods were invoked (particularly the notion of international trade agreements) to bolster, at least on an ideological level, the new US international policy stance.

The Key Currency approach, enthusiastically promulgated by John Williams (Vice President of the New York Federal Reserve Bank), Leon Fraser (President of the First National Bank of New York) and Winthrop Aldrich (Chairman of the Board of the Chase National Bank), who termed the proposal the key nation approach,[73] identified three aspects necessary for postwar international monetary order. First, bilateral stabilisation agreements between the key currencies, sterling and the dollar, since these currencies, it was argued, are the principal media facilitating international trade and are the only ones predominantly used for making international payments. Secondly, non-key currency rates must be permitted to fluctuate and eventually be stabilised in relation to the values of the key currencies. Thirdly, and most significantly, substantial credits should be made available to the UK to aid the stabilisation of sterling as the initial step towards restoring general currency stability. The objective of the Key Currency approach therefore lay in the establishment of an international system wherein only key currencies were generally convertible and only a limited amount of international co-operation in monetary affairs was necessary. Bretton Woods failed (in Williams's eyes) to recognise the importance of key currencies in international trade and therefore, in opposition to the IMF proposals, any extension of credits made by the US should only be negotiated on a bilateral basis, not centrally through an international organisation.

Essentially these proposals represented the New York bankers' solution to the situation of postwar monetary chaos. The solution would attempt to restore the financial and commercial prowess of London co-operating with New York in the joint management of the international monetary system whilst the US loan ($5 billion suggested by Fraser in 1943; $3 billion by Aldrich in 1944[74]), in underwriting the international use of sterling, would act as a financial lever on Britain forcing the pursuit of US style multilateral trade policies. Nevertheless the Key Currency proposals in their pure form implicitly carried a threat of creating currency blocs with their disregard for generalised international economic collaboration. To guard against this threat the State Department allied the principal aspects of the proposals to the more eclectic principles of Bretton Woods resulting in a compromise which depended in reality on close Anglo-American collaboration in line with the Key Currency proposals but which also allowed the US to endorse on an ideological level the generalities espoused at Bretton Woods concerning genuine international co-operation.

By the winter of 1945 the State Department had galvanised a series of dynamic US foreign economic policies to serve as the basis for the American position in the Washington loan negotiations. It is not the case that at this point the United States simply sought 'drastic liberalisation of the world market'.[75] Informed by the Key Currency proposals, the United States principally sought Anglo-American reconstruction of the international monetary system through policies aimed at restoring sterling convertibility and the elimination of discriminatory practices which would enable an integrated multilateral Western European trade and payments system to flourish in the overall context of a multilateral world economic structure dominated by US capital with its superior Fordist accumulation techniques. At this stage US policy focused on European market integration led by Britain and not upon rapid American trade liberalisation since strong protectionist interests still prevailed within the US Congress. Financial leverage, in the form of substantial tied loans to the UK on the basis of the Key Currency proposals, rather than an assurance of major US tariff cuts thus informed the multilateral strategies of US foreign economic policy prior to the Washington discussion.

This chapter has highlighted the nature and complexity of the issues involved in the reconstruction of British capital accumulation as they developed in the early postwar world on the road to the Washington negotiations. Beginning from the observation that capitalist development must be viewed in terms of both political and economic contingencies, whilst acknowledging that economic policies confront and must partially resolve contradictions generated by the uneven reproduction of capital accumulation, it has laid bare the two most immediate economic problems confronting the British state's strategy of capitalist reconstruction: the massive deficit in the external balance of payments expected to develop in the first three or so transitional years, and the massive proportions of the sterling balances and other liabilities accumulated since 1939. In this way the study has clarified the British state's economic rationale for seeking temporary financial help from the United States. It has also highlighted the conditions of the maldistribution in the structure of world production and in the world's demand and supply for essentially internationally traded commodities which left the United States in such a superior postwar position that Balogh assessed the disequilibrium as one 'for which there is no parallel, at any rate since the days of the Roman Empire'.[76]

Within the political context in which Britain sought to fashion an optimal accumulation strategy there existed strong historical precedents favouring Anglo-American economic collaboration. This, in addition to a generalised British belief in the value of multilateralism created an environment conducive to joint US/UK discussions as an initial step towards negotiating a solution of Britain's immediate postwar economic problems. The rise to dominance of the US State Department (and the almost total eclipse of the Treasury Department which had been ascendent and instrumental in laying down many of the articles contained in the Bretton Woods agreements) illustrates the convoluted process through which multilateral integrative strategies became the basis of the American position prior to the loan negotiations. To gain a deeper understanding of the British state's accumulation strategy requires a close consideration of the Washington Agreement itself and a detailed study of British reaction to the loan obligations which was by no means as uniform or concessionary as the formal structure of the document would imply.

3 The Washington Loan Agreement

The Washington negotiations are a central focus of the 'capitulation thesis' view of postwar British development. The British state, according to this view, embraced the tenets of multilateralism outlined in the agreement and established a strategy of accumulation based on accepting a subordinate position in an American-imposed liberal internationalist alliance.

This chapter directly challenges that interpretation. By situating the American loan within the wider context of the state's international trade and payments arrangements it becomes clear that a dual accumulation strategy emerged under Dalton consisting of a *de jure* commitment to multilateralism tempered by a *de facto* commitment to neo-bilateralism. This combination thwarted the ascendant US policy ideals and provided a successful environment for the expansion of British capital in those postwar years characterised by the 'dollar shortage'.

I THE NEGOTIATION OF THE LOAN

Alternatives to the Loan

The previous chapter showed that the British request for aid was based fundamentally (although not exclusively) on the economic constraints facing postwar reconstruction. D. Eccles, Member of Parliament for Chippenham, summed up Parliamentary feeling by asking: 'if we do not get a credit from America where are the goods coming from to fill the gap? It is no use saying that the goods can come from the Sterling Area; they are simply not there.'[1]

Dalton agreed. The rejection of these arguments meant not only 'an economic and financial disaster for this country . . . [but also] . . . a disaster for the whole future of international co-operation'.[2] Whilst subsequent analysts have drawn on Dalton's account and suggested that 'there seemed no alternative but to seek a loan from the United States',[3] we should recognise that at the time there was no such bankruptcy of statesmanship and a variety of alternatives were voiced from many sources.

The principal source of Parliamentary opposition came not from Churchill, who regarded any bilateral alternative as 'utterly fatal' involving a 'prolonged rough and tumble . . . in the economic and financial sphere between the US and the British Commonwealth of nations and the Sterling Area . . . [of which] . . . I am sure we should get the worst',[4] but from his Party colleagues Boothby and Amery.[5] This latter pair expended most energy in criticising the conditions of the loan rather than offering any serious bilateral alternatives. Boothby agreed with Henderson[6] that the convertibility obligation would remove all incentive for other countries to buy from Britain since they could obtain goods more readily from the US. He saw the proposals as a reinstatement of nineteenth-century *laissez-faire* capitalism designed to prise open the markets of the world for the benefit of the United States with extraordinarily little for Britain in return. But in describing Labour's 'economic Munich' in which Attlee was to 'sell the British Empire for a packet of cigarettes',[7] Boothby could offer only a weakly stated alternative of 'the Sterling Area bloc, based upon the British Empire, and fortified by the countries of Western Europe'. Similarly, while Amery derided the agreement as a return to the economics of Cobden and Bright, a single gold standard and the Most Favoured Nation Clause, his only alternative (and that of his group, the Empire Industries Association) was the abolition of the MFN clause substituted by straightforward agreements with foreign nations and the development of Imperial Preference as a definite policy of mutual trade stimulation.[8] Neither of these loosely stated options offered a solution to the immediate problems of the transition period. With America holding a virtual monopoly of the most important supplies, the attractiveness of the dollar rendered any alternative based solely on the Sterling Area as likely to be unworkable and highly unpopular, not least among other Sterling Area members.

The most seriously argued alternative accumulation strategy prior to British and American ratification of the Washington documents derived from Richard Clarke – postwar member of the Overseas Finance Division of the Treasury – in his two papers 'Financial Policy in Stage III' circulated to the Cabinet in June 1945, and 'What Happens If We Do Not Get the US Loan', written on 12 February 1946.[9]

The simplest plan proposed by Clarke and consolidated by Eady –

Joint Second Secretary of the Treasury – was an abandonment of Keynes's 'Grand Design' policies of several years' money, sterling balances, convertibility and non-discrimination, and their replacement by 'Plan 2'. This was a programme based on the creation of as big a multilateral group as possible (Sterling Area, French, Belgian, Dutch areas and Scandanavia) to trade freely amongst themselves (about 75 per cent of prewar world trade[10]) and to pool and allocate their dollars. Allied to this would be an attempt to borrow what dollar credits were available from the US through the Export–Import Bank or by pledging investments. If both could be achieved, Clarke assumed that Britain could proceed to 1948 with only the following domestic and international costs incurred. First, the reduction in food imports experienced throughout the war, falling from an average of 22 026 thousand tons imported in 1938 to 11 032 thousand tons imported in 1944,[11] would continue with retarded recovery in consumption principally because the US was a significant supplier. Secondly, Plan 2 would hamper reconversion of industry because of the need to cut raw materials and machinery supplies together with the retention of basic petrol rationing. The severity of further cuts in, for example, tobacco, film and cotton supplies would ultimately depend on the extent to which Britain could borrow from the US. On the international front many Sterling Area nations would also go short of US goods, with particularly serious consequences for the Colonies, and moreover Canada, who could well be obliged to lend Britain dollars in order to sell her goods and would have to strictly limit her imports from the USA. Finally, as Keynes was wont to point out,[12] the loss of the US loan would severely debilitate Britain's military and political expenditure overseas involving the withdrawal of forces in the Middle East and India and the termination of British finance to European relief and reconstruction schemes with the ending of supplies to Germany. In spite of the drastic political effects of almost total withdrawal of British overseas commitments and the serious economic effects entailed in the loss of US markets for both the UK and the Sterling Area, Clarke nevertheless put Plan 2 forward as a viable option maintaining that 'we could scramble through somehow'.[13]

Clarke's internal Treasury memoranda, and to a lesser degree some of the more publicly expressed criticism of the agreements, increasingly influenced the British state's negotiation, conduct and appraisal of the Washington documents (particulary after Keynes's death in April 1946). Yet these bilateralist strategies could not overcome the principal objection that bringing into the Sterling Area more nations that were themselves in deficit would do nothing to help the UK cover its own deficit.[14] As Keynes had sardonically observed,

'from which countries can we expect to borrow what we have failed to obtain from the United States? . . . the alternative is to build up a separate economic bloc which excludes Canada and consists of countries to which we already owe more than we can pay, on the basis of their agreeing to lend us money they have not got and buy from us and from one another goods we are unable to supply'.[15]

In such conditions, as Pimlott notes, austerity would have been blamed on 'socialism', whilst the lack of dollars would seriously have curtailed the government's socialist programme.[16] Both economically and politically the Labour government required a successful outcome to the loan negotiations, with success judged less in terms of attendant obligations and more in respect of substantial dollar credit. In this sense the British state's negotiations were successful, in spite of the fact that Britain's economic policy apparatus had changed little from its wartime structure.

The Cabinet and Economic Policy-Making

Between the outbreak and the end of the war, the central machinery for economic policy underwent three principal changes (from the Treasury period of September 1939–May 1940; to the period of Committees, May–December 1940; culminating in the period of the Lord President's Committee, January 1941–August 1945), effectively fragmenting the economic policy-making process.[17] With the dominance of the Lord President's Committee structure the Treasury found itself uncustomarily 'under a political shadow which not only diminished its standard privilege and authority but disqualified it from access to the new centres of deliberation'.[18] This wartime structure elevated the control of the labour markets above both finance and production so that, as Middlemas recalls, Bevin stood 'where no Cabinet minister had previously done, rival to the Chancellor of the Exchequer himself'.[19]

The main characteristics of the organisation of central government under the Lord President's Committee stage can be summarised as involving, first, a reliance on interdepartmental co-operation;

secondly, a central focus on the allocation of scarce resources (particularly manpower and materials, with financial decisions largely of secondary importance); and thirdly, in line with point two, the demise of the Treasury and the rise of an external administrative machinery responsible for economic co-ordination. Both Dow and Chester[20] are at pains to emphasise that this system was retained by the incoming Labour government with Dalton becoming Chancellor, Morrison taking up a position as Lord President of the Council with overall responsibility for economic co-ordination, and Cripps becoming President of the Board of Trade. A division of responsibility for economic policy thus existed with financial and budgetary policy the *de jure* responsibility of the demoted Treasury – with both the Economic Section and the Central Statistical Office housed outside the Treasury in the Cabinet Office – and direct planning largely outside Treasury responsibility. This fragmented system was further complicated by the fact that, in addition to his role as economic co-ordinator, Morrison had other onerous tasks as Leader of the House of Commons, chairman of the Future Legislation Committee and chairman of the Committee on the Socialisation of Industries. The lack of a central planning department, a chief planning officer or an economic general staff (all introduced under Cripps's Chancellorship) was only publicly acknowledged during the crises of 1947, yet privately experienced by those concerned with overseas negotiations and balance of payments control throughout Dalton's Chancellorship. Thus, as Cabinet memoranda disclose, with regard to overseas negotiations, 'no organisation [exists] capable of handling this task'.[21] Proposals for a committee consisting of representatives of the Treasury, Board of Trade, Foreign Office, Commonwealth Relations Office, Ministry of Food, Bank of England and the Economic Section of the Cabinet Office to make good this deficiency, appeared only long after the loan agreement had been ratified. Similarly, later proposals for a Sterling Committee to advise ministers on balance of payments issues indicate a significant gap in the early postwar state machinery belying Morrison's 'happy and confident' remarks about the efficiency of economic administration as it existed from Dalton's installation as Chancellor in August 1945.[22]

The Cabinet lacked control over the economic policy apparatus throughout Dalton's Chancellorship. A. Robinson, for instance, now recalls 'how few among all the many were doing the thinking as distinct from uncritically administering policies handed down to them'.[23] As noted earlier, the complexities of negotiating a settlement which concerned Britain's international payments system meant that the task fell largely to civil servants and expert advisers. In the case of the Washington discussions, Keynes and Halifax conducted negotiations almost single-handedly and decided terms. Cabinet members played little part in the proceedings and when pressed on aspects of the agreement showed little understanding of its complexity.

Thus Robbins – assigned as intermediary between the London ministerial term (Dalton, Bevin, Cripps, Morrison, Attlee) and Keynes and Halifax in Washington – recalls the problems of negotiating on two fronts simultaneously 'with the Americans for terms which were not doctrinaire and exacting, and with the Cabinet for a descent from cloud cuckoo land and an understanding of the realities of the situation and the choices which they had to make'.[24] Jay – Attlee's Personal Assistant – commenting on Keynes's proclivity for sending a plethora of witty telegrams, notes that 'on one occasion quoting from one of them Dalton said peremptorily to Bevin: "Foreign Secretary, have you got the telegram?" "I've got 'undreds", replied Bevin, and Bridges trotted round the table to reshuffle the cards for him'.[25] In mid-November 1945 Dalton was still secure in the belief that non-discrimination and convertibility would not begin to operate until after the transition period of several years duration despite Keynes's clear statements dating from July 1945 that Britain would have to abandon this transitional period and accept both obligations from a fixed date of one year after VJ Day.[26]

The Financial Agreement[27] signed between the US and the UK, together with a final settlement of lend-lease, proposals for an International Trade Organisation and the implementation of the Bretton Woods agreements for the setting up of an International Monetary Fund and an International Bank for Reconstruction and Development, constituted in Keynes's view a deal which in the 'light of all factors . . . is the best that could be achieved'.[28] The details of the Financial Agreement must now be analysed.

II ASSESSING THE AGREEMENT

Details of the Loan

First of all, a line of credit was made available to the UK government of $3750 million in final settlement of lend-lease (Canada subsequently granted a credit of US $1159 million on similar lines producing a total of $4909 million – excluding the lend-lease settlement – for Britain's temporary financial easement).[29] The provision for a line of credit rather than a loan meant that the funds would only be advanced as required, thus securing the interests of the US if British reconstruction were to proceed faster than estimated. Article Six of the agreement similarly assured the interests of the US by providing that the credit could not be drawn on to discharge the present obligations of the UK or allow the UK to borrow from other Commonwealth governments before 1951 on terms more favourable to the lender than those offered in this agreement. It was also emphasised that in line with its predecessors, the Atlantic Charter and the Mutual Aid Agreements, the purpose of the line of credit was to assist the UK government to 'assume the obligations of multilateral trade' (Article Three), if not immediately, then no later than within one year of the agreement.

The line of credit was now open to be drawn upon until December 1951 with no payment either of interest or principal to be made for five years and thereafter the interest at 2 per cent (but allowing for the time delay effectively only 1.62 per cent), with instalments of approximately £35 million to be repaid annually over a 50 year period. The interest was to be excused if in any year UK visible and net invisible income fell below £866 million – the average for the years 1936–8.

It is worth noting that the amount offered in the line of credit closely approximated both the estimated transitional deficit figure put forward by Keynes in Washington and his prior assessment of the amount necessary to meet the Justice path of reconstruction. In all this Dalton records, 'the Americans were very generous'.[30] Yet by far the most significant aspect of the agreement concerned the four financial and commercial obligations, which in the view of the *Economist*[31] were to relaunch the British economy prematurely into the icy seas of multilateralism.

The first such obligation (Article Seven) tied Britain to dissolving the Sterling Area dollar pool within one year, thereby allowing sterling receipts for the Sterling Area countries to be convertible in any currency without discrimination. In American eyes this obligation was significant inasmuch as they perceived the dollar pool to seriously discriminate against US exports, since the Sterling Area countries had agreed to deposit their earnings in London and comply with Sterling Area regulations before spending these earnings on US goods. This obligation, from the American perspective, would cut

British control of the dollar earnings of the sterling countries and lead, it was hoped, to the dissolution of the Sterling Area.

The main strictly commercial provision of the agreements obliged Britain to administer quantitative import restrictions (Article Nine) in such a manner as not to discriminate against US imports. This non-discrimination clause, also to be effective within one year, disciplined the UK to restrict importation of foreign goods along the lines of the already mentioned Most Favoured Nation Clause thereby applying an import limitation on the basis of equality to all nations. The implications of this second obligation appeared more onerous for the British state than those concerning the dissolution of the Sterling Area dollar pool. The non-discrimination clause sought to prevent the government from switching overseas sources of supply away from the US, which placed the UK in a difficult trade position since it would have to cut down on purchases not only from America, whose currency it did not possess, but also from other nations whose currencies it did possess. In this way British imports would be determined not by the overall balance of payments with the world at large but by the so called 'dollar gap'[32] (the discrepancy between Sterling Area exports to and imports from the US), hampering trade diversification.

The third proposal in the agreement (Article Ten) concerned the freeing of the blocked sterling balances – accumulated British war debts owed principally to the Sterling Area nations but also to non-sterling members such as Argentina.[33] It announced the intention of the Attlee government to reduce these balances either by releasing instalments for immediate convertibility, releasing similar instalments over a number of years beginning in 1951, and negotiating the adjustment of the balances as part of the Sterling Area contribution to the Allied war effort. For the US it was important to have payments made on the blocked balances free for making purchases in the US, whilst from a British point of view these arrangements were satisfactory in that they closely followed Keynes's original suggestions made in his 1945 government memorandum.

The final and most controversial multilateral obligation (Article Eight) stipulated the general convertibility of sterling within one year of the agreement. This obligation stressed, with potentially serious repercussions, that within one year of the effective agreement neither government would impose any restriction on payments and transfers for current transactions with any other country. The significance of this provision was that it extended convertibility to the nations of

Western Europe and South America whilst obliging Britain to ignore the five-year transition period for general convertibility stated in the articles of agreement of the IMF. Thus from the effective date of the agreement any nation could call upon the UK to supply it with dollars to an amount represented by its favourable balance of payments with Britain. Agreement on this principal was clearly seen by the US as achieving a major goal of American economic policy,[34] and despite British resistance it was a condition that had been expected by Keynes as early as July 1945.

In addition to these obligations Britain undertook to ratify the Bretton Woods agreements, commitments largely complementary to those undertaken in the Anglo-American Financial Agreement,[35] and to support the American proposal for an International Trade Organisation, a proposal based on the US wish to reduce imperial preference and eliminate trade discrimination. This latter proposal was seen as an essential prerequisite for the development of US international economic policy given the views held in the State Department, as expressed privately to Will Clayton, Assistant Secretary of State for Economic Affairs, that 'if you succeed in doing away with the Empire preference and opening up the Empire to United States commerce, it may well be that we can afford to pay a couple of billion dollars for the privilege'.[36]

Taken at face value, the Washington obligations were intended to have a major impact on postwar British accumulation. Mr Spence of the US Committee on Banking and Currency told the House of Representatives in the final debate before the loan ratification that they were fundamental to the success and realisation of American international economic and political objectives.[37]

The obligations concerning convertibility, non-discrimination and, by implication, substantial reduction of preferences, which in Clayton's view formed the three essential cornerstones of the world multilateralism,[38] will be analysed in depth in the following section. It is appropriate, however, at this point to further the discussion begun in the previous chapter concerning developments in the international monetary system by clarifying the American proposal for the dissolution of the Sterling Area dollar mechanism.

The Sterling Area Monetary System

An assessment of the impact of Article Seven dealing with the dissolution of the Sterling Area dollar pool requires a brief investigation into the origins of that mechanism, considered blatantly discriminatory by the US negotiators. Initially it is worth distinguishing between the monetary association of the 'Sterling Bloc' and that of the 'Sterling Area'.[39] As stated in the previous chapter, following the 1931 crisis in the international monetary system when sterling ceased to be directly convertible into gold, there arose a confused state of loosely defined currency blocs. Many nations, constituting the Sterling Bloc, chose to maintain substantial reserves in sterling given the importance of London as a centre for the financing of trade and borrowing, together with the existence of the Gold Exchange Standard and high rates of interest obtainable in the City.[40] However, apart from the fact that trade among Sterling Bloc members could proceed at *de facto* fixed rates of exchange, the bloc association conferred no special privileges upon its members.

With the outbreak of hostilities in 1939 this situation was radically altered. Under an act of mutual convenience a group of nations – the UK, Ireland, Australia, New Zealand, South Africa, Southern Rhodesia, India, Pakistan, Ceylon, Burma, British Colonies, Iceland, Iraq, Egypt, Sudan, Palestine, Jordan and the Faroe Islands[41] – formed the Sterling Area, becoming exempt from British Exchange Control regulations. The Area arose by the force of common interests, convenience and efficiency which the pooling of reserves, the centralisation in London of the essential banking operations for the whole Area, the freedom of payments within it, and the similarity of exchange control applied by each member to all transactions with non-Area countries conferred upon member nations. In essence the Sterling Area could be characterised as a voluntary association of nations without any written constitution or central dictation within which exchange control did not operate. A major purpose of the system was the mobilisation and conservation of the means of purchasing outside the Area, particularly from dollar area nations, for the duration of the war.[42] Out of these circumstances arose the Sterling Area dollar pooling arrangements administered through the Exchange Equalisation Account.

The dollar pooling mechanism regulated the convertibility of sterling within the Area (sterling, of course, was now generally inconvertible for nations outside this area) through the voluntary agreement that all hard currencies earned by members of the Area were surrendered to the pool and allocated according to the individual requirements of member nations. This system ensured that the means of purchasing in dollar countries was centralised in each nation, that any surplus of purchasing power was transferred into a common reserve in exchange for sterling rather than being held independently, and that restraint was exercised in converting sterling to dollars through the use of the import licensing system. Sterling was therefore fully convertible through the dollar pool for licensed purposes, with the regulation of this mechanism solely dependent on the co-operation of the governments concerned. The informal principal of the pooling mechanism was that the reserves of the entire Sterling Area, rather than individual balance of payments positions with the dollar nations, should serve as a guide to the changing severity of dollar import controls of the member states.

In addition, through a combination of informal exhortation and consultation, participating members agreed that only essential requirements would be procured from outside the Sterling area, with drawings from the pool allocated according to need rather than the size of the gold/dollar contributions of each nation. The effect of the dollar pooling mechanism was thus to alter the trading patterns of the sterling countries with the dollar area. Yet the US State Department's interpretation of the mechanism as heavily discriminatory against US goods and under the central control of the UK, failed to appreciate the finer workings of the process. The pooling system in fact increased American exports to dollar deficit nations like India and Australia at the expense of US exports to dollar surplus members such as Ceylon and the Colonies.[43] In terms of trade, the loss to the US was negligible. On this point, therefore, the US objective, as stated in Article Seven, was based on a misinterpretation of the dollar pooling mechanism. Not only was the US diagnosis inaccurate, but the Article itself was superfluous given Article Eight stipulating the general convertibility of sterling. This is the case inasmuch as Sterling Area members would have been reluctant to maintain restrictions on their own dollar imports, less favourable than those in force in non-Sterling Area nations.

In respect of Article Seven this brief analysis vindicates Dalton's view of the mechanism as a largely innocuous voluntary agreement simply designed to cut the demand on reserves of gold and dollars for the whole Area, particularly for the duration of the war,[44] and as such the obligation had little bearing on future British economic policy.

The crux of the Washington document, therefore, rested on the three principles of convertibility, non-discrimination and the implied substantial reduction of preferences. The ultimate objective of US foreign economic policy was to sweep away the nation state as the basis of the European political and economic system and gradually merge Western Europe into a US-dominated world-wide structure of multilateral payments based on the convertibility of all currencies into the dollar. In terms of the Key Currency approach the aim was premissed on the granting of the loan, which made up 40 per cent of the total US disbursements in Western Europe between July 1945 and June 1947 – a total calculated as $10 098 million.[45]

III   NEO-BILATERALISM AND THE LOAN

Aware of these facts, many analysts have concluded that in the face of such powerful obligations the British state simply adopted an accumulation strategy in line with the dictates of the US State Department. 'Capitulation to American hegemony', writes Brett, 'was rapid and complete', with the 'American dominated liberal capitalist alliance' resulting from the loan destructive of the 'possibility of a viable autonomous economic strategy'.[46] Similarly, Van der Pijl sees this as an era in which the Americans successfully developed hegemonic concepts of control consolidating liberal internationalism and allowing the *Pax Americana* to be imposed upon the economic ruins of the defunct *Pax Britannica* in Europe, and Coates sees the US's multilateralist policy impositions eating away at Britain's ability to control its economic destiny.[47] British economic decline, it is even suggested, can be traced to this episode, with the state embracing the tenets of US-style multilateralism, subordinating British capital to the wider integrative objectives of American economic policy. This view, stressing that the loan involved a restructuring of British capital along American lines with the British state strongly tied to US-inspired multilateralism, is nevertheless inaccurate. By placing the Washington agreement within the wider context of international trade and payments arrangements a more complex picture of Britain's accumulation strategy emerges.

The 'capitulation to American hegemony' thesis relies upon an overly literal interpretation of the Washington agreements. The view that US-style multilateralism could simply be established by relief programmes financed in dollars (note the work of the United Nations Relief and Recovery Agency) or straight dollar credits secured on the basis of the Key Currency proposal/Bretton Woods alliance, disregarded both the political will of the Labour government and the

international disequilibria in production and trade. In place of the
view that British postwar economic restructuring was carried out
largely at the behest of the US and involved a subordinated British
state, this account proposes a view of postwar accumulation as a far
more complicated and uneven process, involving a shifting pattern
of temporary Commonwealth and European alliances for short-term
purposes ultimately at odds with US foreign economic policy interests.
Specific political and economic contingencies strangled the US bid
for hegemony and in the course of events enabled the British state
to pursue a plan of accumulation which approximated neither the
multilateralism espoused by the Americans nor the bilateralism of
the critics of the loan, but a dual strategy specifically adapted to meet
the particular political and economic situation existing in postwar
Western Europe.

To begin the critique of the 'capitulation to American hegemony'
thesis it is necessary to chart those political and economic conditions
which were to thwart US foreign economic ideals.

Labour's Domestic Programme

In an abstract sense it is conceivable that a British government may
have implemented the US proposals at the cost of substantially
emaciating their domestic programme. However, the Attlee administration had been elected with a clear mandate to pursue definite
policies of domestic reconstruction. As Attlee recalls, 'people wanted
a positive new policy',[48] and Labour was strongly identified with a
new social agenda premissed, as Dalton records, on the sensation of
'a new society to be built; and we had the power to build it'.[49]
Although there remains a question mark over the extent of the
government's radicalism, it cannot be doubted that the Labour Party
was pledged to full employment and other policies designed to
increase the level of social welfare – policies, generated out of a
critique of the débâcle of 1931, significant enough to be described
by Milward as the 'historical imperatives' underlying the British
reconstruction programme.[50] Contrary to Miliband's claim that 'the
experience of 1931 did not cause any major transformations in the
Labour Party',[51] it is the case that an intensive reorientation of
socialist thought occurred around this period, affecting both Labour's
perception of the capitalist economy and the style and presentation
to the electorate of the Party leadership.

The extent of the theoretical revision which took place after 1931 is shown by the formation in 1932 of the Socialist League whose Executive Committee included Cripps, Bevin, Pritt and the three Labour theorists of the interwar years, Cole, Laski and Tawney. This group focused on the absence of any clear short-term policy as a central problem. Whilst Cole proclaimed the need to rebuild the Party 'on essentially different foundations',[52] Tawney – a major accomplice in the drafting of the 1929 party programme – engaged in self-criticism stressing the need to clarify and order priorities.[53]

The result of this perceived need for a more specific domestic short-term programme was the National Executive Committee's decision in December 1931 to appoint a policy sub-committee which subsequently produced a series of documents concerning, *inter alia*, banking and finance, and domestic and industrial reorganisation, which laid the basis, however incompletely, for the policy orientation of the 1945 General Election campaign. The policy sub-committee of the NEC, dominated by Dalton and Morrison, together with the Economic Advisory Council (chaired by Henderson and closely involving Keynes, Cole, Bevin and Citrine) was joined in 1931 by the Society for Socialist Inquiry and Propaganda, the New Fabian Research Bureau and, in 1932, the XYZ Club, all involving future Cabinet ministers with work directed towards laying down the political programme for future Labour governments.[54] The sharp critique of Labour's own theoretical tradition carried out after 1931, concerning not only the philosophy of socialism but more significantly stimulating an economic policy revision, paved the way for Attlee to claim at his victorious press conference that 'Labour went into this Election on a carefully thought-out programme based on very definite principles'.[55]

The agenda for domestic reconstruction was a first priority in the economic programme of the 1945 Labour government. It was thus essential that any accumulation strategy forged by the postwar British state should support these historical imperatives which underlay domestic reconstruction policies in Britain, rather than simply attempt to promote US-style multilateralism in conditions of a maldistribution in the structure of world production, commodity trade and disrupted money markets. A careful consideration of these historical impera-tives reveals the Labour government's motives for engaging in the Washington discussions. Rather than interpreting this move as one made by the British state as an act of subordination to American hegemony, a study of the political/historical context shows that the Labour government sought the dollar credit in an attempt to avoid abandoning its own domestic programme, which in Dalton's view was the main justification for having a Labour government.[56] As Jay records,[57] the blow to industrial recovery, exports, investments and full employment resulting from non-acceptance of the loan would in the end have been far worse than 'our having to undertake – under *force majeure* – a commitment we probably could not honour'.

A review of Cabinet documents reveals that on many occasions Attlee, Cripps and Dalton urged the Cabinet, not only from economic and financial motives but significantly on political grounds, to accept almost any obligations so long as the dollar credit was forthcoming.[58] Similarly Ellis-Rees, working in the Overseas Finance Division of the Treasury, recalls: '[I] never heard any suggestion that we had even a sporting chance of making a success of the Agreement in its fullness; the only question was how long we could make the credit last'.[59] In this context, therefore, as Attlee later admitted, 'the US and Canadian loans were essentially measures to buy time'.[60] The British State's acceptance of the multilateral obligations was in essence a superficial act taken primarily with a view to securing the much-needed dollar credits and involving a wait-and-see approach towards the attached conditions. The political and electoral motives which lay behind British postwar economic reconstruction must not be underemphasised. The implications of this realisation serve as a direct critique not only of the 'capitulation to American hegemony' thesis but also of functionalist state theories which refuse in many cases to consider the impact of political constraints on accumulation and are content to identify the direction of capitalist development and the actions of the state simply by reference to a logical deduction of the requirements of an abstractly conceived capitalist mode of production.

Such a model cannot explain the actions of the early postwar state, which sought to maximise the opportunities for implementing policies of domestic reconstruction, in addition to forging an accumulation strategy which cut across the requirements of the ideal functioning model of multilateralism. This is the significance of the government's decision to adopt a *de jure* commitment to multilateralism in order to meet the short-term objective of alleviating the dollar shortage which would allow the implementation of their domestic reconstruction programme. For the British state in 1945 it was simply not politically feasible to adopt US-style multilateralism.

Trade Disequilibrium and Multilateralism

A consideration of the economic obstacles preventing the adoption of multilateralism in the early postwar years supports this interpretation. It has already been demonstrated that changes in the international structure of productive, commodity and money capital had severely weakened the position of British capital, particularly in relation to the rapidly internationalised US capital. Between 1945 and 1947 Britain proceeded to accumulate increasing trade deficits with the USA.

The deficit on merchandise trade with the US rose from $764.07 million in 1946 to $950.08 million in 1947, with the overall deficit of Western Europe on visible trade with the US rising from $2356.11 million in 1946 (60 per cent of which was made up of British and French import surpluses) to $4742.14 million in 1947.[61] Gross capital formation consumed 21 per cent of UK national income in 1947 (4 per cent more than in 1938, a year of intensive rearmament), with Britain importing increased amounts of building materials, steel products and raw materials necessary for domestic reconstruction. Coal imports rose from 7000 tons in 1946 to 694 000 tons in 1947 (a total by value of £34 million) of which all but £437 000 worth came from the United States. Quantities of iron-ore and semi-finished steel approached record import levels whilst aluminium imports from Canada rose to twice the prewar total.[62] In 1938 only 19.25 per cent of British imports arrived from the Western Hemisphere. By 1947 this proportion had increased to over 45.5 per cent drawn from dollar regions.[63] These trends continued in 1948 with the import of manufactured goods the highest on record and the total for raw materials exceeded only in 1920.[64]

In the short-term, the deterioration in Britain's balance of trade with the United States was the result of high and increasing levels of imports of food, construction equipment (particularly timber and steel) and raw materials all essential to ensuring rapid British domestic economic recovery but detrimental in the short term to any policy which was supposed to ease dollar dependence.

This trade pattern indicates that the American loan, and subsequent Marshall Aid payments, sustained high levels of British capital investment and maintained rising output and employment. Equal access to trade and the other Bretton Woods multilateral propositions proved largely unworkable in the maladjusted world economic situation simply because they did not allow an easy transition from the industry and trade pattern of the 1930s to a postwar world in which multilateralism did not overly burden reconstruction economies pledged to increasing output and employment. Even in the wake of the 1947 sterling crisis, which commenced well before the agreed date for general convertibility (in which Britain paid out $237 million, as much as the total deficit for 1946, in the last seven days alone before the suspension of convertibility on 20 August 1947[65]), the political and economic objectives of the Attlee administration depended for their implementation not on further cuts in domestic consumption allied to other austerity measures, but principally upon the US making more dollars available to fuel the expanding economy. The $3.75 billion credit, intended to last at least three years, was consumed in just over one. However, it was the success and vigour of the British recovery, not its incipient failure, which exacerbated the balance of payments problem.[66] If multilateralism ever had any potential in early postwar Europe – a proposition I seriously doubt – all chances of the Key Currency/Bretton Woods alliance ended with the suspension of general convertibility in mid-1947.

This second point has emphasised the significance of the economic conditions existing in the early postwar years which, when allied to the political short term policies of the Attlee administration, prevented the path of British accumulation from falling under the sway of the US State and Treasury Departments. Contrary to the capitulation view, it appears that the multilateral trade proposals could not proceed in the postwar environment without a solid basis of international trade underlying them and were objectively unworkable in an environment characterised by serious trade and production imbalance. A view of postwar capitalist development seen in terms of American enforced multilateralism cannot be accepted.

A Dual Accumulation Strategy

Yet, if the established view of postwar capitalist development is rejected, what is the alternative account of capital accumulation in this period? I suggest that neither US-style multilateralism nor the stereotypical view of bilateralism, as presented by the critics of the loan, can adequately portray the British state's accumulation strategy. In the face of large scale productive, trade and balance of payments disequilibria between the world's major trading areas the core of the British state's accumulation strategy in the early postwar years consisted of a web of neo-bilateral monetary, payments and trade agreements which expanded into a successful limited network with relatively flexible controls, consistent exchange rates and relatively non-discriminatory payments mechanisms and trade practices within Western Europe. This network was a series of short-term arrangements which provided a Western European solution to the most pressing Western European problem – the chronic dollar shortage.

The British state's early postwar accumulation strategy thus consisted of two principal elements. First, a *de jure* commitment to US-imposed multilateralism – as outlined in the loan agreement obligations – which released massive dollar injections into the UK economy, enabling the purchase of vital supplies, particularly raw materials and capital goods necessary for the implementation of the sweeping domestic reconstruction programmes on the basis of which the Labour government was elected. Secondly, a *de facto* commitment to neo-bilateral monetary, trade and payments arrangements in the face of the unworkability of US-style multilateralism – monetary and payments arrangements which provided the most feasible system for Western Europe in the absence of a solution to the prolonged dollar shortage. Having considered in detail the first element in this strategy I shall now examine the state's commitment to neo-bilateralism, closely analysing the development of British trading agreements under Dalton's Chancellorship.

Neo-Bilateral Trade and Payments Arrangements

We need to be aware that, contrary to Bareau's opinion,[67] this neo-bilateral network was not simply adopted after the convertibility crisis of summer 1947, which finally laid to rest the early postwar American hopes of a turn to US-imposed multilateralism. Even by 16 April 1946 (only three months after the British ratification of the loan agreement) the UK had secured bilateral agreements with fourteen European nations, seven South American nations, and two Middle Eastern nation states; namely, France, Holland, Belgium, Switzerland, Denmark, Norway, Sweden, Czechoslovakia, Italy, Portugal, Finland, Spain, Greece, Turkey, Argentina, Bolivia, Brazil, Chile, Paraguay, Peru, Uruguay and the nations whom the *Economist* regarded as the most important Middle Eastern trading partners of Britain: Egypt and Iraq.[68] The importance of British trade with these nations is highlighted in that in 1938 they (plus Germany and British Empire nations) supplied 62 per cent of British imports and absorbed over 70 per cent of British export.[69]

I term these arrangements 'neo-bilateral' to distinguish them from prewar Central European bilateralism which was conducted (usually by Germany) on lines essentially different from these postwar arrangements. This earlier form of bilateralism involved both a competitive search for export markets and a large degree of exploitation in which the economically stronger nation (predominantly Germany in prewar Central Europe) imposed increasingly onerous terms of trade on weaker nations (by forcing debit balances, blocking credit balances, arbitrary supply and purchase offers, discriminatory pricing and other such methods), leading to a significant degree of economic and political penetration seriously undermining government policies to expand the trade of the weaker nation. Contrary to this exploitative form of bilateralism the British postwar neo-bilateral arrangements emerged particularly from the search for controlled and balanced imports, and recognised the importance of consistent exchange rates and prices, together with the need to avoid unadjusted payments balances.[70] The objective of these arrangements was to seek a monetary rather than a trade balance with the respective nation, with numerous provisions for flexible clearing methods, capital movements and for transactions with third nations clearly stated in many of the agreements. This was the case inasmuch as the majority of the agreements sanctioned a widening of the trading area beyond the basic two-nation structure. Thus Britain effectively represented and negotiated for the entire Sterling Area whilst agreements with France drew in the nations of the Franc Area, those with Holland drew in the Netherland's colonial areas, and those with Belgium took into consideration Luxembourg and the Belgian Empire.

To gain a deeper understanding of the neo-bilateral aspect of the British state's accumulation strategy we need to look in detail at the precise form of those arrangements and see how apparent contradictions between the signing of such contracts and the strictures of the Washington Agreement were resolved.

Work began on neo-bilateral strategies early in summer 1944, culminating in the first European monetary agreement signed with Belgium on 5 October 1944.[71] By the time Keynes arrived in Washington to negotiate the dollar credit, the UK had signed bilateral agreements with all the major Western European governments listed above, except Portugal and Switzerland, with whom discussions were in progress. The government, the Treasury and the Bank of England took the general view that these arrangements would serve for

Labour's entire term of office with no immediate prospect of reviving full convertibility of currencies under the leadership of sterling or of a return to multilateral world trade.

Although there existed variations, the general pattern of the monetary arrangements can be summarised from the main features of the Anglo-Belgian agreement.[72] First, under this agreement each central bank agreed to sell its currency against the currency of the other at a fixed official rate of exchange. Secondly, except for the Scandinavian nations who negotiated unlimited credit facilities, these sales of currencies had a limit attached to them beyond which sales would be made against gold (the gold ceiling or 'gold points' system). Sterling paid to a resident of Belgium could be freely transferred to another Belgian resident or resident of the Sterling Area, and finally transfer could be extended beyond Belgium and the Sterling Area if the UK government gave its approval (the system of 'administrative transferability'). In other cases, where a nation's currency was deemed not to be of international standing, a payments rather than a monetary agreement was negotiated which was not on a reciprocal basis since all settlements had to be made in sterling. The monetary agreements thus regularised payments relations with an important number of trading countries at a time when the disequilibria in international production and trade between the Western and Eastern hemispheres ruled out the development of a genuinely multilateral system. Administrative transferability allowed sterling a more gradual resumption of its international currency responsibilities without making further inroads into the inadequate British reserves of gold and dollars. It was therefore a successful and ingenious strategy designed to maximise non-dollar trade and provide the most extensive multilateral system feasible in the absence of a solution to the chronic dollar shortage.

Bilateralism and the Loan Obligations

Nevertheless, under the Washington agreements Britain had pledged to removed 'all restrictions on payments and transfers' from the UK to any other nation, and to make the sterling receipts of all Sterling Area countries arising out of current transactions 'freely available for current transactions in any currency areas without discrimination'. These Articles clearly cut across the bilateral arrangements and prompted David Waley, a prominent Treasury official in Overseas Finance, to suggest that the time spent in negotiating the bilateral relations had been wasted and there was no point in proceeding further with such strategies.[73] With the US ratification of the Washington agreements on 15 July 1946 the British state had until 15 July 1947 to prepare for convertibility and non-discrimination – a programme, Ellis-Rees recalls, 'for which we had no relish and we did not really believe in'.[74] Largely under the influence of Cobbold, Deputy Governor of the Bank of England, the government rejected Waley's pessimism and agreed to retain the structure of the bilateral agreements. It was decided to meet the required multilateral obligations not by disregarding but by supplementing the existing monetary arrangements (thus indicating how highly the British state, and in particular the Bank of England, regarded the agreements as part of the UK's overall accumulation strategy).

Beginning, therefore, with Argentina on 3 October 1946 the government negotiated supplementary monetary agreements, leaving the basis of the existing arrangements intact, with all the major trading nations (except France, Denmark and Switzerland, with whom negotiations continued, and various Iron Curtain nations given special exemption by the US government) by 15 July 1947.[75] These supplementary agreements created a transferable accounts system whereby the area in which sterling could be freely transferred (automatic transferability) was extended as more nations became party to the arrangement. The restructuring of the international money markets therefore created a world situation consisting of American account areas – within which sterling was freely convertible into US dollars on demand and freely transferable to other accounts; the Sterling Area – which as stated earlier had always allowed free convertibility of sterling via the dollar pooling mechanism; the transferable accounts area – a gradually expanding area within which sterling was fully convertible via automatic transferability; and a miscellaneous area consisting of nations largely inconsequential to world trade and temporarily exempted from the Washington conventions.[76]

In this way the British state somewhat hesitantly fulfilled the convertibility obligation of the Washington agreements. Yet this situation once again dramatically changed on 20 August 1947 with the suspension of convertibility and the abrogation of the supplementary agreements following the severe drain in Britain's dollar reserves. With this unilateral British action breaching the Washington agreement the international monetary system was thrown into chaos. On the one hand, the privileges of the American account area and the

Sterling Area remained virtually unchanged, with all sterling accruing to American accounts freely convertible (sterling accruing to American accounts was, however, no longer automatically transferable to bilateral account nations) and the British dollar drain therefore continued due to the adverse position of the UK's trade balance. On the other hand, many nations of the former transferable account areas found their rights of automatic transferability withdrawn and the system of administrative transferability reinstated. Thus the withdrawal of the automatic right of holders of transferable accounts to pay their sterling to Americans was the main technical change by which convertibility was suspended.[77]

In addition, a large bilateral account area was recreated through which the original monetary agreements with their stipulated 'gold point' system determined the degree of individual nation's currency convertibility. The post-convertibility world thus consisted of an American account area and a Sterling Area virtually unchanged with free sterling convertibility; a transferable account area regulated by administrative transferability with sterling received by any member nation freely transferable within that country, within the whole area on current account and to the Sterling Area (but not, of course, automatically to the American account area); a bilateral account area similarly regulated by administrative transferability but with sterling received by each nation only transferable within that country or to the Sterling Area without special Treasury permission; and a residual area of nations inconsequential to world trade which remained unaffected by the entire convertibility episode (the Appendix illustrates these complex changes on a nation by nation basis).

In broad outline these were the changes wrought in the international circuits of money capital within the span of Dalton's Chancellorship. The fact that the postwar British state had 'no better alternative than to rely on [these previous negotiated] monetary and payments agreements',[78] highlights the significance of the bilateral arrangements for the state's accumulation strategy. The modifications fashioned in the post-convertibility period were not designed to limit the transfer of sterling as an ultimate end but rather to preclude the loss of gold and dollars to third countries.[79] In fact, as noted previously, the state encouraged the maximum degree of transferability compatible with the preservation of the reserves, aiming if possible to reach equilibrium in trade and payments balances by bringing the shorter side of the account up to the larger, aptly illustrating the concept of 'expansionist bilateralism'.[80]

The realisation that the British state pursued a strategy of accumulation heavily dependent on a system of neo-bilateral trade and payments arrangements, both before and after its brief flirtation with multilateralist full convertibility, invalidates an interpretation of postwar development which focuses on a capitulation to American hegemony. More precisely the foregoing analysis reveals the state pursuing a dual accumulation strategy consisting of an expanded network of neo-bilateral trade and monetary arrangements bolstered by a massive US dollar injection into the UK economy enabling the vital purchase of supplies, raw materials and capital goods necessary for economic recovery and the implementation of the sweeping programme of domestic reconstruction on the basis of which the Labour government was elected.

To consolidate the view that the British state adopted a dual accumulation strategy in this period, ultimately at odds with the early postwar wishes of the US administration and involving an ambivalent attitude towards European integration, it is necessary for this chapter to consider finally how the two remaining 'enshrined principles of the Loan Agreement'[81] – non-discrimination and the elimination of preferences – fared under Dalton's Chancellorship.

The Application of Non-Discrimination and the Elimination of Trade Preference

The suspension of convertibility presented the British state with severe tactical problems, in regard both to the newly negotiated bilateral agreements and to the application of Article Nine of the Washington agreement – the non-discrimination clause. As indicated above, the piecemeal negotiation of the supplementary monetary agreements allowed many nations the right of convertibility several months before the official commencement date of 15 July 1947. Thus, for instance, Belgium, Luxembourg, the Netherlands and Portugal advised exporters that they could invoice in convertible sterling from 27 February 1947.[82] Contrary, therefore, to Jay's latest recollection[83] that the 'loan began to melt away' on the establishment of convertibility in July 1947, we should be aware that convertibility had a much longer time span covering almost a six-month period for many nations.

It is wrong to assume that the 1947 balance of payments crisis resulted simply from the convertibility obligation. The dollar drain had its origin in a number of factors.[84] A substantial rise in world prices affected British imports from December 1945 onwards (the US wholesale price index rising 40 per cent between December 1945 and March 1947). The fuel crisis of February 1946 (estimated to have cost £200 million worth of exports), disappointing domestic agriculture production, excessively slow military demobilisation and miscellaneous but significant dollar costs in occupied Germany all intensified the drain on resources. The strictures of the convertibility obligation, estimated to have cost the UK government over $500 million in sterling conversions, supplemented but did not precipitate the dollar drain. When convertibility was suspended on 20 August 1947 only $400 million of the US credit remained undrawn. Investigations now show that over 70 per cent of the drawings were to meet liabilities incurred by the UK in its own visible and invisible trading transactions with a further 20 per cent to meet the needs of the rest of the Sterling Area and only approximately 6 per cent accounted for by third nation sterling conversions.[85] Nevertheless, the US Treasury still regarded the loan agreement as the basis of the postwar international economic order. With the failure of convertibility, attention shifted to the issue of non-discrimination. Pumphrey of the US Treasury stressed that 'the convertibility provisions had never been as seriously taken as the non-discrimination provisions'.[86]

Following the demise of convertibility and the temporary failure of the Key Currency approach, the US administration throughout the rest of Dalton's Chancellorship focused increasingly on the significance of further concessions on imperial preference linked to non-discriminatory trading as outlined under Article Nine, even to the extent of threatening blackmail about further financial assistance and the unfreezing of the $400 million worth of undrawn credit.[87]

Again, to argue that these obligations imposed increasingly onerous pressure on the Attlee government ultimately forcing British capitulation is not accurate. The non-discrimination clause, which proposed that Britain must not buy goods which could be obtained from the US or elsewhere at slightly cheaper prices, was effectively ignored by the British state in trade transactions. Thus Attlee later commented that 'with regard to non-discrimination the provisions of the Loan Agreement have hardly been operative at all'.[88] Despite publicly expressed fears that the minor nuisances of the clause (Britain had curtailed the import of periodicals from Australia and revoked certain open licenses for the import of particular fruit and vegetables)[89] might become serious hardships following the balance of payments difficulties of 1947, the British government had since April 1947 repeatedly stressed to the Americans that Article Nine did not precisely define non-discrimination and its interpretation, therefore, was always subject to ambiguity and negotiation.[90]

This recalcitrant British attitude to the agreement initially led the US administration to examine carefully the rights assured them under mandate conventions, trusteeship agreements and other international acts. Yet confrontation over the issue was avoided by the State Department who subsequently agreed that, in conditions of a substantial imbalance in world trade, 'a too strict interpretation of the clause did not make sense'.[91] Indeed, when in 1949 the British government asked for an official cancellation of Article Nine, the US Treasury – a little bemused at the request – asked why Britain was raising the issue of the clause 'when we had so far been allowed to discriminate without objection from them'.[92] The 'under the counter' arrangements hitherto practised in connection with Article Nine woud be endangered and held up to ridicule if international public attention became focused on the clause, as would necessarily be the case in the circumstances of an official cancellation.

Dalton's remark, made to the House of Commons, that 'we [the British government] have punctually kept our word . . . because . . . [as] part of the British way of life . . . when we sign a document we keep to it'[93] was a long way from the truth. As Playfair of the Treasury privately admitted, 'we have broken our agreements right and left . . . in substance we are very far wide of the loan agreement . . . [and the only remaining question is] how far we can prudently dress it up to look as if we were inside it'.[94]

A similar fate befell the US efforts to reduce British trade preferences. In spite of American claims that British concessions on preferences failed to meet any legitimate expectations,[95] it is far from clear that the US Congress were at this stage willing to sanction serious tariff liberalisation. Following the failure of the Marshall Aid integrative strategies the US administration did not seriously attempt to promote European integration via policies of trade liberalisation until 1949 as the following chapters will demonstrate. In the immediate postwar years covered by Dalton's Chancellorship, this reticence on the part of the US over tariff concessions was met by an ambiguous British response, resulting in a virtual stalemate on the general subject of preference reduction.

On the one hand, the widely shared views, voiced for instance by the Federation of British Industry, that concessions should be made only on receipt of a comparable value in return with no question of unilaterally abandoning present Commonwealth agreements,[96] were tempered by early British Treasury estimates that 'there would be great advantages to us from a general clearance of trade barriers'.[97] Indeed, despite US claims to the contrary, close analysis of the British Imperial Preference system established at Ottawa in 1932 (allowing duty-free status on approximately 80 per cent of all imports from the Empire) shows that although the US lost ground due to the operation of the system in New Zealand markets (the smallest of the major Empire markets), America maintained its overall share of the UK and Indian markets whilst actually increasing its share in commerce with South Africa and Australia.[98] The issue of trade preference was unresolved throughout Dalton's era with neither the US nor the UK certain of the consequences of early tariff reduction, and strong lobbies in each case preventing the realisation of the agreements regarding preferences signed in conjunction with the loan agreement at Washington.

The potential contradictions inherent in claiming that the British state pursued a dual accumulation strategy consisting of a *de jure* commitment to multilateralism and a *de facto* adoption of neo-bilateral trade and monetary arrangements are therefore resolved when it is realised that the multilateralist obligations of the loan agreement were largely ignored by the UK given the postwar environment of a serious maldistribution in the structure of world production and in the world's demand and supply for internationally traded commodities. Analysis of the loan agreement reveals that the development of a genuinely multilateral accumulation strategy depended less upon internationally agreed principles of currency convertibility and non-discriminatory trade and more fundamentally on the underlying pattern of trade arrangements and the international structure of productive capital.

Given an appropriate condition of balance in world production and trade, the multilateral flow of trade and payments can function as an automatic regulator to effect the constant adjustments in production and trade throughout the world necessary to maintain this balance. The First World War had however thrown the multilateral system out of balance by disrupting the productive capacity and the gold reserves and foreign investments of Europe, whilst simultaneously stimulating an equally immense development of production in the United States. In the interwar period the US was reluctant to see the balance restored via large increases in her imports or decreases in her exports. A favourable US balance of payments was therefore maintained by reconstruction loans and private overseas investment which sharply declined from 1929 onwards as world economic conditions deteriorated and there was a return to restrictive bilateral trading.

The economic effects of the Second World War repeated the pattern of 1914–18 but on an even more immense scale. The United Kingdom's great need in 1945 was to have a breathing space in which to develop a strategy to meet the needs of reconstruction, in international circumstances where a balance in world production and trade was lacking. With the aid of dollar credits the British state could begin to restore equilibrium in its balance of payments and slowly expand international trade within a neo-bilateral system protecting inconvertible sterling.

The US State Department, however, feared the discriminatory practices which the war had done much to encourage and attempted to instigate policies which would force the UK to make an immediate contribution to the creation of full world multilateralism. With apparent indifference to the imbalanced world economic situation the US sought to force the issue on the removal of discrimination against the dollar whilst amassing annual balance of payments surpluses with the rest of the world of approximately $8 billion.

The negotiation of the Washington agreement thus turned less for the Americans on supporting British economic reconstruction and more on securing conditions for the removal of discrimination against the dollar.

In a situation where the future direction of British external financial policy had not been conclusively decided, the Americans insisted on sterling convertibility as the prime condition of dollar assistance. Britain's acceptance of the terms of the loan (and the deferment of other possible objectives of external financial policy such as the abandonment of sterling as an international currency or the construction of an exclusive international system based on sterling), was taken with the full realisation that the conditions were simply 'paper concessions' made at the time when Britain desperately needed dollars and it was clear that the State Department objectives for Britain were economically and politically 'unobtainable'.[99]

The economic chaos of the postwar period and the dollar shortage, of which the UK's persistent deficit was a manifestation,[100] made it impossible for the British state to adhere faithfully to any condition for removing restrictions from the transferability of sterling. Without Sterling Area viability, more general equilibrium between the dollar and non-dollar areas, considerably higher foreign currency reserves and more concessionary American financial policies, the British state considered convertibility 'a Utopian idea'.[101]

Nevertheless, the state was aware that the international standing of sterling could be used as a strong bargaining counter to extract American assistance. In the negotiations on sterling balances, for instance, the state emphasised the idea of the international role of sterling in three ways. First, they opposed any arrangement for the creation of more than one class of sterling (sterling accumulated before a particular date and that accumulated after this date). Secondly, the state opposed the US wish to arbitrarily cancel or block balances of foreign holders; and thirdly, they recommended that negotiations with foreign holders over the amount to be released 'should be on the generous side'.[102]

Although the UK therefore privately dismissed the reintroduction of convertibility in the immediate or near future, it took steps to restore confidence in the international position of sterling whilst accepting the principle that sterling in non-resident hands could not be wholly inconvertible (hence the 'transferable' and 'administrative' sterling arrangements). Exploring the tension between these principles gave Britain sufficient latitude to extract immediate dollar aid from the US whilst retaining control over the transferability of sterling and consequently blocking State Department objectives.

In the wake of Britain's dual accumulation strategy the US administration shelved the Key Currency/Bretton Woods approach. 'Convertibility', the US Treasury informed Truman in September 1947 'in the old sense was dead and would remain so for some time to come.'[103] It now began to promote a more flexible European Recovery Programme less dependent on clauses such as non-discrimination, and aimed more directly at British-led European integration, administered through such agencies as the Committee of European Economic Co-operation and its descendant, the Organisation for European Economic Co-operation. This takes the analysis beyond Dalton's Chancellorship, which ended ignominiously on 13 November 1947, towards a study of Britain's economic strategy under Cripps.

4 The Marshall Offensive

It is generally argued that by the autumn of 1947 Britain faced an imminent economic collapse that was only averted by timely American assistance offered in the form of Marshall aid. The view that Britain, and more generally Western Europe, faced an 'impending economic catastrophe'[1] in late 1947 was expressed by Clayton in May 1947, who concluded: 'without further prompt and substantial aid from the United States, economic, social and political disintegration will overwhelm Europe'.[2] Similarly, Oliver Franks, chairman of the Committee of European Economic Co-operation, set up on the 15 July 1947, took the view that 'in the spring of 1947 the economic and social state of Western Europe was far graver than in the thirties',[3] whilst Dean Acheson defended foreign aid in terms of 'our duty and our privilege as human beings' facing 'the facts of international life . . . [which] . . . mean that the United States is going to have to undertake further emergency financing of foreign purchases if foreign countries are to continue to buy in 1948 and 1949 the commodities which they need to sustain life and at the same time rebuild their economies'.[4] Subsequent interpretations have portrayed this 'annus horrendus',[5] the 'crisis year of unrelieved disaster'[6] as a turning point forcing the Labour government to yet further levels of subordination and capitulation to American interests.

We are led to believe that, faced with a seemingly intractable economic crisis, the British state eagerly grasped the 'economic lifeline'[7] offered in the form of Marshall aid and thereby 'accepted American leadership in the new world economic and political order . . . subordinating British interests to American, but maintaining those roles and commitments which the Americans found useful'.[8] The consolidation of American hegemony in the North Atlantic area, it is claimed, went beyond Britain simply assuming junior partner status in a US-dominated world economic structure, and involved 'a concrete transformation of the European class structure along lines of the US model'.[9] In short, 'through the Marshall offensive, the *Pax Americana* was imposed on the economic ruins of the defunct *Pax Britannica* in Europe'.[10]

The initial purpose of this chapter is to evaluate this interpretation. Both aspects of the position – first, that Britain faced acute economic

71

disaster in 1947, and secondly, that Marshall aid involved further British capitulation to American hegemony – will be explored in detail. In keeping with the overall emphasis of the book this account will begin with an analysis of the British economy as it developed from 1946 to the middle of 1948, before turning to analyse the foreign policy manoeuvrings of the US administration as they materialised in the form of the Marshall Plan. The British state's reaction to the Marshall Plan in the context of the dual accumulation strategy developed under Dalton's Chancellorship will then receive attention. This will take the form of a close study of Britain's attitude towards US integrative policies, developments in the sphere of productive capital, changes in intra-European trade and payments arrangements, and an analysis of the structure and workings of the European Marshall aid agencies, the CEEC and its descendant, the OEEC. The basis and the effects of Marshall aid will then have been sufficiently clarified to enable a more precise interpretation of the state's economic strategy in this period to emerge. Specifically this chapter will propose that, far from 1947 being seen as the turning point in British recovery with Marshall aid halting Britain's deterioration and enabling a 'great economic leap forward'[11] to occur, Marshall aid disbursements to Britain were primarily used for food imports releasing resources to enable the already widespread domestic reconstruction programmes to continue. This is a conclusion which supports the so-called 'European revisionist' view of the impact of Marshall (most impressively presented by Milward (1984) on whose argument this chapter draws), which must be argued in detail, given Kindleberger's opinion that it is 'supported neither by evidence . . . nor by recollection' (Kindleberger (1987) p. 252).

In contrast to the orthodoxy represented by Kindleberger which sees 1947 as the economic watershed, it is in many ways more accurate to view the early 1950s as a more significant turning point in British accumulation, with a redirection of British industry away from an overriding concern with exports towards the development of a large-scale domestic consumer market based on relative surplus value productive techniques occurring under Butler's Chancellorship.

This is not to suggest that the Marshall offensive did not aim to lay the foundations for an Atlantic economy based on the generalised export of American accumulation conditions. This clearly was a primary aim of the US administration. Contrary to the majority of accounts, however, this objective was not achieved by the Marshall Plan. Specific factors constrained the export of US capital to the UK in the Marshall period and the insignificant US investment which did occur under Cripps's Chancellorship never carried with it the implication that Britain had become subordinated to an Atlantic economy dominated by the United States. Close analysis shows that the mechanisms of the Marshall offensive by which the US sought to achieve hegemony were continually undermined by the actions of the British and French states which sought, as in previous negotiations, to extract the maximum benefit from the US aid whilst incurring the minimum loss of economic or political sovereignty.

Contrary to those accounts which insist on simplifying the development of the postwar international economic order by claiming that the latter can either be understood in terms of the 'Bretton Woods system' or the 'capitulation to American hegemony' thesis, this chapter further develops the alternative argument presented in the previous sections. This view indicates that the British state forged an accumulation strategy which had little to do with the New Hampshire talks, and which constantly sought to thwart US foreign economic policy ideals involving an uneven series of temporary alliance and short-term compromise measures designed to support the growing British economy as European nation-states scrambled for dollars.

I THE 1947 CRISIS

A confusing tendency amongst contemporary analysts is to study the impact of American aid in relation to Western Europe as a whole. This results in an artificial conflation of the individual crises experienced by Western European states and leads to imprecise judgements on the impact of Marshall. This confusing conflation is not simply the product of retrospection.

The belief in the US State and Treasury Departments that the piecemeal *ad hoc* approach to reconstruction had broken down by late 1946 substantially contributed to a failure on the part of the US administration to distinguish between the scale of Western European crises in 1947. State Department archives indicate that decisions on the allocation of aid and the basic question of who should qualify as primary beneficiaries were still contested with the Treasury Department more than eight months after Marshall's address (see Kindleberger (1987) p. 252). Isolating the precise nature of Britain's economic crisis is therefore a prerequisite to assessing whether

Marshall dollars were necessary or incidental to British economic and political reconstruction.

The existence of 'grave economic distress',[12] identified in Clayton's memorandum, carried the implication of total imminent economic collapse. This implication on which Marshall based his Harvard address (and largely taken at face value by analysts since) is simply not borne out by a review of British economic indicators in that year.

Production and Trade Prior to Marshall

British capital between 1946 and 1950 achieved rates of growth of industrial production which have never been sustained since. The index of industrial production (average 1946 = 100) for all industries, achieved a monthly average throughout 1947 of 108 points despite the disruption experienced in February and March resulting from the coal shortage aggravated by the harsh winter.[13] By September 1947 – a period of imminent collapse, according to many analysts echoing Marshall's assessment – the index of industrial production had risen to 115 points, climbing in November to 123: almost a 25 per cent increase in industrial production over the 1946 level. This trend continued throughout 1948 and 1949 which averaged indices of industrial production of 121 and 129 respectively[14] enabling overall industrial production levels to rise by approximately 7–8 per cent annually between 1946 and 1950.

By early 1948 (before Marshall aid payments began to reach Britain) production targets had been attained for deep-mined coal extraction and had been exceeded by 9.5 per cent in open-cast coal mining. Similarly, shipbuilding exceeded its production target whilst the output of steel ingots, sheet steel and iron castings averaged a figure of 3.5 per cent in excess of estimated production.[15] The production of motor vehicles had risen from a weekly average of 1586 in 1938 to a figure of 10 377 per week in September 1948. The weekly output of passenger cars totalled 6926 in September 1948 of which 5046 were produced for export in addition to 1984 commercial vehicles a week exported, producing a record export level for the motor vehicle industry.[16]

A review of the building and civil engineering industries reveals similar trends. With over 1 005 000 operatives employed in these industries in September 1947, a total of 460 000 homes (including 149 000 permanent houses, 127 000 temporary houses and 181 000 conversions and repairs) had been created by autumn of that year, compared with a total of 5500 homes 'fit for heroes' provided in the two-year period following the First World War.[17] An impressive programme of capital investment had also been achieved in this period with, for instance, £14 million of new machine tools produced for the re-equipment of the engineering industries and a gross capital investment figure for 1946 as a whole, including both maintenance and new construction, in excess of £1300 million.[18]

For British productive capital an uneven but unmistakable increase in overall productivity and output had occurred since 1946 and gained momentum despite intermittent fuel shortages throughout 1947. The theory of Britain's imminent economic collapse therefore cannot be explained in terms of industrial stagnation.

Furthermore, despite Clayton's view that 'millions of people in the cities are slowly starving',[19] the estimated calorific value of daily per capita food consumption in the UK increased from a figure of 2800 for the crop year 1945–6 to 2900 for the crop year 1946–7, with the index of weekly wage rates for all industries increasing in proportion, but not falling behind, the retail price index for 1947.[20] When the performance of British exports is examined a similar upward trend emerges. The dynamic nature of productive capital was reflected in the increase in the value of exports of UK goods in 1947 which was, apart from 1920, the highest on record and nearly two-and-a-half times the 1938 figure. Allowing for price rises since 1938, the volume of exports in July 1947 had increased to 26 per cent more than in 1938 with the fourth quarter volume index figure approximately 117 points – showing a substantial improvement on the first two quarters' figures of 101 and 102 respectively, which were particularly affected by the fuel crisis and adverse weather which disrupted the transport of goods for export.[21] Exports of machinery and electrical goods reached record levels. In the second half of 1947, 88 per cent of exports were mainly manufactured articles, 2.5 per cent raw material exports, and 6 per cent food, drink and tobacco article exports.[22]

This vigorous upward trend of British exports continued throughout 1948 with a 32-point upward movement in the index of the volume of exports recorded in the second quarter of 1948 over the comparable 1947 figure. By July 1948 the index stood at 149 points (1938 = 100), exceeding the target figure set for export-led economic recovery by the government in late 1947, without Marshall aid in any substantial form having reached the UK.[23] The claim that Britain faced imminent economic collapse cannot draw support from this second indicator of economic development, the level of exports.

Domestic Reconstruction and the Sterling Crisis

The 'crisis' of 1947 can now be clarified. Full employment, capital reconstruction and rising domestic welfare had been pursued with a certain indifference to the diminishing levels of gold and dollar reserves held by the postwar state.[24] Dalton's frequent Cabinet warnings that 'we are racing through our US dollar credit at a reckless, ever-accelerating speed'[25] illustrate this orientation of the Attlee administration. The decision to link expanding output to increased exports in an attempt to sustain an ambitious dollar-fed domestic reconstruction programme had – as Milward (1984, ch. 1) points out – predictable, and at times severe, implications for the level of British foreign currency reserves in a world economic context of dollar shortage and US near-monopoly of vital raw materials. Before the UK had financed large trade deficits with the US via a high level of invisible earnings plus the earnings of dollars in third markets, predominantly in the underdeveloped world. By 1947 Europe was running a cumulated deficit on those invisibles of $0.6 billion[26] and the inconvertibility of sterling outside the Sterling Area and the US effectively closed off third-market dollar earnings, intensifying British dollar demand.

The real 'crisis' of 1947, therefore, had its origins not in industrial stagnation, starving populations or restricted exports but in the ambitious and successful domestic reconstruction programme pursued by the British state, that had been fuelled largely since 1945 by US and Canadian loans (Milward (1984) ch. 3). By 1947 this aid was almost exhausted. The British state faced a temporary but serious problem of diminishing foreign reserves. A survey of the direction of British exports, the magnitude of British imports and the crisis in the state's currency reserves will elucidate this interpretation.

Whilst the volume of British exports increased substantially throughout 1947 their destination had changed little from that of 1938. While in 1938 17 per cent of UK exports went to hard currency areas in the Western hemisphere, with 42 per cent directed to the Sterling Area, 36 per cent to Europe and approximately 4 per cent to the rest of the world, this pattern had changed little by 1947 with 16 per cent directed to the Western hemisphere, 47 per cent to the Sterling Area, 30 per cent to Europe and 5 per cent to the rest of the world.[27] The overall regional distribution of exports remained skewed in favour of the Sterling Area and Western Europe, drastically limiting the British state's dollar earning capacity in hard currency markets. This problem was compounded in that the regional distribution of imports to the UK had changed significantly since 1938 with the UK drawing in far more imports from the Western hemisphere. The prewar figure of imports from hard currency areas had totalled 30 per cent, with the Sterling Area supplying 31.5 per cent, Europe 34 per cent and the rest of the world approximately 4 per cent. By the second quarter of 1947 45 per cent of UK imports derived from hard US currency areas, with 30.5 per cent arriving from the Sterling Area, 4 per cent from the rest of the world and Europe supplying a diminished 19 per cent.[28] Imports from the Western hemisphere had increased from a monthly average of £25 million in 1938 to £83.1 million in July 1947.[29] The strain which this pattern of trade imposed upon Britain's foreign currency reserves (even taking into account the US and Canadian dollar credits) substantially contributed to the economic crisis of 1947 – the dwindling dollar reserves of the British state. The origins of this crisis have often been misunderstood and need careful study.

The Impact of the Convertibility Obligation

It is often suggested that the introduction of convertibility in 1947 marked a key episode in British economic history leading to a major crisis and provoking a decline in UK productive capital at the behest of the interests of the City of London which, it is claimed, were victorious in preventing 'national' industrial reconstruction and investment policies from receiving high priority. It is said that the interests of the national economy were scuppered by the victory of City interests forcing the acceptance of the reintroduction of the UK into a US-dominated liberal capitalist alliance.[30] In all these accounts the introduction of convertibility plays a key role in explaining the 1947 crisis. Thus Brett maintains that 'without the crisis created by convertibility, the huge reserve losses . . . would have been avoided'.[31] Yet the claim that 'the enforced attempt to introduce convertibility in July . . . led to a major crisis'[32] is largely untrue. Close analysis reveals that the net monthly drain in British gold and dollar reserves accelerated from $31 million in the first quarter of 1946, rising to $124 million in the fourth quarter of 1946 and reaching a figure of $322 million by March 1947.[33] A significant dollar drain had therefore begun before a single supplementary monetary agreement enabling sterling convertibility had been signed. With the official convertibility date, 15 July 1947, some four months away, the UK had already experienced a substantial drain in its dollar reserves. An examination of the UK drawings on the US credit provides interesting reading for those who give a high priority to the impact of the convertibility obligation.

In the last six months of 1946 the UK's total payment for its own commitments (including those of the Sterling Area) taken out of the US credit amounted to $510 million. In the first six months of 1947 this figure stood at $1630 million and in the final seven or so weeks until 23 August 1947 the total payment by the UK for its own commitments together with those of the Sterling Area taken out of the US credit amounted to $970 million.[34] In all, over $3350 million of the US credit had been drawn by the end of August 1947. A breakdown of the drawings reveals that 70 per cent were made to meet the liabilities incurred by the UK in its own visible and invisible trading transactions, with a further 20 per cent of the drawings made to meet the demands of the rest of the Sterling Area. Contrary to popular opinion, the operation of the convertibility clause (enabling currency convertibility to be extended to some South American nations and the majority of Western European countries) accounted for not more than 6 per cent of the drawings of the US credit (the conversions by Belgium, often singled out as a major contributor to the crisis, were later established to have been only $208 million).[35] Thus, whilst the convertibility clause drew widespread attention to the British dollar drain thereby supplementing the real crisis with a crisis of confidence in sterling, it is not the case that the rapid exhaustion of British gold and dollar reserves was brought about by the enforcement of the convertibility obligation. The two most important phenomena revealed by a study of the relevant public documents: that the drain began in a significant way before any supplementary monetary agreements had been signed, and that only 6 per cent of the drawings on the US credit can be traced to the operation of sterling conversion, indicate that the real causes of the foreign reserve crisis must be sought elsewhere.

The central explanation of the crisis in the British state's currency reserves must be related to the expanding industrial and domestic reconstruction programmes initiated under Dalton. The high demand for imports of raw materials, food, construction goods and other commodities essential to sustain this expansionist strategy coincided with the loss of dollar earnings in third markets and a contraction of invisible trade, making the possibility of dollar shortages ever more likely. The failure to increase exports to the hard currency areas

together with the necessity to increase imports from the Western
hemisphere in the wake of the destruction of many of the traditional
European and East European sources of imports began the rapid
exhaustion of UK foreign currency holdings.

The currency reserve problems resulting from the industrial and
commodity trade imbalance between the Eastern and Western hemispheres (the US trade balance on goods and services for instance in
1946 gathered a surplus of $7 billion increasing to $10.7 billion in
1947[36]) were compounded for Britain by the substantial rise in the
US index of wholesale prices which rose 40 per cent between
December 1946 and March 1947. This reduced the buying power of
the US credits by almost $1 billion from the time of the negotiation.[37]
The price paid for imports in early 1947 was therefore in excess of
260 per cent of the 1938 figures whilst the price of exports had
increased to only 210 per cent of the 1938 figure. This deterioration
in the terms of trade had a crucial impact on British foreign currency
reserves. Allied to this major cause of the crisis it is possible, as
indicated in the previous chapter, to cite the February fuel shortages,
estimated to have cost £200 million in lost and disrupted exports,
British dollar costs in Germany under the terms of the Fusion
Agreement which by mid-1947 was making a demand of $150 million
above UK estimates,[38] and the disappointing levels of domestic
agricultural production (linked to the generalised European failure
of recovery in primary production) which increased world price
inflation and accentuated the European dollar scarcity. To summarise,
contrary to the claims that the convertibility obligation led to the
crisis of 1947 it can be demonstrated that the major cause of the
rapid exhaustion of the US credit lay in the overseas expenditure of
the UK and the Sterling Area in its own visible and invisible trading
transactions in a context of dramatically rising US wholesale prices
and massive dependence on US sources of supply which placed an
undue strain on British foreign currency holdings.

The position of British capital accumulation in 1947 has thus been
sufficiently elucidated for this study to discount the view that Britain
was in the throes of a generalised economic paralysis, and to replace
Clayton and Marshall's erroneous opinions with a more precise
interpretation of the crisis which was precipitated by specific developments in Atlantic trade and intensified by expansionist domestic
reconstruction policies. Although, as I shall indicate, the British state
responded to this crisis by proposing to cut their planned investment
programme for 1948 by 18 per cent (a proposal which was never

carried through) and impose a more rigorous import policy, the fact remains that in large measure the reconstruction strategy continued.

Far from Marshall aid 'saving' a deteriorating economy, its resources were actually used by the state to ease balance of payments constraints enabling the economy to continue expansion without a return to the deflationary policies of the 1930s. Marshall dollars served to release resources for capital accumulation which otherwise would have lain idle; that is to say, they acted in a capital liberating rather than capital transfusing fashion.[39] The orthodox account that Marshall aid 'presented socialist Britain with an economic lifeline'[40] forcing the UK to new levels of subordination to US hegemony can only be refuted by close analysis of the policy ideals of the US together with a study of the amount and form of US aid to Britain, the structure and organisation of the European aid agencies, and the British state's objectives as they developed in response to the Marshall offensive. It is to these issues that the study must turn.

II   AMERICAN AND BRITISH ATTITUDES TO MARSHALL

The Key Currency Solution Discredited

With the suspension of sterling convertibility in August 1947 and the failure of the non-discrimination clause to be applied with any seriousness, Clayton acknowledged that 'the entire foreign economic policy of the United States was in jeopardy'.[41] The intensifying European dollar shortage indicated that the whole United States international economic programme would have to be written off as one country after another experienced dollar difficulties. As later recounted in a US Commission on Foreign Economic Policy report, by the second half of 1947 it had become painfully evident that the US's immediate postwar foreign economic policies grounded in the 'Bretton Woods/Key Currency proposal' alliance had been based upon 'incorrect political and economic assumptions'.[42] The assumptions that, first, in the transition phase the emergency needs left by the war could be met by orderly assistance programmes (by the British loan, credits extended in connection with other lend-lease settlements, loans from the Export–Import Bank, credits from the Bretton Woods institutions), and secondly, that after the transition phase private foreign investment would revive and together with the apparatus of the International Bank for Reconstruction and Development furnish an international monetary network suitable for an expanded world economy, proved a grossly inadequate appraisal of the international economic and political postwar situation. Yet the achievement of a system of multilateral world trade based on the twin pillars of sterling convertibility and non-discrimination in trade remained the driving force behind US foreign economic policy theorising. Although the Key Currency/Bretton Woods approach to achieving these aims had been thoroughly discredited by the summer of 1947 the aims themselves remained intact with the US Treasury continually pressing the British state for an outline of the methods by which the UK hoped to attain the agreed objectives – particularly that of convertibility.[43]

The need for a new approach to attain these objectives and simultaneously safeguard America's strategic political and military interests in Western Europe was intensified in 1947 not only by the extension of Soviet military power into Eastern Europe but also by the need of the US to maintain its colossal export surplus in the face of a predicted domestic recession. The lack of available international credit, the planned tapering off of US aid programmes and the depletion of foreign currency reserves made a sharp decline in US exports look inevitable.[44] To many in the administration, including Walter Salant and John Snyder of the President's Council of Economic Advisors, the US export trade – $14.7 billion in 1946 rising to $19.7 billion in 1947[45] – was much more than a cushion for any minor recession. Rather, they saw exports as a critical prop to the entire domestic economy.[46] Likewise, the State–War–Navy Co-ordinating Committee under General Hilldring (instructed by Acheson to investigate the world's need for further military and economic aid in conjunction with State Department representatives) concluded that any substantial decline in the US export surplus would have a depressing effect on business activity and employment in the US, with any significant drop in European purchases having serious implications for both world recovery and political stability.[47] The withdrawal of the UK from Greece and Turkey in February 1947 had also indicated to the US that military expenditure would have to be increased in the postwar period as the US, via the Truman doctrine, replaced Britain as the key defender of world liberal (and, in many cases, not so liberal) capitalist relations.

The US response to this crisis in foreign political and economic policy was to switch emphasis away from a focus on Britain as the sole key to economic recovery for the rest of the world towards a view that the integrated development of Europe as a whole was vital to world recovery and a prerequisite to achieving the general aims of US commercial and financial policy. Stressing the role of the economic recovery of West Germany, the substitution of a regional for a nation-by-nation approach to Europe's problems, and that there should be no substantial diversion of European resources from recovery to rearmament, the American administration sought to weaken the nation-state as the basis of the European political and economic system and attempt an integrated reconstruction of Western Europe under the banner of a 'recovery programme'. As Kindleberger, writing in 1950 of his experience working with the European Recovery Programme in the State Department recollects, it was designed to produce much more than economic recovery. With the issue of Western European integration pressing, the Marshall Plan was regarded as a golden opportunity to introduce a new era of European unification, since lack of European cohesion was 'held responsible for many deep-seated European ills' (Kindleberger (1987) pp. 47–8).

The turn towards the policy of European integration as a method of solving the German problem, maintaining capitalist relations in Europe, sustaining the US export surplus, halting Soviet advance and promoting US-style multilateralism under the apparently politically neutral guise of aid for increasing productivity and prosperity, had strong support in the US administration, echoing the much earlier co-operative internationalist schemes of Woodrow Wilson.[48]

This orientation of US foreign economic policy had been dormant during the Second World War when it was believed that a regional grouping in Western Europe could possibly destroy the universalism that was the objective of American postwar policy and that constituted the basis for American insistence on the creation of the United Nations.[49] In January 1947, however, it received a new impetus when John Foster Dulles called for the reconstruction of Europe along federal lines, including a decentralised German confederation, under American leadership.[50] The momentum for this type of solution gathered pace throughout 1947 and was consolidated by Acheson's speech that became the precursor to Marshall's Harvard address, in which he asserted that 'Europe's recovery cannot be complete until the various parts of Europe's economy are all working together in a harmonious whole . . . the achievement of a co-ordinated European economy remains a fundamental objective of our foreign policy'.[51]

Thus, by early June (prior to the Harvard address of 5 June) Acheson and Clayton had informed the British state that 'the piecemeal approach of fixing up one country after another will not receive political support and must be abandoned'.[52] The Bretton Woods/Key Currency solution had been 'thoroughly discredited' and Acheson and Clayton admitted that in the present situation they now 'had to eat practically every word that they had uttered before Congressional Committees during the past three years'.[53] The future lay in an integral plan of economic co-operation worked out for Europe as a whole, even if a temporary consequence of such integration in the context of a world dollar shortage would be discriminatory against the United States. The key to restoring European productivity, it was claimed, lay in a massive recovery programme transcending national boundaries and founded on the principles of collective action, maximum European self-help and mutual aid, the pooling of information and resources, and the reintegration of Germany which, it was emphasised, even in defeat 'is still the potential heart of Europe'.[54]

The US administration therefore advocated a form of free trade customs union in which the restrictions on the movement of capital would be removed from a particular area thereby maximising efficiency, output and income, allowing Europe to reach similar levels of productivity and prosperity to that already attained in the US, ultimately restoring the equilibrium in world trade without which US-style multilateralism was impossible. The Marshall offensive, it was claimed, would improve Western Europe's capacity to earn dollars both through increased exports and by an expanded inflow of US investment. This would create a situation in which the restoration of multilateralism, price stability and the recovery of production could be achieved whilst also realising the close link between the economic integration of Western Europe into one large market and the achievement of a stable, loyal political bloc.[55]

Before analysing the role planned for Britain in this new American approach it is important to consider the immediate British response to Marshall.

Britain's Strategy of Non-Committal Co-ordination

Many analysts report Bevin's initial reaction to the Marshall offer – 'it was like a lifeline to sinking men . . . we grabbed the lifeline with both hands'[56] – as an indication that the British state wholeheartedly

accepted the co-operative integrationist American terms and thereby
allowed the US to synchronise ruling-class hegemony in the North
Atlantic area.[57] But the interpretation outlined, for instance, by Bob
Lovett, US Under-Secretary of State, that 'the special wartime
position for Britain . . . [was] now inconsistent with the concept of
Western European integration and the other objectives of the
European Recovery Programme',[58] simply was not accepted by the
British state and was a position by no means taken for granted in the
US administration. The often invoked but little understood notion
of 'special relationship' could not be abandoned in the wake of the
Marshall offensive (even if successful), principally because it had a
material foundation which rested upon the US's continued reluctance
to assume the role of the world's financial centre. Convertibility and
the position of sterling as the world's premier currency were issues
which remained unresolved in the Marshall aid scheme and therefore
termination of the special relationship seemed premature to many
participants. The fact that the Overseas Finance Division of the
Treasury were studiously contemplating 'hammering out the basis for
a UK/US economic partnership' in March 1950[59] clearly indicates
that the economic integrationist aspect of the Marshall offensive was
never considered a viable proposition by the British state.

Britain's position on integration was clarified immediately after
Marshall's 5 June offer in a memorandum which explained:

> there are special considerations affecting the United Kingdom, as
> a world trading power, in any conception of this kind not only
> because we may be pressed to contribute towards the needs of
> Continental Europe goods which it is in our better interest to
> export elsewhere, but also because the whole conception of
> European 'integration' needs to be reconciled, if it can be, with
> our stated objective of a return to multilateral trade.[60]

If pressed on the issue, the UK delegation was informed to take the
line that there is no time, at least in the early stages, for more than a
rough and ready co-ordination of European requirements. In the
context of the view that 'it is not the policy of His Majesty's
government to participate in a federal regime in Western Europe
and in forms of integration leading up to such a system',[61] the British
state approached the Marshall offensive with an attitude of obtaining
maximum dollar aid whilst at the same time sufficiently safeguarding
the multiple interests and responsibilities which the UK had estab-

lished worldwide. Although fully aware that by accepting Marshall aid 'we might find ourselves involved in a subordination of our economic policy to the United States',[62] the British state avoided any such eventuality by a series of manoeuvres designed to save face with the Americans (thus ensuring dollar aid) whilst relinquishing no control, either to a European union or transatlantic ruling class alliance, of any major aspect of economic policy. Bevin's rather off-the-cuff Foreign Office view – now the received wisdom – which maintains that Britain simply grabbed with both hands Marshall's offer and was drawn, albeit reluctantly, into an integrationist position, does not stand close scrutiny. Rather, the strategy adopted by the British state in response to Marshall is best characterised as one of non-committal co-ordination. This was a policy developed by Britain in response to US charges of obstructionism. To benefit from US aid the UK took the initiative in European co-ordination gaining key positions in both the CEEC and the OEEC and thereby preventing the implementation of some of the wider US strategies whilst retaining full control of domestic policy making. A consideration of how the state viewed Marshall's offer in the context of the crisis in Britain's currency reserve levels further supports this interpretation.

The State's Search for Dollars

As outlined above, the crisis in the state's reserve holdings did not reflect an overall crisis in production or distribution. The crisis arose, the Cabinet had deciphered by October 1947, 'not because we cannot produce enough in the UK to pay for the supplies we need but because we cannot sell our goods in the market from which our supplies alone can come'.[63] The large proportion of foodstuffs and raw materials imported from the Western hemisphere could not be matched by a sufficient export of UK goods to dollar markets to bring about a dollar balance. Moreover, in the context of the world shortage of dollars and the inconvertibility of sterling, the earning of dollars via UK surpluses in third markets was an avenue now largely blocked. The Cabinet therefore concluded: 'whatever we do to maximise our production and so our exports, even if we greatly exceed our target, we shall be met by the same, for us, insuperable difficulty'.[64] In this situation the British state welcomed dollar aid from any quarter so long as it did not violate two essential conditions. The débâcle of the Anglo-American Financial Agreement led the government to vow privately that 'we shall never again accept a commitment which we do not honestly believe that we can carry out and maintain', and secondly, 'we shall not accept any commitment to come into operation at some particular date in the future. Circumstances can change and 1947 taught us (and one hopes the USA) a bitter lesson in this respect.'[65] The state's acceptance of American aid 'must depend on the form in which it may be given, and the conditions which may be attached to it'.[66] Given such provisos the flexible Marshall aid scheme, with its vague and ambiguous notion of integration, its grant-in-aid rather than loan status and its wide-ranging general nature appealed to the government as a way of gaining dollars in the wake of the rigid, rapidly timetabled, precisely conditioned loan previously secured from the US.

We should recognise that the Marshall offer represented only one avenue that the state explored in late 1947 in an attempt to ease the foreign currency crisis. In a series of manoeuvres, including investigating the possibility of enlisting the services of private financier Sir Clarence Sadd to arrange a dollar credit between a consortium of British and New York banks,[67] the UK Treasury unofficially assessed how the foreign reserve balance could be improved. In addition to attempting to amend the regulations of the IMF to enable two years' drawings to be made in one lump sum, the Treasury pronounced on various measures of 'subterfuge'[68] principally involving the Reconstruction Bank, in a complex effort to gain dollars whilst maintaining a finely balanced tactical position both in regard to the Marshall proposals and the application of Article Nine (non-discrimination) 'so as to give no legitimate excuse to the American government for arguing that we had not fulfilled the assurances we had given them'.[69] This tactical strategy included the ploy of drawing heavily upon British foreign currency reserves to resensitise Washington to the British crisis, thereby creating a situation in which the plain evidence that the UK was down on its reserves might jerk the State Department into a more rapid timetable for Marshall.

Whilst the Cabinet was aware that there would be no further substantial aid to anyone except within the ambit of the Marshall Plan, and that this would be given to each country as a result of bilateral negotiations which themselves would form part of a more general plan, the open-ended nature of this general plan was easily reconciled both with the continuation of Labour's domestic reconstruction programme and with the provisos underlying the British state's financial policy. US dollar aid, it was assumed, would flow more easily to Britain as part of a general plan than through a separate renegotiation. This assumption proved accurate. To chart how the British state refashioned the US understanding of Marshall into a less threatening dollar aid scheme incapable of imposing US hegemony on the UK we need to analyse how the vague Marshall proposals evolved into a series of fact-gathering, dollar-distributing, technical co-ordinating committees largely dominated by UK representatives.

III THE ADMINISTRATIVE APPARATUS

Setting up the CEEC

The notion that upon hearing Marshall's 5 June offer Bevin 'moved into action . . . with zest and speed' creating a 'new basis for the political and economic development of the North Atlantic world'[70] is a pleasant enough myth for those who believe in history as a succession of events enacted by 'great individuals of the era', but nevertheless is an entirely false interpretation. In late May the Attlee administration had been informed of a US aid programme for an integrated Western Europe[71] and by 2 June Acheson and Clayton had made it clear that Britain should take 'a more vigorous lead in trying to bring Western European countries together'.[72] In view of the British state's opinion that 'the UK cannot participate in any wide expansion of preferential tariff systems or in any European integration fund',[73] the motivation behind the British initiative lay in gaining control of any 'integrative movement' in order to defuse the most disagreeable aspects of such a scheme.

A second related myth which should be dispelled is the opinion that Marshall intended his offer to extend to the Soviet Union and Eastern Europe. Marshall's statement that 'our policy is directed not against any country or doctrine but against hunger, poverty, desperation and chaos'[74] is often taken at face value to infer that 'the offer was made to Europe, not just to Western Europe. They did not wish to divide Europe: responsibility for that must lie with the Russians'.[75] Yet the insistence that US aid depended on a co-ordinated European response leading to European economic integration obviously prevented Soviet acceptance. This was eminently clear (and eminently acceptable) to the Attlee government who recognised on 6 June that 'Marshall's "new plan" is explicitly anti-Russian'. However, for publicity purposes 'we presumably want to make the "new plan" look as Pan-European and as little anti-Russian as we can'.[76] The Soviet Union's view that European countries should put up their requirements individually without a co-ordinated programme was made the point of great contention by the British and French states, eventually leading to Molotov's withdrawal and the Soviets objecting that the preparation of an overall programme meant that smaller European states were being subject to big power domination which would threaten national sovereignty. The British and French insistence on a co-ordinated programme, Molotov prophesied, would not result in the unification or reconstruction of Europe but rather beget divisiveness.[77] It is clear from this episode that neither Bevin nor Bidault wanted Soviet participation, and equally clear that Marshall breathed 'a sigh of relief when Molotov refused to play' (Kindleberger (1987) p. 100). The fact that Britain and France eventually presented a series of individual 'shopping lists' under a weak guise of co-ordination to the US administration for the distribution of aid (on a basis hardly inconsistent with the original Soviet proposal), shows without doubt that the Soviet Union was excluded from participation in the Marshall Plan on political grounds at every level of its execution. Moreover a primary reason for setting up the Committee of European Economic Co-operation (CEEC) as the European counterpart to the US Economic Co-operation Administration (ECA) (headed by Hoffman who saw his purpose as 'saving the world from the gang in the Politburo' compared to whom 'Hitler was a baby'[78]) in preference to working through the UN's Economic Commission for Europe, was that the Soviet Union had six out of the seventeen votes in this latter body and it would therefore have been difficult to marginalise the Soviet Union or draw up the necessary co-ordinated programme without the formation of a new body.[79]

Following a series of Bevin/Bidault discussions it was decided to set up a 'temporary organisation'[80] for co-ordinating US aid in the form of a 'Committee of Assistance' which would regulate the work of technical sub-committees dealing with subjects such as food and agriculture, fuel and power, iron and steel, transport and manpower. Sixteen nations – Austria, Belgium, Denmark, France, Greece, The Netherlands, Eire, Italy, Luxembourg, Norway, Iceland, Portugal, Switzerland, Sweden, Turkey and the UK – convened the CEEC under the chairmanship of Oliver Franks. Each member nation could contribute to the work of the sub-committees which aimed at collecting and collating technical data on the basis of lengthy questionnaires. The supervision of these committees eventually fell to an Executive Committee of no more than five nations chaired by the UK which, together with France, 'hand picked' the other Executive members (Italy, Holland, Norway). Only Italy chose a representative of ministerial status for the Executive Committee. Contrary to the view that the CEEC 'was a major step on the road to European recovery and unity',[81] analysis of the CEEC's constitution reveals that the low level of national representation together with the firm orientation to focus on technical data and leave untouched wider questions of European integration, set the stage for a fundamental opposition between the far reaching objectives of the United States and the machinery of the CEEC which had been fashioned to comply with the conditions for dollar assistance whilst resisting these wider US ambitions.[82] The significant divisions between the US and Europe (and between European nations themselves) on such key issues as the future political and economic position of Germany, the mechanisms of intra-European trade, and the specific economic problems of Italy, meant that none of the member countries fully supported American aims for the CEEC. The concept of integration therefore remained unexplored as national transient alliances developed on specific policy issues among the member nations each of which hoped to use elements in the new US strategy to further its national reconstruction programme.

The glib official assessment that, in response to the American wish that the CEEC should make recommendations concerning the size and distribution of dollar aid to Western Europe, the CEEC simply 'recognising that their economic systems are inter-related and that the prosperity of each . . . depends on the prosperity of all . . . completed its task at the end of September',[83] hides a multitude of tensions, ambiguities and machinations which characterised the body and which served to illustrate both the extent of national divisions amongst members and the international obstacles thwarting the political and economic aims of the US. The history of the 'September report' illustrates this last point. An advance draft of the report infuriated the State Department since the European bid for $29 200 million over a four-year period contained no provision for any 'continuing organisation' or any recommendations for achieving European integration.[84] Bob Lovett explained to Marshall on receipt of the draft, 'progress so far is disappointing in that all that has come out is sixteen shopping lists which may be dressed up by some large-scale but very long-term projects such as Alpine power'.[85] After frenzied meetings between Clayton (plus other high officials of the US administration) and the Executive Committee, the bid for aid was reduced to $17 billion of which $5300 million would be available in the first year. The report was substantially rewritten under US pressure and by the time of publication included a proposal that participating nations would take effective steps to create internal monetary and financial stability along with the reduction of trade barriers and, despite British opposition until very late in the day, also included the clause that a permanent organisation expressing the 'common objectives and joint responsibility' of Western Europe would be created.[86]

Amid such diplomatic rhetoric the Convention of the Organisation for European Economic Co-operation (OEEC) was thus signed on 16 April 1948. Whilst the agreement, dubbed by Bidault 'unique in the history of our Continent',[87] pledged the sixteen signatories to 'close and lasting co-operation', it nevertheless carried over into the new organisation the tensions and divisions which had marked the CEEC. Before analysing how the British state subverted this second US attempt at providing effective machinery for European economic integration it is instructive to consider the British state's management of the bilateral treaty signed with the US which ensured the continuity of dollar assistance beyond the first quarter payment which had begun on 3 April 1948. Such an analysis will demonstrate both how the Americans attempted to use Marshall as a political lever and how the UK state successfully resisted such manoeuvring.

British Resistance to the Economic Co-operation Agreement

Whilst many have interpreted the Marshall episode as a clear case of British capitulation to American hegemony, others have focused upon Marshall's key sentence that 'it would be neither fitting nor officious for this government to undertake to draw up unilaterally a programme designed to place Europe on its feet',[88] and concluded that 'the Americans did not assert dominance over Europe by the formulation of the Marshall Plan'.[89] This chapter denies the validity of either of these interpretations and has stressed that, although the US clearly sought to impose their 'new plan' to restructure the Western European economies in the interest of extending American dominance, this strategy was successfully resisted by the European (and especially British) states who sought their own solutions based on programmes which would enable the retention of economic sovereignty and the expansion of domestic reconstruction. A review of the negotiations surrounding the British acceptance of the Economic Co-operation Agreement[90] signed between the UK and the US on 26 June 1948 supports this latter interpretation.

The view that US aid was founded on the principle of non-interference in national sovereignty of the recipient nation is quickly dispelled by studying the draft US agreement circulated in May 1948 which, as the Treasury recognised, gave 'the United States very wide possibilities of interference in our economic and financial policy'.[91] As a whole the draft version threatened to limit the British state's economic policy-making in the areas of external commercial policy (including imperial preference and non-discrimination), export policy, exchange policy and industrial policy including nationalisation and the ending of subsidies to production. Outside of economic policy, the draft contained articles effectively transferring aspects of British law to the International Court of Justice which Rowan described as 'unprecedented and undesirable'.[92] Specifically Article V of the draft agreement, dealing with trade policy, attempted to infringe British economic freedom in a manner beyond the ambit of the recovery programme. It required the UK to accord US trade most-favoured-nation treatment running until mid-1953, with an undertaking not to increase Commonwealth preferences above their existing level nor to discriminate in import restrictions against US goods beyond the extent permitted in the International Trade Organisation Charter. At the same time the USA would remain free to reject the Charter obligations, reverting to higher tariff policy at will.[93] In addition, the UK would be called upon to accept a similar most-favoured-nation obligation for trade with Germany, Japan, Trieste and Korea. Finally, the Article required the UK to prevent trade and business practices which were considered detrimental to European recovery, in a way which 'condemned all restrictive practices as harmful unless proved otherwise and obliging us to prevent any particular practices the US may specify'.[94] These provisos threatened to extend considerably the existing UK commitments established under the loan agreement which the UK had so far failed to observe without penalty, and under the ITO Charter and the General Agreement on Tariffs and Trade which had failed to produce the results required by the US and from which the UK could withdraw at 60 days' notice. Balancing provisions present in the ITO Charter which enabled nations to waive the Charter rules in the event of severe inflationary pressure in world trade, and outlines that tariff reduction and export subsidisation must be by negotiation only, were moreover omitted in the draft US agreement.

In addition, Article X attempted to weaken national control of gold and exchange policy by enabling the United States to put severe pressure on the UK to alter the exchange rate whenever deemed desirable. It thus appeared to the Treasury that as a reaction to the unilateral British decision to end convertibility in 1947 the US now wished to bend the existing rules of the IMF more completely to its own purposes and 'to use it to intervene in crucial areas of national economic policy-making'.[95]

The British state's resistance to these measures was unfaltering. Since without the UK any 'continuing organisation' would have been totally ineffective, the US was forced to delete these provisions whilst gaining a commitment from the UK to discuss the question of most-favoured-nation treatment for Germany and Japan in a manner which would not involve its being linked to the bilateral agreement.[96] For its part the UK made minor compromises. Private American investments in Britain under the ECA could be converted back into dollars and offset against recovery programme grants whilst 5 per cent of the total appropriation would be set aside for the purchase of strategic materials for the American economy. (A clause was also inserted requiring 50 per cent of the goods shipped under ERP to be carried in American bottoms at US freight rates.[97]) Nevertheless, the draft agreement episode indicates that the political leverage of the USA via Marshall was severely restricted and whilst minor concessions were granted the British state managed to resist (and thereby help other recipient nations to resist) the more significant US incursions into areas of national economic policy-making. The view that Britain capitulated to American interests via Marshall is simply not borne out by a study of the CEEC or the bilateral Economic Co-operation Agreement. However it is only by analysing the final form in which Marshall aid came to be organised in Europe – that of the OEEC – that a definite position can be established.

British Dominance of the OEEC

American inflexibility over the concept of a 'continuing organisation' measured the importance the State Department attached to the OEEC as a final attempt to achieve their multilateral ideals via the integration approach. Whilst many US officials involved with the OEEC recollect that it was 'a real force tending to pull national policies constantly into a more European pattern',[98] its organisation marked the limits rather than the extension of US influence. The US attempt to co-ordinate the national economic policies of Europe floundered on the same series of obstacles encountered by the CEEC, notably the wide differences in domestic economic recovery policies reflecting fundamental differences of economic situation. Although dollar aid attempted to solve the financial aspect of the crisis inasmuch as the payments crisis was temporarily eased allowing further domestic expansion, the vague nature of the American concept of integration enabled nations to gain dollars under the guise of co-ordination whilst in reality remaining fundamentally divided.

Despite American hopes, shared by Sean MacBride – Eire's Minister for Economic Affairs – that the OEEC would lead the economic integration of Western Europe, becoming an 'Economic government for Western Europe',[99] the British state's position was uncompromisingly outlined by Cripps: 'we do not envisage the OEEC should assume any authoritative control over any nations' plans'.[100] To ensure that the British view prevailed, steps were taken to maintain tight control over the constitutional structure of the organisation in a manner practised by the UK in its handling of the CEEC. As in the earlier body, the OEEC functioned via an Executive Committee composed of representatives from seven nations (the UK, France, Italy, Sweden, Switzerland, Turkey, The Netherlands) under which a number of technical committees were classified either as 'horizontal' (handling general subjects over a wide field such as Programmes, Balance of Payments, Trade and Payments, Manpower) or 'vertical' (dealing with specific commodities such as oil, steel, coal, textiles). Constitutionally the Executive Committee was responsible to the supreme body of the OEEC, the Council, on which all sixteen member nations were represented. However, in practice the Executive Committee held the real power of the organisation partly for the reason that it was the only section to sit in fairly continuous session.[101]

The UK's position of dominance within this overall structure rested not only on the fact that Britain held the chairmanship of the Executive Committee in the person of Hall-Patch (a devotee of Bevin and a continual source of annoyance particularly to Averell Harriman, the Special Ambassador of the ECA, whom Hall-Patch dismissed as a superficial careerist simply using the ECA appointment to foster his personal publicity both in Europe and the US[102]) but also in that Britain invariably had key representatives in each of the different bodies set up to deal with specific tasks. For instance, the UK held the chair of the Programmes Committee, had a decisive representative in the 'Group of Four' (UK, France, Netherlands, Italy) which worked out the first allocation of American aid, chaired the 'Committee of Five' (UK, France, Belgium, Greece, Norway) which supervised the balance of payments negotiations surrounding intra-European payments schemes, and held the chairmanship of the Balance of Payments Committee. In addition, for work on the OEEC's long term programme the UK held the most influential position since the central decision-making unit fell under the guidance of the chairman of the Executive Committee, disappointing the French who were increasingly suspicious (and rightly so, according to Hall-Patch) that Britain 'also have the Swedish vice-chairman of the Executive Committee in their pocket'.[103]

To the continual chagrin of the Americans, the British state displayed a remarkable ability to 'produce the right man for whatever task was most important at the moment',[104] thereby sidestepping any proposal which would either threaten UK economic sovereignty or reduce UK dollar aid. The UK willingly endorsed benign OEEC objectives such as that which stated that 'in developing the means of co-operation between them the individual nations shall retain their freedom to adopt techniques of economic administration that are appropriate to their general economic and political objectives'. However, specific suggestions that national investment programmes should be collectively examined were forthrightly rejected by the UK, on the grounds that 'the scale and direction of our investment programme is a central feature of our full employment and general economic recovery policies and we cannot thus accept any appreciable loss of control over it'.[105] Given the British state's high level of activity in and substantial influence over the OEEC as a whole, it is hardly surprising that in response to American criticism Bevin would not consider enlarging its scope or amending its constitution (except in the direction of Clarke's suggestion[106] that whilst it was essential for the UK to retain the chairmanship of the Executive Committee it might after all be advantageous to have the chair of any committee the Americans sought fit to propose, such as that of a new Economic Policy Committee).

Low-level, British-dominated, inter-governmental co-ordination thereby characterised the UK state's strategy in response to the American wish to achieve US-style multilateralism via European integration. The precise methods by which the US sought to fashion an OEEC-led European economic integration, adamantly deciding that the OEEC should recommend the allocation and distribution of dollar aid and forcing the OEEC to produce a common long-term programme for European economic recovery, failed to achieve this aim. Not only did the Americans meet strong British resistance to any extension of the scope of the organisation in a 'supra-national' fashion, but the OEEC as a mechanism could not overcome the barriers thrown up by the other nation-states in regard to such fundamental issues as the role of Germany, the operation of the Monnet plan in France, the apprehensiveness of the Italian government with regard to a free capital market, the gross Dutch international deficits, and the preparedness of the Belgians to allow a direction of investment shaped by international patterns of comparative advantage.[107] The multilateral world aim of the US could not be sought via a vehicle which, whilst left in the hands of the Europeans, eventually managed only to strengthen individual economies (by easing foreign currency reserve problems) thereby reinforcing a world economic structure fundamentally based on the nation-state.

It has thus been argued that in 1947 British capital was not in the grip of a general malaise but rather that the British state was experiencing specific difficulties in its foreign currency reserve management because of the widespread dollar shortage. The dollar problem was intensified by the government's pursuit of expansionist domestic programmes in the context of a maldistribution in the world's resources further aggravating balance of payments problems caused by the superior productive structure of the USA. The Marshall Plan eased the British dollar position. Yet the European agencies set up to administer US aid could not produce the integrated European capital circuits which the Americans needed to further their own export surplus and wider multilateralist aims. Contrary to popular opinion, US hegemony was not established over the British state or economy by the Marshall offensive. Despite the application of considerable political pressure, the British state refused to relinquish any meaningful aspect of economic sovereignty, replacing the US wish for integration with a much more benign version of non-committal European co-ordination within which the principle of national economic and political decision-making autonomy was duly inscribed. The constitutional structures of the CEEC and the OEEC together with the proposals informing the bilateral Economic Co-operation Agreement reflected the successful application of the British state's strategy. Britain did not accept American leadership in a new world economic order via the Marshall offensive. The account of the British state slowly sinking to new depths of capitulation to US interests simply does not stand close scrutiny.

It would, however, be foolish to leave an appreciation of the impact of the Marshall offensive on British accumulation at this level. Whilst we can discard the grand 'capitulation' thesis, it remains for this chapter to assess the precise affect of the Marshall offensive – US aid disbursements, direct Anglo-American government and industrial links, US policy for sterling – on the development of the British economy in the context of Cripps's austerity Chancellorship up until sterling devaluation (which will be considered in the following chapter). To accomplish this task the remainder of this chapter will assess the key developments which took place in the British economy under the auspices of the Marshall offensive, whilst charting the precise role played by dollar aid in the overall accumulation process.

IV   ASSESSING THE IMPACT OF THE MARSHALL PLAN

Industrial Restructuring and the Marshall Plan

The UK's national programme for economic recovery submitted to the OEEC in December 1948[108] outlined the intention of the government to bring about a rapid recovery in the general economic situation by means of an increase in production, the elimination of inflation, the expansion of exports and invisible earnings, the diversion of purchases away from the Western hemisphere and the adjustment of imports to a level consistent with the expected long-term capacity to pay for them. The success of this programme depended on the continued expansion of industrial production to meet the priorities outlined by Cripps whereby 'first are exports, second is capital investment in industry, and last are the needs, comforts and amenities of the family'.[109]

The British state's concern to increase production struck a deep chord not only with the US administrators of Marshall but also with the US Chamber of Commerce and key American industrialists. With simplistic political and economic reasoning the US position was exemplified by the likes of Ray Gifford, Chairman of the Borg-Warner International Corporation and adviser to the US Department of Commerce, who concluded, 'the spread of Marxian doctrines may be stopped [in Western Europe] by bettering the world's standard of living through the direct application of many of the same methods that have been so conspicuously successful in the world's most productive free society – the United States'.[110] The American belief that the greatest service the USA could render to Britain (outside of dollar aid) would be 'to give them our industrial management and technical aid in the modernization of their plants and methods and processes',[111] prompted Hoffman and others of the US administration to attempt a restructuring of British productive capital along Fordist lines.

But the claim that the Marshall plan laid the material foundations for an Atlantic economy based on the generalisation of Fordism by injecting purchasing power for innovative production in Western Europe,[112] cannot be accepted as an accurate interpretation. Although the US undoubtedly wished to carry the dollar-led Marshall offensive further by the widespread export of American accumulation conditions in 1948, private US investment did not materialise in the Marshall era. The narrowness of markets, exchange control obstacles, non-convertibility of sterling, ineffective Anglo-American productivity meetings and the very low level of dollar aid received by Britain (together with the inappropriateness of many of the USA's productive techniques to a British economy geared to export rather than mass consumer domestic markets) all constrained American attempts to restructure British productive capital. An analysis of two prominent attempts to refashion the UK industrial sector – one on an inter-governmental basis, the other on an industry-to-industry basis – will highlight the validity of these remarks.

The Anglo-American Productivity Council

The US interest in exporting American accumulation conditions to Europe is often seen as a political move effectively disguised behind the façade of the supposedly apolitical politics of productivity.[113] This interpretation holds that the theme of productivity acted as a substitute for the harsher questions of allocation stressing that by enhancing productive efficiency, whether through scientific management, business planning, industrial co-operation or other corporatist tendencies, the American strategy could transcend the class conflicts that arose from scarcity. Whilst great store was set by moving Europe from the 'realm of material necessity' to the 'realm of abundance' it is inaccurate to claim that the US administration 'viewed the transition to a society of abundance as a problem of engineering, not of politics'.[114] The political justification for increasing productivity – to prevent the 'lure of communism' – was always prominent in the productivity rhetoric with the more perceptive US officials acutely aware that class conflict arose from the process of production itself and was not therefore simply a question of distribution. Hoffman, for instance, objected to any state encroachment on private capital, claiming in the wake of proposals for steel nationalisation, 'they should not use our dollars to engage in social experimentation . . . if they start playing ducks and drakes with their economy . . . we are going to hold up the investment'.[115]

This line of thought led to the establishment of the main inter-governmental agency by which the US, under the auspices of Marshall, sought to restructure British productive capital – that of the Anglo-American Productivity Council. Hoffman's allegations that British management required a new attitude to technical efficiency, new American productive techniques, a worker-acceptance of new methods, greater output per man and mobility of labour, 'otherwise Congress may be reluctant to provide funds',[116] prompted a swift response from Cripps. With Board of Trade backing he agreed to set up a Council 'to exchange views on the question as to whether there are ways in which the United States industry could co-operate in assisting increased productivity and to take such steps as are consistent with this programme and with similar objectives of the Economic Co-operation Administration'.[117] A series of initial meetings began in London on 25 October 1948 during the course of which various sub-committees dealing with standardisation of productivity, specialisation of industry, economic information, the maintenance of productive plant and power, plant visits and the exchange of production techniques were appointed. The Trades Union Congress had emphasised its support for the Council by stating:

> it cannot be too clearly brought before the members of affiliated organisations that the only means of carrying these national overhead charges (brought about by the shorter working week, a weeks holiday with pay, increasing old age pensions, raising the school leaving age, consolidating the NHS) is by greater production . . . and by removing the chief obstacle to the improvement of productivity . . . the attitude of suspicion and hostility of the workers concerned.[118]

Yet, although these sub-committees were staffed with trade union leaders such as Deakin and Lawther, it is a mistake to assume that

American assistance was immediately forthcoming or that the UK industrial sector welcomed such a strategy.

The Board of Trade and the Ministry of Labour had identified factors which would contribute towards increasing productivity. They cited an increase in technical efficiency involving the use of improved materials, machinery, processes and an ample and continuous supply of power as well as improvements in the efficiency of management and the labour force. None the less, specific constraints halted the British adoption of Fordist accumulation strategies in 1948. Work towards laying the basis for such conditions had been taken via the establishment of the Department of Scientific and Industrial Research, via the support given to the British Standards Institution, the British Institute of Management and the regional bodies fostering Joint Production Committees. Yet these steps were largely cosmetic throughout the life of Cripps's Chancellorship and were mainly prompted by the British realisation that 'there will undoubtedly be trouble if the Americans think that we are not sufficiently interested in productivity or that we are not making use of the assistance which they can give us'.[119] Stressing that 'the relation between workers and employers in this country is quite different from that in the United States', the real Treasury view was that 'it is essential to avoid an unregulated stream of Americans coming over here, either individually or in groups, making superficial investigations and ill-considered reports'.[120]

While the British state was pledged to increasing productivity, the position of the British economy in the Marshall period was not conducive to the widespread adoption of American Fordist strategies. The problems facing manufacturing in the two countries were by no means identical. In particular, the vast US home markets calling for mass produced consumer goods were absent in the UK where many potentially home-based industries were handicapped because their product was considered inessential whilst their export potential was limited by foreign import restrictions. In addition, shortages of raw materials (particularly steel) and the need for restraint in capital expenditure (in line with Cripp's priorities) all acted to hold down total output below the level which would justify planning for mass production. Furthermore, it was widely believed that any large scale attempt to impose American methods of time and motion study would result in hostility leading to industrial stoppage rather than increased output. While the British economy remained geared to an export-led recovery in the context of exchange control obstacles, inconvertibility of sterling, raw material scarcity and low home market demand, the application of Fordist accumulation techniques was simply not a viable proposition.

American Council of Aid to European Industry

Energetic attempts to establish US productive techniques on an industry-to-industry basis, rather than relying on government initiative, ran up against the same obstacles whilst also encountering the British industrial sectors' distrust and disapproval of American enforced restructuring. An approach by Charles Davis, President of Borg-Warner (one of America's largest producers of automobile parts and equipment whose officials were actively identified with both the US National Association of Manufacturers and government commerce agencies), canvassed by Ray Gifford on the basis that 'government loans are about the poorest form of risk, whereas advances on an industry to industry basis if handled properly are generally rapid',[121] is worth reviewing in this context. Gifford's principal recommendation was to set up an 'American Council of Aid to European Industry' to provide the services of the USA's top industrial executives, sub-executives, engineers, production and marketing experts and technical specialists to the sixteen European nations which were beneficiaries of Marshall aid. The purpose of the plan was the raising of living standards 'to resist the lure of Communism',[122] and it attempted to combine sections of the Federation of British Industry with the US National Association of Manufacturers to render a real service to the ECA.

Yet by 16 November 1948 Gifford's initiative had failed, almost entirely due to FBI distrust and lack of interest. The only material manifestation of the negotiations was the suggestion by Gifford that Borg-Warner open a plant in the UK to concentrate on the production of standardised gear boxes.[123] To the UK manufacturers specialising in the production of a variety of gear types the suggestion was anathema and raised thoughts that Gifford was angling to set up a UK factory without new plant simply to assemble American-made parts – a move which would have brought little benefit to UK industry (a fear which continues to haunt the minds of British industrialists). Norman Kipping – Director General of the FBI from 1946 to 1965 – bemoaned Gifford's 'patronising attitude' throughout the negotiations and decided that British industry should not entertain 'visits of

American professional business consultants of whom the FBI had no very high regard'.[124]

Alongside the accumulation conditions of British productive capital, which precluded large scale import and adoption of American Fordist strategies in the Marshall period, must also therefore be added the UK industrial sectors' implicit distrust of such techniques. The claim that the Marshall offensive laid the material foundations for an Atlantic economy based on the generalisation of Fordism appears to be inaccurate in the case of Britain. The agencies designed to accomplish a restructuring of British productive capital appeased the American demands for action on productivity (and thus maintained the flow of dollar aid to the UK) yet were considered cosmetic operations by the British state having little tangible effect upon industry for the variety of reasons outlined above. Furthermore, while the UK's net receipt of aid for 1948–9 totalled $935 million, this represented only 2.8 per cent of national income of which only 8.3 per cent was allocated to the import of machinery and vehicles – the latter category accounting for only 0.4 per cent of all 1949 imports.[125] Specific constraints worked against the export of Fordism and the minuscule funds allocated from Marshall to machinery and vehicle imports had no significant effect on the structure of British productive capital. Before offering a conclusion on the precise effect which dollar aid had overall on the British economy it remains for this chapter to investigate the key developments which took place in trade and finance under the Marshall offensive in this first stage (that is, up until devaluation) of Cripps's Chancellorship.

European and American Perspectives on Trade and Payments

It is often overlooked, even by those who wish most strongly to emphasise the hegemonic dimensions of the Marshall Plan, that the Americans sought to achieve their integrative ideal not only by insisting on European co-operative agencies, bilateral negotiations and incursions into the industrial sectors of recipient nations but also by close inspection and direction of European trade and payments arrangements. Any moves that facilitated intra-European trade and payments were welcomed by the US as a step towards a regional multilateral system based on the model of a European clearing union. The leverage Marshall aid gave the US in directing such issues warrants close scrutiny.

With the termination of sterling convertibility the limitations on intra-European trading prompted many nations, particularly Belgium, who were net creditors to Europe but debtors with extra-European nations to seek a solution which would enable them to mobilise their credits in Europe to discharge their debts with the Western hemisphere. The interests of nations in this position, together with the British state's realisation that, in the wake of Marshall's offer, 'the Americans would never be content with a scheme which enlarged, say, European demands for American steel if those same countries were unable for financial reasons to purchase Belgian steel',[126] led to the canvassing of four proposals aimed at expanding intra-European trade and payments. The UK proposal centred on enlarging the credit margins of the existing agreements to aid the movement of goods between the participatory nations. Yet this proposal was specifically turned down by the creditor countries who showed themselves afraid of unrequited exports. Alternative schemes such as that of a US dollar stabilisation fund and a dollar aid transferability scheme were indefinitely shelved whilst a solution based on the mutual transferability of European currencies took shape.

This latter scheme, established by Benelux, Italy and France, became the First Agreement on Multilateral Monetary Compensation signed on 18 November 1947. The signatories agreed to a system of automatic multilateral offset of balances where this was possible without increasing anyone's liability of gold payments. For example, if France owed Italy $3 million, Italy owed Belgium $5 million and Belgium owed France $4 million, a central office (the Bank for International Settlements (BIS) at Basle was named as agent) could cancel France's debt to Italy, reduce Italy's to Belgium to $2 million and Belgium's to France to $1 million. Automatically offsetting debts in this way (called 'first category compensations') would expand trade whilst reducing the need for gold and dollar payments in trade amongst participatory nations.[127] Eight other nations including the UK joined as 'occasional members' of the agreement since they were not at this stage prepared to agree to third country transfers without their consent. Although the British state had adopted a system of automatic transferability within the Sterling Area and the American account nations and administrative transferability over a much wider area, she was not prepared to relinquish administrative control within Europe for the sake, as the Treasury saw it, of improving Belgium's overall dollar position. The UK interest, the London Committee on European Economic Co-operation clarified, 'lies not so much in tight and rather artificial obligations of convertibility to a group – arbitrarily chosen from the economic point of view – of countries inside the Marshall Europe, but in expanding the international use of sterling throughout the world as a whole', when Sterling Area viability, dollar and non-dollar area equilibrium and higher reserve levels could be established.[128]

After the convertibility débâcle the British state, although committed to convertibility in the long run, was not going to entertain a premature general reintroduction of automatic transferability (in however limited a form). The UK diagnosis that no financial panacea could cure miscellaneous deep-seated economic ills proved correct and the initial Benelux agreement managed to compensate only $1.7 million out of a bilateral debit balance total of the participating countries amounting to $762.1 million.[129] The limited obligations of occasional members, the frequent need for specific consent before transactions could be carried out, the attractions of bilateral bargaining, the fear of losing gold through the workings of the clearing mechanism, and the tendency for a handful of nations to emerge as creditors or debtors to the group as a whole all prevented this simplistic agreement from accomplishing a European clearing arrangement on the multilateral lines sought by the US administration.[130]

Nevertheless, the Americans had viewed the Benelux initiative as 'an encouraging indication of greater economic co-operation'[131] in Europe, and decided to link the Marshall aid payments with a new trade arrangement in the form of the First and Revised Intra-European Payments and Compensations Agreements of 16 October 1948 and 7 September 1949. These arrangements were modelled on the idea of redistributing Marshall aid on the basis of 'drawing rights'.

Belgium had expressed the opinion that 'we do not want Marshall aid for ourselves; we want it to cover our needs by our own exports; therefore we want our customers to receive Marshall aid and pay us the dollars we need.[132] Influenced by this suggestion, it was decided that any expected difference in the balance of payments between a specific pair of countries would become the debtor country's drawing rights on the creditor. For instance, if as a result of negotiation it was agreed that Italy expected to export to France $11 million more in goods and services than France would export to Italy, then under the payments agreement Italy would grant France drawing rights of $11 million, deducted from the Italian Marshall aid allocation.[133] In effect, the drawing rights represented dollar gifts from one OEEC nation to another. Britain, therefore, having a large trade surplus with France, embarked on tough bargaining sessions to save dollars which would escape via the operation of drawing rights.

Seventy-eight sets of bilateral negotiations were finally concluded on this basis which had the result of cutting Britain's dollar aid from $1 239 million to $935 million for 1948–9 representing a 25 per cent loss due to the operation of drawing rights.[134] By freeing sterling balances held by OEEC nations, Britain contributed a total of over $500 million to financing intra-European trade in this one year alone whilst the UK's surplus exports, both visible and invisible, amounted to not more than one-fourth of this figure.[135] Although Britain thus viewed the arrangements as less than equitable the state was consoled by the fact that the new agreement did not in any sense eliminate the neo-bilateral basis upon which Dalton had constructed the UK's accumulation strategy. The OEEC dubbed the arrangements 'a superstructure' resting upon bilateralism with the systems of gold ceilings and dollar points together with other provisions of the bilateral agreements remaining in force.[136]

Overall, the operation of the First Agreement was constrained by many of the factors which had blocked the original Benelux initiative, and continued to thwart the Revised arrangement from achieving a more multilateral European trade and payments system. Drawing rights financed only approximately 8 per cent of trade among OEEC members during the twelve months ending June 1949 and automatic first category compensations as a means of settlement remained extremely modest with OEEC member turnover reaching only $160 million from October 1948 to June 1950 – less than 2 per cent of the gross surpluses incurred during that period.[137] As the British Treasury had foreseen, the calculation of the amount of aid needed by each nation on this basis surpassed the wit of man.[138] Despite complex revisions, $260 million of the drawing rights 'finally established' remained unused at the expiration of the agreements with the proportion of the bilateral deficits financed by drawing rights ranging from 0 per cent for Italy to 89 per cent for Austria and the proportion of the bilateral surpluses from 0 per cent for Greece to 68 per cent for Belgium.[139] Faulty forecasting produced arbitrary financial results. In addition, a system calculated on a purely bilateral basis disregarding the development of each nation's overall creditor or debtor position in Europe, produced unstable and paradoxical consequences adding, for instance, $300 million to France's net surplus and shifting the UK from a small surplus of $30 million to a large deficit of $290 million.

Moreover, the agreements in some cases fostered a contraction of trade since once the drawing rights had been established the beneficiary countries had a definite incentive to make use of them even if better or more essential imports became obtainable at lower prices from other sources. The danger of losing the benefit could act as a deterrent to the readjustment of policies which might reduce the nation's deficit below the level of the drawing rights which had been allocated.[140] To the chagrin of the ECA it slowly became clear that, far from Marshall aid forging a new European multilateralism, America was actually providing dollars to increase the flexibility of the neo-bilateral framework Dalton and others had established in opposition to US wishes.

Despite the fact that the Revised Payments Agreement of September 1949 included, after fierce resistance from Cripps, a clause providing for transferability of drawing rights up to 25 per cent that is to say one-fourth of the total drawing rights could in principle be used to settle deficits with other participating countries as well as with the grantor itself – the operation of this minor multilateralising aspect in the context of the continuing neo-bilateral framework proved demonstrably ineffective. Since the bilateral portion of the drawing rights (75 per cent) had to be fully used before tapping the multilateral portion, the system tended to remain conspicuously bilateral for the entirety of the Revised agreement. The use of drawing rights against countries other than the initial grantor amounted to only 9 per cent of the total drawing rights used under the Revised arrangement,[141] whilst the sudden flood of devaluations experienced before the end of September added to the confusion and unreliability of the system.

Whilst the US therefore applied immense pressure to alter the trade and payments arrangements of Western Europe – 'never before had Mr Harriman and his expert advisers taken such a direct and active part in a decision under the Marshall Plan that the European leaders were obliged to make'[142] – the neo-bilateral accumulation strategies proved resilient to this latest multilateralist onslaught. The British state had no intention of seeing convertibility reintroduced by the circuitous route of a European payments agreement[143] yet was obliged to join the arrangements to benefit from dollar aid. By taking the initiative in organising the institutional machinery which decided the form of the arrangements, the UK managed to resist the main ambitions ECA had for restructuring the European trade and payments system whilst benefiting, albeit not to the same extent as France, from Marshall dollars. Nevertheless, the price paid by the British state for this stubborn resistance to the US demands for backdoor convertibility was a calculated campaign focusing upon trade liberalisation which laid the basis for the next thrust of US foreign economic policy.

Trade Liberalisation as a Countermeasure

As early as March 1949 Cripps realised that the way to resist US pressure successfully was to make constructive counter-proposals to distract the ECA from pushing through maximum transferability of drawing rights which would involve further dollar loss to European nations given the UK's trading pattern. Cripps therefore put before the Cabinet a proposal for 'a general relaxation of import controls in Western Europe with a view to diverting US pressure for new European payments arrangements which would involve us in a loss of dollars'.[144] This would take the form of Open General Licences (permitting any person to import the goods in question without limit, thereby amending the Import of Goods (Control) Order of 4 June 1940) for imports of specified goods from specified nations.

Whilst proposing to take the lead in import relaxations, Cripps stressed that Britain could not continue them on the initial scale unless other countries followed the principle. This resolve was consolidated in mid-June with the Cabinet recommendation that 'OEEC nations should take steps to progressively eliminate quantitative import restrictions between one another, to achieve a complete liberalisation of intra-European trade by 1951'.[145] This proposal, taken up by the OEEC and developed in the form of the European Payments Union, will be analysed in the following chapter. However within the context of the Marshall offensive it has been necessary to introduce the subject of trade liberalisation since it was clearly a compromise action taken by the British state to avert further demands for sterling convertibility being pressed on the UK. In the event it was a successful manoeuvre. Rapid British growth experienced after devaluation put British capital on a footing from which a cautious European-led multilateralisation of intra-European trade and payments was judged to be warranted and beneficial to the UK economy.

The grand designs the ECA had fostered for a rapid achievement of their integrative Marshall-led ideals through a manipulation of intra-European trade and payments had met with the same failure that characterised their other schemes involving the structure of the European aid agencies, the bilateral agreements and the incursion into the sphere of productive capital. Yet the pressure the US brought to bear had opened up a new route through which their multilateral ideal could be sought, that of trade liberalisation. Any assessment of the Marshall offensive must recognise this point amid the generalised failures of the US administration on most other fronts. It remains for this account of the impact of the Marshall offensive on British accumulation to analyse the precise role played by dollar aid in the overall process of capital accumulation and thereby move towards an assessment of the claim that 'it is inconceivable that the economic and social policies of the Attlee government could have survived without this massive platform'.[146]

Cripps's Domestic Measures to Reduce Dollar Spending

The central priorities for dealing with the drain in foreign currency reserves had been established by Dalton long before the chaos of August 1947. By March 1947 Dalton had stated that an export target of 140 per cent of the 1938 volume was to be reached by the second quarter of 1948 and a diversified import programme for 1947–8 was to reduce food imports from hard currency sources by at least £80 million.[147] In the wake of the rapid exhaustion of the US dollar credit Cripps consolidated and expanded these priorities, proposing that physical output be increased to a third above its prewar level, whilst exports were to be expanded almost 40 per cent above the 1947 level (150 per cent of the 1938 volume) and imports would receive much more drastic cuts than envisaged under Dalton.[148] To these basic measures Cripps announced that, in order to increase rapidly the volume of exports in the near future, labour, coal, steel and other materials would have to be switched from manufacture for the home market to manufacture for export and this would result in the 'postponement of certain investment projects'.[149]

This proposed cut in capital investment would mainly fall on construction and investment in plant and machinery, reducing the gross amount of domestic investment from a projected figure of £1600 million for 1948 to £1320 million (an overall reduction of 18 per cent in the forecast for fixed investment for 1948).[150] Finally, with regard to budgetary practice, Cripps developed the notion of 'disinflation' which he defined as 'the reduction of an undesirable degree of inflation', as opposed to deflation which 'is not merely the removal of undesirable inflation but is the creation of a positive degree of deflation below the normal in order to accomplish some particular end' (in terms of Cripps's motor tyre analogy, 'if it is pumped up too hard you disinflate it to the right level, but when you get a puncture you deflate it altogether').[151] Although such explanations amused contemporary commentators, the reasoning behind the rhetoric was clear in that, since inflationary pressure would be increased as exports expanded, consumption had to be limited and a policy of wage restraint (linked to increased productivity) was essential if Britain's relative cost and price structure was not to move too far out of line with those of the US and other foreign economies.[152] Cripps thus took steps to prevent the development of a dangerously inflationary situation by combining high direct taxation on personal incomes and distributed profits (applying equally to the lower earned incomes via the introduction of PAYE tax and indirect taxation increases) with a TUC-backed policy of wage restraint consolidated by announcements proclaiming that 'there is no justification at the present time for any rise in incomes from profits, rent, or other like sources and rises in wages or salaries should only be asked for and agreed upon in exceptional cases'.[153]

A definite structure had therefore been established under Cripps for expanding capital accumulation whilst reducing the strain on the British dollar deficit. Yet despite these measures, the Cabinet decided on 23 June 1948 that further drastic action would have to be taken to reduce the dollar drain if Britain received no Marshall aid.[154] The economic consequences of receiving no aid, it was claimed, would be manifest in no further purchases of US tobacco, abolition of standard petrol, reduction of the dollar food import programme to Canadian wheat only, reductions in general food rationing to a level 10 per cent below the prewar average, reductions in consumer goods, industrial dislocation, and a 12 per cent cut in the raw material import programme.

Marshall Aid – an Economic Lifeline?

It has been on the basis of these assessments that many analysts have claimed that Marshall aid 'presented socialist Britain with an economic lifeline'.[155] Pointing to the indispensability of Marshall aid, it is assumed that Britain 'tied herself – with ever increasing servitude – to the USA',[156] with low rates of investment a key aspect of the British 'decline'. The Attlee government, it is claimed, in the context of the dollar drain and Marshall credits, failed 'to create the kind of climate [necessary] for large scale investment and rapid increases in productivity'.[157] This interpretation, however, does not give an accurate picture of the role of Marshall aid in British economic reconstruction.

To understand the weakness of the 'economic lifeline' view two points must be emphasised. First, it is not adequate for an analysis of actual economic development to rely either on government command papers or upon unpublished state documents which merely attempt to *estimate* future trends or consequences. In this context both Cripps's 1948 pronouncements and Cabinet future trend estimations are unreliable and insufficient as sources for an assessment of the importance of Marshall aid. For instance, while Cripps was *proposing* an increase in physical output over four years to a third above its prewar level, in actual fact output in late 1948 *already* exceeded 20 per cent of its prewar volume. Similarly Cripps's 'ambitious' aim to expand exports was in fact very modest since they already stood in 1948 27 per cent higher than the 1947 level. Fixed investment provides another example, in that Cripps expected an increase of only 17 per cent between 1947 and 1953 but, unknown to the Treasury, investment in 1948 was already considerably higher than that attained in 1947.[158] Although these state papers give a view of the British economy as one requiring general overall improvement, in reality capital was in the early stages of near-boom conditions and the only economic crisis facing accumulation in general was that of the dollar shortage. The unreliability of the government estimates indicates that the Treasury had not perceived the underlying strengths of the British economy and their premature assessment of the economic consequences of receiving no aid must be read with a critical eye.

The second area of weakness in the 'economic lifeline' view concerns the position of the British state with regard to capital investment cuts. Despite the fact that the Investment Programmes Committee drew meticulous statistical tables proposing, first, an 11 per cent cut and then, after the FBI suggested a 25 per cent cut, deciding on an overall 18 per cent reduction for fixed investment in 1948,[159] no cuts in capital investment occurred in that year. The fact remains (apparently unknown to those who bemoan investment cuts, lack of productivity and neglect of re-equipment) that as 1948 progressed the programme outlined in the command paper 'Capital Investment in 1948' was rendered obsolete and the volume of fixed investment rose £200 million between 1947 and 1948, climbing to higher levels throughout 1948–9.[160] While Morgan states that 'not until 1953 did new capital investment in Britain reach the level of

1938', a close review of the actual figures demonstrates that whilst there was a shortfall on the 1938 level of nearly 20 per cent in 1946 (even though that year saw a 150 per cent rate of increase over 1945) the prewar level was regained in 1948 and continued to rise throughout the life of the Attlee administration to a level roughly twice that of 1938 by the end of 1949.[161] Contrary to those who argue that the British state failed to create a climate conducive to productive investment, it was a cardinal principle of the investment programme to reduce, should reductions prove necessary (and in 1948 they did not), 'elements in the programmes which contribute to the amenities or the domestic standard of life, rather than on productive industry'.[162]

These two facts – first, that the government in early 1948 was by no means fully aware of the underlying strengths of the British economy and was therefore subject to major errors of judgement regarding projected consequences, and secondly, that fixed capital investment actually rose in 1948 by approximately 8 per cent whilst there had been a planned reduction of 18 per cent for the same year – although interesting in themselves, transform the estimation of the importance of Marshall aid to Britain when seen in the context of the composition of aid received by the UK.

Calculating the ratio of Marshall aid received by Britain (which between 1948 and 1951 totalled approximately $2695 million) to gross domestic capital formation reveals that the dollar aid could potentially contribute no more than 10 per cent of capital formation in the first two years of receipt, falling to 6 per cent in the final period of receipt (suspended from 1 January 1951 when it was phased into Mutual Security Assistance).[163] The claim that 'Europe would have been Communistic if it had not been for the Marshall Plan'[164] is bizarre indeed in the light of the above calculation which shows that the Washington assistance was capital-liberating rather than capita-transfusing, 'like the lubricant in an engine, not the fuel',[165] enabling the existing structure of UK capital to continue expansion, investment and reconstruction without a return to the deflationary policies which characterised the 1930s. The percentage of national income represented by the net dollar aid after the operation of drawing rights amounted to less than 2.4 per cent for the 'crisis' period from July 1948 to June 1949, with imports funded by Marshall dollars only 11.3 per cent of all British imports in 1949, falling to 7.5 per cent in 1950.[166] With regard to the constitution of these imports, over 42 per cent of all imports were food imports (machinery and vehicle imports accounting for only 0.4 per cent of the total by comparison) with over 32 per cent of Marshall dollars allocated in 1949 to the import of food.[167]

It is quite plain that the UK used Marshall aid to bolster food imports thereby releasing other funds to enable domestic reconstruction, investment and industrial productivity to continue expansion in line with the 'historical imperatives' which underlay the postwar government's general accumulation strategy. The planned reduction of capital investment – premissed on the need to reduce imports of timber, steel and other materials – never took place and the raw material import programme increased throughout 1948 rising again 17 per cent by value the following year (initially calculated to support at least a 7 per cent increase above 1948 in industrial production).[168] A large raw material margin was thus left for domestic investment and consumption, since the amount of raw materials going into exports in 1949–50 did not overly exceed that of 1948, contrary to the government estimates made in late 1947 and early 1948. Capital investment therefore proceeded apace because Marshall aid helped support a large dollar food import programme easing balance of payments constraints (particularly in the first year of receipt) and loosening bottlenecks which otherwise would have slowed the recovery process.

That many analysts incorrectly see the British state introducing capital investment cuts whilst relying on Marshall dollars to support a generally ailing economy leads them to overrate the contribution of the Marshall Plan to British accumulation. In reality the Marshall Plan was not indispensable to the Attlee government's economic objectives. By restraining food supply to the calorific intake of 1947 there would theoretically have been no need to expend massive dollar reserves on food imports.[169] Yet Marshall enabled the ambitious economic and social policies of the British state to proceed without undue alteration and without requiring politically unacceptable levels of austerity to be imposed on the British population. Whilst it is inaccurate to assume that Marshall aid had no beneficial effect on British accumulation (a position which with some qualification could be advanced with regard to Sweden or Belgium) it is wrong to claim that it acted as an economic lifeline for the UK economy. The British state employed Marshall aid (in much the same way as they expended the US dollar loan) to ease balance of payments constraints, selectively bolstering the food import programme, enabling the expansionist reconstruction policies to continue without having to risk an unacceptable political price being paid at the next General Election.

The conclusions of this chapter are three-fold. First, the British economy was not 'saved' from total collapse by Marshall in 1947. No overall state of economic paralysis existed. Capital was moving towards record levels of expansion. The 'crisis' of 1947 was a crisis in British foreign currency reserves which had its origins not in a general economic malaise but in the expansionist domestic reconstruction programmes on the basis of which the Attlee administration had been elected. These programmes were premissed on maintaining full employment, capital investment, reconstruction and rising levels of domestic welfare. In the context of a world dollar shortage, which reflected the United States near-monopoly of raw material and food supplies, they had the predictable consequence of rapidly exhausting the US dollar loan. In conditions of tight exchange control and inconvertibility of sterling, Britain could not return to prewar patterns of trade and was thus unable to finance large trade deficits with the US via a high level of invisible earnings or the earning of dollars in third markets. With a substantial rise in US wholesale prices in 1946 and other miscellaneous events (outflow of dollars to Germany, February fuel crisis) the foreign currency drain was intensified. Whilst in the popular imagination the balance of payments crisis came to be blamed on the convertibility obligation, in reality the working of this obligation accounted for not more than 6 per cent of the drawings on the US credit. The receipt of Marshall aid, when it arrived in April 1948, sufficiently eased the dollar drain to enable the government to abandon its proposed capital investment cuts and continue its expansionist programme without significantly cutting domestic food consumption. By using the US dollars principally to bolster food imports, Marshall aid benefited the Attlee government more on a political than an economic level. Whilst releasing dollars for use elsewhere, Marshall aid was not indispensable for the continuation of the government's economic policies since a tighter control and rationing of food imports and consumption would have obviated the need for dollar expenditure precisely in the region where Marshall dollars were expended. A minor capital investment cut together with a major restraint of food imports would, in other words, have eased the dollar drain in a way similar to that achieved by the actual receipt of Marshall aid. Yet the political consequences of such action would have been significant for this first majority Labour administration, particularly with the MacDonaldite débâcle of 1931 still alive in the memories of the Cabinet and the electorate, and still serving as a benchmark by which the actions of the Attlee government were judged.

Secondly, the British government's receipt of Marshall aid cannot be construed as an act which subordinated the British state to American interests. American hegemony was not established over the UK, neither did the Marshall offensive tie Britain to junior partner status in a new US-dominated world economic order, or lead to a concrete transformation of the British class structure along the lines of the US model. The idea of an American-dominated, multilateral world trading system based on the twin pillars of sterling convertibility and non-discrimination remained the driving force behind US foreign economic policy despite the discrediting of the State Department's original 'Bretton Woods/Key Currency' strategy. Yet the revised programme spearheaded by the ECA of an integrated regional multilateral clearing system fusing Western Europe into one large market achieving the economic and political stability necessary for later insertion into a world multilateral structure met strong nation-state resistance at every stage and was ultimately transformed (largely on British initiative) into a European notion of non-committal co-ordination which was coaxed into displaying sufficient signs of co-operation to enable US dollar aid to flow. British domination of the constitutional structure of the CEEC and the OEEC thwarted the aggressive integrative ideals the US sought to impose via these organisations. The position of Britain in the world economy (its policy to take the initiative in European affairs and its strong Sterling Area base) lent the UK state sufficient power to restrict severely any political leverage the US hoped to employ via Marshall. Concerted American attempts, for instance via the bilateral Economic Co-operation Agreement, to make incursions into areas of British economic policy-making met with a resolute British refusal to comply, forcing the US to abandon this approach and accept the more benign British version of non-committal co-ordination within which the principle of national economic and political decision-making auton-omy was inscribed. This chapter dismisses the Marshall offensive version of the grand 'capitulation' thesis as confidently as the previous section discarded the Anglo-American loan capitulation thesis.

Thirdly, an assessment of the impact of Marshall aid on the British state's accumulation strategy demonstrates the inaccuracy of the claim that the Marshall offensive began a significant export of American accumulation conditions to Britain by injecting purchasing power for innovative production, restructuring British productive capital along US Fordist lines. Whilst the US government and industrialists sought to 'halt the spread of Marxian doctrine' by raising British living standards via an export of Fordist accumulation techniques, specific constraints worked against such an export. Private US investment in the UK failed to materialise in the Marshall era since the narrowness of markets, exchange control obstacles, inconvertibility of sterling and the UK industrial sector's distrust of the aims and methods of American professional business consultants all constrained large scale export of US industrial machinery. The overall orientation of the British economy under Cripps's Chancellorship, towards production for controlled export and domestic austerity policies, made the export of American accumulation conditions largely unnecessary. In contrast to manufacturing in America, the vast US home markets calling for mass produced consumer goods were absent in the UK where many potentially home-based industries were handicapped because their product was considered inessential and the continued shortage of raw materials together with the need to reconstruct factory premises (plus the need for restraint in capital expenditure in line with Cripps's economic priorities) all served to hold down output below a level which would have justified planning for domestic mass production. Many of these constraints had lifted by the mid-1950s when Fordist strategies became relevant with a redirection of productive capital away from an overriding concern with exports to the development of a large scale domestic consumer market based on relative surplus value production techniques. The accuracy of this assessment is confirmed by an analysis of the use of the Marshall dollars which shows the UK employing Marshall aid for food imports whilst in 1949 only 8.3 per cent of dollar aid was allocated to machinery and vehicle imports, with this latter group accounting for only 0.4 per cent of all 1949 imports. No significant export of American accumulation conditions resulted in this first stage of Cripps's Chancellorship whether in the guise of Marshall aid or otherwise.

Finally, a study of the leverage the Marshall offensive gave the US in restructuring the British state's financial and commodity policies indicated that the grand designs the ECA fostered for a rapid achievement of their integrative Marshall-led ideals through a manipulation of intra-European trade and payments mechanisms met with the same overall failure that characterised their other incursive strategies. Far from Marshall aid forging a new European multilateralism, American dollars ended up strengthening and adding longevity to the neo-bilateral framework of trade and payments arrangements set up in opposition to State Department wishes by the British state under Dalton's guidance. Nevertheless, the pressure brought to bear on this framework – and the Treasury's realisation that America was attempting to reintroduce convertibility under the guise of transferable payments agreements with ever widening jurisdiction – prompted the British state to pre-empt ECA action by offering a programme of co-ordinated trade liberalisation. To understand the importance of this proposal both to the expansion of British accumulation and the limited achievement of specific US policy ideals, it is necessary to place it within the context of sterling devaluation and the formation of the European Payments Union.

5 The Revision in State Strategy

The final phase of Cripps's Chancellorship from late 1948 to mid-1950[1] saw a fundamental reorientation of the British state's accumulation strategy – a reorientation which is often obscured by analysts who simply equate the period with devaluation.[2] Whilst a discussion of devaluation is indispensable in disclosing Cripps's short-term policy alternatives, the state's overall accumulation objectives cannot be revealed by so narrow a focus. As in the preceding sections this chapter will therefore elucidate the state's relation to accumulation by charting the political and economic constraints on state action via an analysis of economic developments from mid-1948 to the end of the first quarter of 1950. This reveals that, whereas Dalton's dual accumulation strategy had successfully nurtured capital accumulation through the trials of the immediate postwar years, a revision of state policy was essential in the final phase of Cripps's Chancellorship if capital expansion was to be ensured.

This revision occurred principally in the area of trade and finance and took the form of a reappraisal of future multilateral international economic co-operation involving fundamental discussions on the cardinal issues of convertibility, discrimination, trade liberalisation, UK/US relations and the plausibility of alternative currency areas in the wake of continental plans (customs unions, Finebel) to exclude the UK from a European trading system. The trade and payments structure established to supersede the neo-bilateral framework erected under Dalton represented a concession by the UK towards European multilateralism which reflected both the pressure brought to bear on Britain by the ECA and other American agencies, and the growth of UK foreign currency reserves experienced after the third quarter of 1949. It will be shown that this period marked the end of the US attempt to subordinate the UK into a single large European market and brought the realisation that although the UK would remain committed to a single world multilateral system, Britain's global associations meant that the UK would continue its position of international ambivalence towards Europe and the US. In American eyes the most satisfactory option now lay in the pursuit of European integrative schemes which could be fashioned without

116

the participation of the UK. In terms of US capital expansion this policy had two distinct advantages. First, the retention of Britain within a single world system (finally laying to rest US fears of an autonomous Sterling Area soft currency bloc) meant that the major obstacles preventing New York financial markets from becoming the world financial centre could be circumvented in the short term by using the London financial system while continually pressing for general convertibility. Secondly, a more integrated European structure (even without the UK) would relax many of the constraints immediately present on US capital export whilst reinforcing Western Europe against the 'westward thrust of communism' which even at this late stage threatened, particularly in Italy, to undermine vital US interests.

Detailed analysis of major changes in British state policy, and American policy as it affected British accumulation, must proceed initially on the basis of a clearly charted account of developments in the UK economy from the close of 1948 to the balance of payments crisis of the first half of 1949.

I A NEW STERLING CRISIS

Economic Growth under Cripps

The previous chapter identified the events which fuelled the economic crisis of 1947 and concluded that the crisis did not reflect a fundamental weakness of British productive capital. The expansion of UK industrial production continued throughout 1948 reaching a new peak in October of that year 27 per cent above the 1946 monthly average.[3] Although the industrial population increased by only 2 per cent, industrial production as a whole rose 12 per cent above the 1947 figure, 16 per cent above prewar.[4] Manufacturing industry as a whole expanded its output by over 13 per cent above 1947, with steel production reaching a record level of 14.9 million tons, 17 per cent above 1947. Increased supplies of steel enabled the engineering industries to raise output by 16 per cent over 1947, to a volume over 50 per cent greater than prewar. Likewise production of bread grains was nearly 40 per cent more than prewar and other grains increased 20 per cent over 1947. Textile production showed a marked increase in output with the production of cotton rising to 20 per cent above 1947 and rayon output registering a figure 24 per cent greater than

1947.[5] The maintenance of nearly full employment contributed to this rising trend of industrial production, with unemployment among the total industrial population never reaching 2 per cent, as did the notable decline in industrial stoppages which reduced the number of working days lost owing to trade disputes by 20 per cent in comparison with the previous year.[6]

Gross domestic investment in fixed capital rose by 5 per cent in real terms in 1948 above the previous year and Cripps was now in a position not only to increase expenditure on housing and social services but also to 'place primary emphasis on investment in the basic and manufacturing industries where lower costs or increased production will contribute directly to our recovery'.[7] Overall gross fixed investment represented 13 per cent of the gross national product in 1948 compared to a figure of 10 per cent in 1946.[8] Close analysis of productive capital in 1948 reveals a vigorous pattern of expansion which rather belies the assessment that 'low investment was the key problem, and it was the failure of British governments to create the kind of climate for large scale investment and rapid increases in productivity that was most striking'.[9] Despite the popularity of this interpretation of British 'decline', it is simply untrue to claim that 'whenever something went wrong with the balance of payments, domestic investment was hit on the head'.[10] As I shall later demonstrate, industrial expansion continued throughout 1949 (a year of acute balance of payments crisis), exceeding the 1948 levels of industrial production by some 7 per cent and enabling gross fixed investment to continue to increase to a figure of 13.5 per cent of gross national product in that year.

This expansion was reflected in the volume of British exports, which increased from 9 per cent above 1938 in 1947 to 30 per cent above in the first half of 1948 and 50 per cent in the second half.[11] This overall increase of 39 per cent above 1947 was principally accounted for by the substantial improvement in metal goods and textile exports, with exports of vehicles (including locomotives, ships and aircraft) 45 per cent above the previous year and exports of cotton yarns and manufactures achieving a 68 per cent improvement over 1947. Nevertheless, the regional distribution of exports failed to show any significant alteration from the previous pattern, with 50 per cent of UK produce still being directed to the Sterling Area, 16 per cent to Western hemisphere nations and 34 per cent to other countries. The policy of switching purchases from dollar to non-dollar sources of supply had, however, begun to have an effect on imports in 1948. Whereas almost one half of UK imports derived from the Western hemisphere in 1947, this proportion had been reduced by 1948 to only 30 per cent with imports from the Sterling Area and other nations equally making up the balance. The level of imports, although increasing three points in terms of the volume index, continued to show changes which had been apparent since 1946. Food, drink and tobacco imports had fallen from 47 per cent to 42 per cent of the total, matched by an increase in the percentage of raw material imports from 27 per cent to 33 per cent with the remaining 25 per cent of total imports consisting almost wholly of machinery and processed materials for industry, with only a negligible proportion of articles ready for direct domestic consumption. This slow reorientation of imports had been an essential condition for higher levels of production and had contributed towards balancing overseas payments.

With regard to the state's currency reserves, the UK had reduced the gold and dollar deficit, which stood for the whole Sterling Area at approximately £1024 million in 1947 to a net deficit of £423 million by the end of 1948.[12] The drain in currency reserves had apparently diminished (via financing by US/Canadian credits, IMF purchases, the South African gold loan and Marshall Aid) to a third of that experienced in 1947, and in the first quater of 1949 the reserves stood at a figure of £471 million compared to a low of £437 million calculated for the third quarter of 1948. Moves towards the restoration of the dollar balance of payments and the attainment of 'viability' by 1952, independent of dollar aid, had however been almost imperceptible. Nevertheless, the British state had defined the first priority of economic policy as the restitution of dollar viability before the end of Marshall aid, with Cripps constantly reaffirming that unless an external balance was achieved there could be 'no prospect of a firmly based independent economic life'.[13] Towards this end the state had promoted policies to expand production, increase visible exports, restore invisible earnings, regulate the volume and constitution of imports, and select markets from which dollar savings would accrue.

UK trade with Western Europe produced an overall average annual trade surplus of approximately $57.8 million between 1946 and 1950. However, trade with the United States in the same period amassed annual deficits of over $600 million.[14] Cripps's 'positive and expansive'[15] methods of solving the dollar deficits – expansion of trade with the dollar world; acquisition of gold and dollars from trade with the gold-producing areas of the Commonwealth and gold-earning

Colonies; and the development of alternative sources of supply in the UK itself, in the Commonwealth and in the rest of the non-dollar world – could only attain precarious advances in an unbalanced structure of international trade and production. The scale of the problem in 1948 is starkly illustrated by the fact that less than half of UK imports from the Western hemisphere were covered by British and Sterling Area earnings in that region.[16]

The Resistance to Early Devaluation

The most pressing task facing the British state in late 1948 was that of finding an effective means of reducing the dollar deficit which threatened the economy with recurrent financial crisis, if possible by drawing on the soft currency surpluses continuously gathered since 1946 whilst maintaining full employment and a high level of public expenditure, both seen as indispensible by the Attlee administration. In a prescient paper Richard Clarke, of the Overseas Finance Division of the Treasury, outlined one – at the time unorthodox – method of achieving this aim via price manipulation.

Recognising the futility of mere exhortation to buy in non-dollar markets, Clarke noted that, whilst raw materials and food from Western Europe were 50–100 per cent dearer than materials from the USA, 'the working of the price calculus gives us all the wrong answers in relation to our objectives'.[17] Efforts to establish dollar-saving in the UK, find soft currency supply sources and guide exports to dollar markets merely had the effect of 'swimming against the stream' by asking people to abstain on patriotic grounds from action which was in their financial interest. Clarke thereby proposed in February 1948 a sterling devaluation to reach a sterling/dollar parity of between \$2.5–3.0 to produce a situation where, in terms of sterling, dollar imports would be dearer than those from any other source and exports to the dollar area would become financially attractive. A fall in the sterling/dollar rate would help to adjust UK consumption, production and trade patterns whilst having a beneficial effect (if other European nations followed suit) on the relative prices of sources of supply and the diversion of exports for Europe as a whole. Without this action, Clarke prophesied, 'I would expect another instalment of dollar crisis (even with ERP) some time in 1949'.[18]

Whilst few argued with Clarke's prognosis there was at this stage general disagreement on the efficacy of his solution. George Bolton, a Director of the Bank of England, took the view that no adjustment of the rate of exchange could have any substantial effect on the dollar shortage 'which is the expression of a production problem' reflected in the persistent large favourable balance of payments of the USA.[19] Price manipulation, the Bank argued, would have little effect on the breakdown of channels of trade and the comparative lack of production outside the USA, and could even 'precipitate an exchange crisis of unpredictable magnitude'[20] whilst turning the terms of trade further against the British economy.

Most Treasury officials and Cabinet members took a similar view. Cripps, for instance, as late as June 1949 was adamant that 'you cannot possibly find any solution to our present problems by juggling with money incomes or finances or fiscal measures'.[21] The only way to meet the dollar shortage, Cripps maintained, was to increase the efficiency of production without lowering wages or lengthening hours of work. With improved salesmanship UK goods would become more competitive in dollar and home markets: 'we want our money to be worth more in purchasing power and not less . . . that is *our* policy for solving this difficult problem'.[22] Clarke's diagnosis, and the support of Herbert Morrison who repeatedly argued that the 'temptation to defer action until it is publicly dictated to us by events should be resisted if we are to retain and maintain confidence',[23] failed to convince Cripps or the Bank of England. In 1948 it was generally agreed that it was premature to devalue when exports had not lost momentum and when there was consequently little in hand to permit a redirection of exports to dollar areas. Nevertheless, as Cairncross, economic adviser to the Board of Trade, points out,[24] it was obvious that at some point in the postwar years it would be necessary to reconsider the sterling/dollar exchange rate and this point was rapidly approaching in early 1949 when exports began to lose momentum and the prime requirement was not simply to expand the total but to effect a redistribution of exports between dollar and non-dollar markets.

Having reviewed the expansion of accumulation throughout 1948 and examined the early controversies surrounding state management of sterling, we can chart the economic and political developments which led to the 'marked change of view' amongst state officials who by mid-July 1949 had 'come round to the position that devaluation would make a valuable contribution towards easing dollar difficulties'.[25] The importance of this discussion lies less in bringing to light the technical process of policy making and more in tracing the constraints on the state's economic policy, whilst contextualising the

British decision to devalue, which became a vital component in later transatlantic discussions concerning the future of multilateralism.

II DEVALUATION AND MULTILATERALISM

Causes of the Sterling Crisis

Despite continued expansion of industrial production throughout the first quarter of 1949, with the index of industrial production of all industries reaching a record level of 131 in March of that year (a clear 8 point increase over the December 1948 level),[26] it was becoming evident that, in contrast to the overall progress made in 1948, exports were now losing momentum whilst imports maintained a steady increase. By April the monthly average of UK exported produce had fallen from a figure of £159.2 million for January to £137.4 million, with the UK now exporting a smaller proportion of produce to North America than before the war. This last point was the most significant. In the first four months of 1949 the rate of exports to the USA fell 14 per cent lower than the rate for the last quarter of 1948 while British exports to the entire dollar-earning markets of the Western hemisphere fell from a figure of 16 per cent of total UK exports in January to 12 per cent by April 1949.[27] Retained imports nevertheless continued to rise with the volume index, which stood at 81 points in 1948, increasing to the mid-90s by the end of the second quarter of 1949 (93 in June, 96 in August), and the proportion of imports from the Western hemisphere continuing to constitute approximately 28 per cent of all UK imports.[28]

This deterioration in the UK balance of trade, particularly with the dollar area, contributed to a balance of payments crisis which posed a threat to the British economy more serious than that experienced in 1947. The drain in British gold and dollar reserves, which stood at £471 million in March 1949, was accelerated by the mounting trade deficit of the Sterling Area with the United States, which almost doubled in the second quarter of 1949, increasing from a deficit of $159 million to $280 million.[29] The dollar reserves proportionately decreased to £406 million in June, £368 million in July and £348 million by August – a fall of 26 per cent in just over five months.[30]

Throughout the convertibility crisis the Treasury had been of the opinion that 'it is unsafe to allow the reserves to be drawn down to below £500 million'.[31] Yet with the reserves down to £330 million by 18 September 1949 it was little wonder that Cripps believed if the problem could not be solved 'then it does mean a division of the Western world into two economic groups and very likely collapse of the economy of Europe, which is balanced on a knife-edge'.[32] The gravity of Cripps's prediction demands that we review the origins of this decline in detail.

Many analysts pointed to the new sterling crisis as the manifestation of the 'contradictory uneconomic objectives' pursued by the Labour administration involving high public expenditure and full employment without deflationary policies – 'which cannot be made to work at all except at the height of a world boom and only then with the aid of a dollar subsidy'.[33] A more cogent explanation, however, must make reference to the inventory recession which took place in the United States during the first half of 1949. American imports from OEEC nations declined more or less continuously from January 1949, when they stood at $85 million, to July 1949, when they amounted to $50 million with the share of imports from the UK only 62 per cent of the comparable figure for July 1948.[34] This decline coincided with a significant fall in the US industrial production index from 191 in January to 161 points by July – a parallelism similar to that experienced in the temporary US business decline of 1938. The most clearly identifiable aspect of the 1949 recession was the fall in inventories, with manufacturing output suffering an 8.5 per cent decline between July 1948 and May 1949 largely because goods were supplied by running down existing inventories.[35] Although in respect of the total value of Western Europe's foreign trade the decline in exports to the US was only marginally important in absolute terms, for the UK the decline had a devastating effect. This indicates important differences between the trade of the UK and the rest of Western Europe which are worth elaborating.

Britain's Exclusion from the Intra-European Trade Boom

The total value of Europe's extra-European trade in 1949 had failed to increase beyond the level of the last quarter of 1948, with the Sterling Area continuing to absorb over half of UK exports and the nations of Western Europe less than one quarter. By contrast intra-European trade amongst the developed Western European nations (excluding the UK) accounted in 1948 for 55 per cent of the total exports of France, Italy, Germany and Benelux (hereafter referred to as 'Little Europe') with the value of intra-Western European exports in 1949 increasing 28 per cent above the 1948 level. By 1949 intra-European trade was booming, with France experiencing an increase in the value of its intra-European exports of 42 per cent. Exports to Western Europe as a percentage of all exports showed a similarly high level for Denmark (79 per cent), West Germany (76 per cent), Benelux (61 per cent) and Sweden (60 per cent), whilst in the same period British exports to this market experienced an increase of only 4.9 per cent.[36] The fact that the traditional structure of British trade left Britain supplying a wide variety of markets with very different requirements and low effective demand for high levels of many manufactured exports must be considered by any study reviewing British 'decline'. Yet within the context of the present discussion it is highly relevant in explaining why Western Europe as a whole was largely sheltered from the effects of the US recession whilst Britain experienced a severe sterling crisis.

With the UK excluded from the intra-European export boom, United States imports by value from the Sterling Area fell by 17 per cent in 1948–9 with the sales of five key Sterling Area commodities (rubber, tin, cocoa, diamonds and wool) suffering a serious depression as their sales dropped by half over the period December 1948 to June 1949.[37] This sharp fall in the earnings of Sterling Area primary products, plus the reduction in UK exports to both the US and Canada and a 38 per cent increase above the 1948 level in UK import expenditure in the US (and to a lesser extent attempts to move capital from sterling holdings by running down working balances), made a significant contribution to the exhaustion of UK gold and dollar reserves. To these factors must be added, first, the loss in dollar income attributable to the declining efficiency of the sterling exchange mechanism – whereby the use of 'cheap sterling' in New York to finance Sterling Area commodities had deprived the Sterling Area of dollar income – and secondly, the effect of speculation when the expectation of devaluation led to the deferment of purchases payable in sterling and of actual disbursements in sterling. In addition to the internal British debate on devaluation, formalised as early as the beginning of 1949, Sweden had approached the UK in the OEEC concerning currency realignment in November of that year, whilst the US Treasury, the ECA and the Federal Reserve Board made numerous references to the efficacy of the move in various public hearings. By June 1949 *The Banker* was reporting 'the almost universal belief in the City that devaluation was inevitable'. The resultant two-way pressure on sterling (deferment of purchases and sterling conversions) could have accounted for almost half the deterioration in the net dollar deficit between the first and second quarters of 1949. Cripps came to this conclusion when he realised that the loss of reserves up to 18 September was higher than in the second quarter, and in the last thirty days before devaluation amounted to £42 million, compared to £65 million for the whole of the second quarter.[38]

The 1949 sterling crisis demonstrated the fragility of Britain's postwar economic recovery and indicated the possible long-term drawbacks of concentrating commodity export in the traditional trade markets of the Sterling Area to the detriment of intra-European trade expansion. In contrast to 1947 this latest crisis was almost entirely a British affair with many of the other Western European nations increasing hard currency foreign reserves over the crisis period. This led the ECA to consider what had been inconceivable up until that point: Western European integration without a British initiative or even without British participation. Before analysing the development of US policy on the future of Western Europe in the context of achieving US multilateral ideals before the exhaustion of Marshall aid, it is essential for this chapter to detail the British state's changing response to the sterling crisis. This response focused not only upon the narrow but important issue of stemming the dollar drain, but encompassed much more wide-ranging discussion concerning Britain's commitment to multilateralism and its accumulation strategy with regard to Europe, the Sterling Area and the United States.

The Implications of Devaluation

The state's decision to devalue, taken in Cripps's absence (while the Chancellor attended a Swiss sanatorium) and communicated to him on 8 August 1949, was more than a simple 'step towards currency stability' or a 'natural and proper' readjustment to the markets of the world.[39] It represented the consolidation of the British commitment to find a 'way towards a one world economy'[40] and a final rejection of the notion that the UK should establish an international system of its own based upon sterling. Whilst careful discussion on the feasibility of a sterling soft currency bloc was carried out by the Cabinet as a course of action if all else should fail, the decision to devalue reinforced the economic, political and strategic considerations which favoured convertibility as a final objective.

Since the signing of the American loan in December 1945 the viability of a 'two-world trading structure' had increasingly declined with the Treasury now arguing: 'we favour convertibility as a objective for the basic reason that one cannot insulate our international system based on inconvertible sterling from the rest of the world's system based on gold and dollars. The two trading systems are inextricably tangled, and there must be some means of settling payments between the two'.[41] This was an argument that had been advanced by Cripps in various public debates since 1947. Thus in October 1948 Cripps stated that the progressive restoration of multilateral trade 'is an essential condition of world prosperity and the only satisfactory long-term solution to Britain's own trade problems'.[42] Similary, in his keynote speech to the Imperial Defence College one month later, Cripps stressed that the UK 'cannot operate in isolation . . . for a nation with an open economy like ours success depends on the maintenance of a high level of activity throughout the world leading to a high level of demand for our exports especially in the Western hemisphere . . . and in the progressive expansion of multilateral practices in overseas trade as rapidly as circumstances allow'.[43]

But it was not until the completion of the debate around the 1949 sterling crisis that the spectre of a soft currency sterling bloc was finally banished from the agenda of the Attlee administration. Devaluation itself was recommended by Gaitskell (in the company of Wilson and Jay) on the grounds that exchange control had not prevented the drain whilst the controls over dollar expenditure exercised by the Commonwealth nations were ineffective. Since no special US help would be forthcoming there was a real danger of currency collapse if the reserves continued to fall.[44] Cripps and Bevin in the final stages of the crisis displayed an unusual fluctuation of opinion on devaluation, with Cripps 'much more doubtful about the value of the step at all, at first, but later appeared strongly to support it', and Bevin's line 'changing as he talked'.[45] Nevertheless, the increasing speculative pressure on sterling swayed the Cabinet in favour of Gaitskell's recommendation, with Cripps believing that the argument based on the need to create more confidence in the pound was more valid than the argument that devaluation would enable Britain to earn more dollars. On the psychological side, he claimed, 'there is no doubt whatever that since last Spring a very wide expectation has grown up that sterling would be devalued and this has militated against the stability of sterling and has caused a certain degree of strain upon our reserves'.[46] Yet it was not at all clear that the effect of devaluation, while it might increase the volume of the country's exports to the dollar area, would be sufficiently great (in view of the smaller number of dollars which would be earned) to help close the gap. 'It would be quite impracticable', Cripps advised, 'to give any indication of what extent devaluation would assist exports, and any guess could soon be checked against published trade figures'.[47] By late July, therefore, the Cabinet was agreed that sterling (largely because of the atmosphere created in the United States) could not achieve stability without devaluation. However, as Cripps explained to a meeting of Canadian and US ministers, 'we do not regard devaluation as a miracle working device which can put matters right by the wave of a wand';[48] only as part of a joint transatlantic package would devaluation be an advantage to the UK.

State Action to Halt the Dollar Drain

The overall state strategy developed in response to the sterling crisis turned not only upon a 30 per cent fall in the parity of sterling from $4.03 to $2.80 announced on 18 September after consultation with the US on 7 September. It also involved specific internal and external manoeuvres designed both to halt the dollar drain and, as Morrison pointed out, to reaffirm 'confidence in the government's leadership which would automatically improve the chances of the US administration accepting unpalatable measures on their part to ease our difficulties'.[49] This, it was also hoped, would renew the British public's confidence in the Attlee administration with the General Election imminent.

Although the Cabinet absolutely rejected the suggestion that 'our external difficulties could be directly related to high levels of public expenditure and taxation at home', Attlee agreed, at Cripps's and Morrison's behest, to a review of government expenditure 'with the object of securing such economies as can be obtained without prejudice to major government policy'.[50] Attlee thus issued a directive calling for Heads of Civil Departments to curtail services not essential to major government policy and to begin a more economic administration of the policies which must be retained. Morrison had calculated that public expenditure was now running at an annual figure of £3000 million, and concluded that 'it does not make sense that in such an immense total we cannot find say, 5 per cent worth of expenditure which could either be pruned off or spread over a longer period without serious consequences'.[51] A reduction in the rate of net expenditure by 5 per cent was thereby proposed in conjunction with a study of the reductions which could be made in the government's investment programme.

The principal rationale for this proposed internal measure of reducing public expenditure consisted of three elements. First, the publicly announced commitment to counter any inflationary tendencies which could develop in the near future. Secondly, and rather more significantly, to demonstrate to the USA that 'the UK were ready to help themselves to get out of their difficulties and were not merely waiting for assistance from others',[52] or as Morrison more revealingly expressed it, 'to look as if we know where we are going and how to get there'.[53] Finally, the proposal was intended to renew domestic support for the government in the wake of the oncoming General Election, since the Cabinet agreed 'if there is one thing the British will not easily forgive it is a "mess" '.[54] Prompt and convincing action was thereby prescribed as a remedy to sweeten both the forthcoming Washington negotiations and prepare for the domestic Election under the official guise of taking steps to curtail inflationary tendencies. In an attempt to dissociate these three aspects the Cabinet concluded that the reductions in state expenditure should not be discussed as a condition of any assistance offered by the US government and that 'in any public announcement that might be made cuts in public expenditure should not be presented as connected with any agreements reached in those talks'.[55] The blatant political intentions behind this seemingly internal economic manoeuvre (contrast, for instance, the strong economic rationale behind the Healey/Jenkins state expenditure reductions of 1976[56]) can be further clarified by a review of the fate of the proposed reductions.

Political Considerations Influencing Internal Measures

·As demonstrated in the last chapter it is common for analysts to argue that 'British decline' is predominantly the result of low levels of investment in domestic manufacturing industry. It is largely beyond the scope of this book to address in detail that proposal.[57] However, we can show the weakness of those accounts which cite the 1947, 1948 and 1949 proposed capital expenditure cuts as examples of the suggestion that 'whenever something went wrong with the balance of payments, domestic investment was hit on the head'.[58] Eatwell, for instance, notes the government's public statement that 'investment at home in engineering products should in 1950 be slightly less than in 1949' and concludes that investment fell significantly between those dates. Yet close study of state policy over that period shows how misleading an out-of-context quote can be and how it can bring an analysis to a patently false conclusion. After a report from the Investment Programmes Committee in August 1949 Harold Wilson (at the Board of Trade) concluded, 'there is no easy way of reducing inflationary pressure by cuts in investment without major changes in government policy', changes affecting, for instance, full employment and the reorganisation and re-equipment plans for the socialised industries which would not under any circumstances be sanctioned by the Attlee administration.[59] The opinion of the Investment Committee was that the investment programme made a valuable contribution to economic recovery and the reduction of costs, and should consequently be affected as little as possible. The Cabinet agreed with this suggestion and as a result total fixed investment for 1950 did not decline but, as in previous years, increased, in this instance by £100 million, with gross fixed investment reaching a record figure of 14 per cent of gross national product by the early 1950s.[60]

With regard to the public expenditure cuts in general, the views of Thorneycroft and Eden[61] that they represented 'make-shift arrangements got together . . . by . . . harassed men', 'scratched together' and still 'sketchy and indefinite', were nearer the mark than the official pronouncements. The final total for expenditure cuts fell short of its target, reaching only a proposed £122.5 million, of which £79 million was to be gathered by reducing feeding stuffs, defence and additional profits tax; £28 million accounted for by administrative economies; and £10 million for the levy of one shilling on prescriptions (later revoked in April 1950).[62]

A review of the internal economic measures proposed by the state to accompany devaluation leaves little doubt that the official stance that the measures were employed to counter inflationary tendencies conveyed less than the true justification for the strategy. As an attempt to reduce inflation (which posed little problem until the effects of the outbreak of the Korean hostilities began to be manifest in late 1950) the final form of the state expenditure reductions was plainly inadequate. The Cabinet would not entertain discussion of deflation since it was perceived that such measures would threaten the very basis of the government (principally its fundamental objectives of maintaining full employment and rising living standards), and thus they decided under the banner of disinflation to announce proposed cuts, the effect of which was calculated to be more political than economic. The extent of the political success of this manoeuvre, particularly its effect on the American administration, can be judged by considering the development of the external strategies adopted by the state in the face of the dollar drain, strategies directed not only towards the British Commonwealth but also designed to reduce the large US balance of payments surplus and to effect an increase in trade discrimination.

External Policy Negotiation

Following the state's initial measures to check the dollar drain by reducing the total value of dollar imports by 25 per cent over the twelve months to July 1950 (from a proposed figure of £1600 million to £1200 million), the first move to consolidate this strategy via external policy was made after a meeting of Commonwealth Finance Ministers ending on 18 July 1949. Stressing that the UK and the Sterling Area's primary objective must be 'the achievment of a pattern of world trade in which the dollar and non-dollar countries can operate together within one single multilateral system',[63] the meeting decided on a variety of emergency measures to stem the current drain. These included pledges to increase efficiency in production, co-operation in the use of resources, expansion of sales in dollar markets, and the decision that Commonwealth nations would follow the example of the UK by instituting a comparable 25 per cent reduction in their dollar expenditure. This measure proved beneficial to the UK, particularly when seen in the context of the decrease in the extent of trade control (via trade liberalisation programmes and reversion to private trade practices carried out in 1949) in the non-dollar world, significantly reducing imports from the dollar area by commodity class from a figure of 22 per cent for 1949 to a record low for the 1940s and 1950s of 18 per cent in 1950.[64] Evidence of public expenditure cuts and reductions in dollar imports also had a political pay-off for the British negotiators who were now able to seek the assistance of the USA and Canada in supporting these remedies and 'in taking others in the external field which are not wholly within our power'.[65] The study will now review these other measures in the external field since, as I shall demonstrate, the September tripartite discussions led to important policy developments on both sides of the Atlantic, having major repercussions for Britain's accumulation strategy which persisted well beyond the life of the Attlee administration.

A cursory reading of the joint British and American/Canadian discussions held in Washington on 7 September 1949 is apt to disclose little of their real significance. At face value the discussions appear to have been simply concerned with issues such as oil production in the US, a commodity agreement for tin, joint discussion on shipping and US agriculture support prices. However, closer analysis reveals that the tripartite talks clarified many of the most significant topics concerning the world economy, including the British position on convertibility, non-discrimination and dollar viability, and the American response to Britain's candid assessment of its relation to Europe.

The British state delegation arrived remarkably well prepared for the Washington consultations. In addition to being able to point to the proposed domestic expenditure cuts and dollar import reductions, the announcement by Cripps that 'the best policy for us to pursue in the interest of the solution of our common problem is to embark forthwith on a sterling devaluation'[66] clearly gave the British the initiative in the discussions (Bevin earlier had advised Cripps: 'you can use this as a bargaining counter'[67]), which impressed upon the Americans the nature of the British resolve and even suggested a new basis for Atlantic co-operation.

The Treasury's view that the UK must 'attain viability and freedom from dollar aid at the earliest possible moment'[68] was translated by Cripps in the discussions into the precise statement that the UK saw no solution in 'more aid for Britain' and indeed, the UK now required that the sterling system increase its dollar earnings 'so as to pay its way by 1952'. Whilst recognising, as Hall-Patch later confirmed, that 'for some time Washington has been in one of those periods of gestation in which the policy makers are debating amongst themselves fundamental issues',[69] the British team expressed its considered opinion on the basic topics of convertibility and non-discrimination in an effort to gain 'the establishment of the greatest identity of views possible between the three governments'.[70]

Cripps forthrightly rejected the popular American claim that British dollar difficulties could be related to internal UK policy. The provision of full employment and improved social services 'was essential if fundamental social upheavals were to be avoided'[71] and to lay undue stress on UK internal policies missed the more primary point that 'an approximate condition of balance in world production and trade is lacking'.[72] This imbalance, due in considerable part to the failure of the US to adopt a sufficiently liberal import policy, had a serious impact in the UK because of its position as the repository of the main monetary reserves of the non-dollar world. Following this diagnosis the British position on the 'agreed objectives' of external financial policy was relatively clear.

First, it was stressed that convertibility and greater multilateral trade must be the results of equilibrium in trade and not be seen as steps towards it. Consequently, if the UK could not convert its favourable balances, 'we must spend them where they are spendable'; that is to say, in an absence of world production and trade balance resulting in inconvertible sterling, the UK must conduct the majority of its trade in sterling markets and this 'inevitably means more discrimination'.[73] Non-discrimination in present conditions was adjudged to be 'nonsense' and could only in the future follow convertibility, not precede it. As liberalisation proceeds, the British state had diagnosed, UK import policy would necessarily become more discriminatory against the US. Discrimination against US imports would be vital, 'for this is how the world structure of consumption and trade is moulded for dollar-saving'.[74] The agreed direction of external financial policy was clear – 'the question is not *whether* we make sterling convertible into gold or dollars, but *how much* and *under what conditions*'. Yet moves towards this objective could only in the visible future proceed on the basis of organising more discrimination, particularly in Europe where 'the need for dollar-saving structural change is not realised enough'.[75]

Consequences of the Tripartite Talks

This frank assessment on the part of the British state had three principal consequences, one of which was clearly unintended by the Cripps mission. First, the realistic exchange of views yielded some tangible benefits for the UK in terms of alteration in US and Canadian external economic policy. The joint communiqué issued at the end of the tripartite discussions stressed that the consultations had 'resulted in a clear understanding of the character of the difficulties to be faced and an increasing realisation that a fully satisfactory solution will necessitate continuing efforts in many directions'.[76] As part of such an effort the USA and Canada agreed to reduce obstacles to the entry of goods and services from debtor nations, realising that high tariff rates were 'clearly inconsistent' with the present position of creditor countries. A resumption and acceleration of stockpiling was also agreed upon, particularly with reference to rubber and tin purchases, and a revision of US policy on drawings from the IMF and the Export–Import Bank was also instituted. Finally, by the way of tangible benefit, the USA agreed to broaden the use of ERP funds allocated to the UK, specifically allowing ERP financing to be used for purchases of Canadian wheat, and they agreed to a review of government measures to encourage US and Canadian investment in the UK. Although many of these points appear rather technical and perhaps peripheral to the promotion of British recovery, they were undoubtedly concessions on the part of the US administration and reinforced the second major consequence, that of re-establishing the basis of the 'special relationship' between the UK and the USA outside the ambit of the OEEC.

State documents reveal that the UK viewed the tripartite talks as a major step towards consolidating UK/US economic ties, to the exclusion of further intra-European links. Whilst prior to the discussions close American links had been forged mainly via foreign policy with Bevin feeling 'morally committed to Acheson to take no strong unilateral action',[77] following the tripartite consultations the British state was led 'to favour the idea of a US partnership in the sense of having a common objective and conducting economic policy in order to reach it'.[78] Recognising the suspicion generated in Europe concerning the status of the Washington talks, Gaitskell suggested that continuing meetings 'must be kept as informal as possible' since the UK 'must resist any proposal for enlarging the tripartite talks by inclusion of other OEEC countries'.[79] The discussions had thus consolidated the Cabinet view that the UK 'by reason of its geographical position and of its political and economic relations with the Commonwealth and the United States could not enter into any exclusive political or economic association with Continental countries'.[80] There can be little doubt that by this stage the British state had rejected any scheme for UK participation in European integration. Whilst opinion remained divided in the US (as I shall shortly clarify) the Washington talks represented for the US Treasury in particular a significant moment in the evolution of US integrative policy, in terms of the realisation that the UK was now fully committed to independent viability within a one-world economic system. Ambiguity, however, remained in the overall American assessment of Britain and European integration until the establishment of the European Payments Union, which, as I shall later show, was created only after major policy concessions by the

US, concessions which had their origins in the Washington consultations.

The final consequence of the talks lay in the discussions concerning non-discrimination. The persuasive British argument for more discrimination was accepted by the US and then pushed to a conclusion which the British negotiators never anticipated. The British state had suggested 'we are ready to move away from bilateralism in certain conditions'.[81] When allied to the argument for discrimination this proposal presented the US administration with a gilt-edged opportunity to press the UK for closer collaboration with the non-dollar world in forming a regional multilateral system. This aspect of the development of state strategy forms the second part of this chapter and thus it suffices at this stage merely to point out that Cripps's reluctance to sanction the terms of the EPU was constantly undermined by American reference to this aspect of the Washington declaration.

The Revival of Sterling

The state's response to the 1949 sterling crisis had thus been protracted and complicated, involving an analysis of issues which related not only to the dollar drain but concerned the very fundamentals of UK accumulation strategy. By the final quarter of 1949 it was clear that the deterioration in dollar reserves had been reversed, with a study accumulation discernible from October onwards. By January of 1950 the reserves had climbed to approximately £450 million (£648 million in new rates), and April registered a figure of some £525 million (£759 million), the first time the reserves had risen above the Treasury 'minimum safety level' since March 1948.[82] While the increase was clear, the causes of the amelioration were rather less so.

The government, of course, claimed success for its measures, particularly that of devaluation, yet the restoration of exports approximately to the 1948 level in the first half of 1950 is attributable in large part to the recovery in the US economy rather than simply to the devaluations. Polak notes that the devaluations increased the volume of exports to the US by an amount little more than enough to offset the fall of about 15 per cent in dollar export prices, whilst causing a 10 per cent increase in the dollar value of Western Europe's exports to other markets in the Western hemisphere, and concludes that 'only an improvement of 5 per cent in the devaluing countries' exports to the US can be attributed to the devaluations'.[83]

Furthermore, whilst the 25 per cent reduction in dollar imports lessened the pressure on the British dollar reserves, it should also be recognised that the return of Western Europe, particularly West Germany, to prewar levels of output had improved the European supply position. Dollar economies, which to the chagrin of the US continued after the period of crisis, and improved European sources of supply turned the Sterling Area deficit on dollar account from $31 million in the final quarter of 1949 to a small surplus of $40 million by March 1950, increasing to $180 million for April–June quarter.[84] By April 1950 the amelioration was so complete that, in addition to the fundamental objectives of full employment and higher living standards, Gaitskell added a new objective: 'the accumulation of gold and dollar reserves at the expense of the USA'.[85] Our 'great achievement since the devaluation', the Treasury boasted, 'has been to put the whole of our ERP assistance to reserve'.[86] Recognising that the Americans must soon end a situation in which the US taxpayer was contributing $750 million to British reserves, the Treasury concluded that assistance was no longer required since 'bankruptcy was almost definitely behind us'. (It was with such a realisation that ERP to Britain ended on 13 December 1950.)

III   A REVISION IN STATE STRATEGY

The resolution of the 1949 sterling crisis had created a number of conditions which, although largely unintended by the British state, were conducive to the development of a substantially revised UK accumulation strategy. Devaluation made almost inevitable a major rebuilding of the already unsatisfactory European trade and payments arrangements arrived at in early September. A neo-bilateral scheme whereby balance of payments forecasts were the basis on which drawing rights were established was now irreconcilable with the economic changes which characterised Western Europe following devaluation and the sterling crisis. The growth of British foreign currency reserves called into question the framework of neo-bilateralism which by early 1950 was shown to be insufficiently elastic, absorbing far more credit than was desirable if each nation's debits and credits could have been offset against one another. Maximum transferability, the Treasury now argued, was 'in our fundamental long-term interest – it enables us to match deficits with surpluses and it removes fetters from the use of sterling without which the whole of our external policy remains an uphill struggle'.[87]

Whilst the neo-bilateralism established under Dalton had nurtured and facilitated the recovery of European trade, and had been of especial benefit to the UK, whose dollar reserves required the complex protective mechanisms characteristic of neo-bilateralism, a turning point had been reached by 1950 when the British state recognised that 'transferability and trade liberalisation make it progressively more meaningless to seek to deal with trade and payments problems by bilateral negotiation. We need a multilateral solution in any event'.[88]

The amelioration of the British position had not been lost on the United States who now took the view, with increasing justification following the Washington talks, that unless the UK could give some indications of positive future action, Britain's 'chances of obtaining Treasury co-operation in modifying US policies will be much reduced'.[89] William McChesney Martin, Assistant Secretary of the US Treasury, specifically cited the example of the 25 per cent reduction in Sterling Area dollar imports introduced as 'an emergency measure that had now become permanent policy' and called upon the British state to 'make experiments' to indicate that British actions were 'directed towards our agreed aim'. The UK Treasury had decided that 'both on merits and tactically in relation to the US we must show willing'[90] and for that purpose believed that a gradual and controlled introduction of a degree of convertibility in Europe represented the most fruitful form of progress in the financial field, allied to progressive action in the trade field which had been initiated via the programme of trade liberalisation. A combination of factors – European dissatisfaction with a restrictive bilateralism now thrown into confusion by devaluation; British acknowledgement that increased reserves of foreign currency could sanction expanded accumulation; and American pressure – prompted the British state to reassess future economic strategy. Whilst the expansion of currency reserves following the sterling crisis had laid the necessary objective conditions for a revision of state economic strategy, varying political imperatives made it unclear what form this redirection would take. To assess this realignment of state policy the remainder of this chapter needs to focus on the struggles which characterised the British and American administrations, indicating the opportunities for British and US capital expansion which resulted from the final compromise.

A New ECA Policy Approach to Multilateralism

The uneven adjustment of the American administration to the rapid political and economic developments in Western Europe in the closing half of 1949 produced a series of often contradictory strategies for the attainment of the common goal of US foreign economic policy. The establishment of a US-dominated world economy, capable of sustaining domestic demand and a large export surplus, characterised by non-discriminatory multilateral trade based on the general convertibility of sterling, remained the constant long-term objective. Nevertheless, the thorough discrediting of the Bretton Woods/Key Currency proposals for achieving this objective had now been followed by the discrediting of the ECA proposal to move towards the common goal via an OEEC-led Western European integration. The September Washington discussions had further convinced the US Treasury that the UK and the Sterling Area had an importance for US strategy which went beyond that of simply leading Western European integration – a route which, it was quite clear, the UK would not in any case pursue. Arguing that the ECA integrative strategy was based upon a serious contradiction in that it assumed a high level of US business activity whilst co-terminously sanctioning a sharp reduction in European imports from the US, the Treasury's strategy was to press the UK on a 'dash for freedom' programme involving an immediate restoration of sterling convertibility and an abandonment of trade restrictions and protections in a bold effort to achieve early viability. The Treasury 'solution' was, however, blocked by the State Department and the ECA who both recognised its impracticality and had drawn rather different conclusions from the Washington discussions concerning future policy.

Whilst the ECA acknowledged that European integration could not be achieved on an institutional OEEC basis using Marshall aid as leverage, the administration, encouraged by UK initiatives to liberalise trade, now focused upon a strategy of harmonising national trade and payments policies with a view to creating a regional multilateral payments union and authority which would ultimately meet the ECA goal of European integration but via a rather more subtle route than approached earlier. The belief that European viability could only be premissed on the creation of a large domestic market with no internal trade barriers had now led the ECA towards analysis of the most effective payments mechanism which would permit 'full automatic transferability of European currencies (not just drawing rights) and controlled convertibility of net surpluses on intra-European accounts into dollars'.[91] This revised ECA strategy for European integration via manipulation of trade and payments arrangements nevertheless still embodied a simplistic evolutionary scheme for the achievement of American aims.

By multilateralising trade on a regional basis Europe would have abandoned bilateralism whilst retaining discrimination and trade control towards the rest of the world, particularly the dollar area. The gradual liberalisation of intra-European trade and payments, the ECA believed, would exert a downward pressure on European costs and prices in at least four ways. Initially, the introduction of full multilateral settlement within Europe would result in price reductions by enabling the cheapest import source to predominate, thus eliminating the generation of uncompetitive 'abnormal' profits. Trade liberalisation would led to the gradual elimination of high-cost marginal firms due to exposure from outside competition, whilst the removal of trade restrictions would almost certainly affect the pattern of new investment resulting in a more economical allocation of resources. The establishment of industrial plant incapable of sustaining 'unprotected' production would be guarded against whilst the introduction of low cost plants at present unbuilt because of inadequate markets would be significantly encouraged. Finally, to the extent that import restrictions vary amongst European nations, many countries may become exposed to US competition as a result of trade and payments liberalisation creating a less sheltered European environment.[92]

Trade liberalisation under the auspices of a European Payments Union (EPU) would, the ECA claimed, operate to lower European costs and prices, increasing competitiveness and moving the continent to a situation of viability whereby there would be an end to trade discrimination *in toto*, a subsequent restoration of sterling convertibility and the introduction of full world multilateralism. The accomplishment of this plan, Hoffman had assessed, depended on the creation not only of a European Clearing Union whose actions to liberalise trade and multilateralise payments would be necessary within the time-span of Marshall aid, but also upon the establishment of 'really effective machinery for direct co-ordination of national policies by agreement or by some international control over actions of governments and central banks'.[93] This machinery was proposed in the form of a European Monetary Authority which ultimately 'should be transformed from a co-ordinator of the monetary policies of its member countries to a central bank . . . [underlining] . . . its supra-national character'.[94]

While the ECA solution obtained Congressional approval, the American administration could not obscure the controversy surrounding the strategy. The US Treasury maintained that a European Payments Union would increase the difficulty of the dollar problem, diminishing the prospects for an early return to full sterling convertibility. For the EPU to succeed, trade discrimination with the Western hemisphere would have to be increased to prevent the liberalisation of intra-European trade resulting in an unwanted increase in European imports from outside sources.[95] Following visits to the Treasury and the State Department, Hall-Patch detected the 'weakness' of the US administration as regards foreign economic policy noting that, whilst 'there is no support for integration outside Washington among the people we saw', even within the Washington circles 'there are strong sections inside and outside the Administration who recognise our special position and wish to buttress it'.[96] The fact that the original ECA integrative strategy had in even more propitious circumstances resulted in failure did not augur well for the success of this revised effort, particularly since it ignored the 'problem of Germany' within European reconstruction and the obvious confrontation which would ensue with the UK over the position of the Sterling Area in a regional multilateral structure. The limitations of the ECA strategy can be assessed only in the context of the negotiations over liberalisation and the EPU, particularly as they affected the British state, to which this study must now turn.

British and American Assessments of the EPU

The initial step towards the formation of the EPU was taken in December 1949 with discussion of the ECA proposals for full intra-Western European currency transferability in payments settlements on current account, with settlements to be made in gold.[97] All participants recognised the freeing of a wide range of invisible payments in addition to payments on commodity account, together with a clause further reducing quantitative restrictions by the date set for European transferability – 1 July 1950. Despite Hoffman's initial enthusiasm that a clearing union would be in operation within 90 days[98] the British state's early assessment of the proposals threatened serious deadlock.

The UK position that Britian should not involve itself in the economic affairs of Europe 'beyond the point at which we could, if we so wished, dis-engage ourselves, and we should therefore treat with strict reserve any schemes for the pooling of sovereignty or for the establishment of European supra-national machinery',[99] had not been modified since the Washington talks. In fact, the Cabinet's position over this issue had become more inflexible as a result of the consultations, since the UK could see no attraction in long-term economic co-operation with Europe in the face of the traditional UK/Commonwealth trading partnership which had been considerably enhanced via the new-found political and economic understanding reached with the USA. By January, Bevin and Cripps had decided that Britain could not surrender its sole responsibility for budgetary policy or the level of foreign currency reserves. Action could not be undertaken which might sacrifice opportunities for dollar saving or earning in order, as Cripps saw it, to make it easier for other European nations to accumulate dollars.[100] Understandable fear of another sterling crisis had led the British state to reaffirm Dalton's dual accumulation policy as the optimal strategy in conditions of dollar scarcity. By the end of January 1950 Britain's position was clear. 'It is a cardinal point in the policy of the UK', Cripps declared, 'that the multilateral facilities offered by sterling shall not only be maintained but increased'; however, 'it is essential that any new scheme that may be evolved should leave undisturbed the existing monetary arrangements entered into by the UK, and we could not agree that they should be subordinated to, or superseded by the EPU.'[101]

The British conception of the EPU therefore differed significantly from that of the ECA inasmuch as the UK viewed any union as a lender of last resort, so that settlements through it would relate only to those deficits and surpluses which could not be settled by recourse to the payments arrangements already in existence between European nations. The American interpretation of the Union as the sole lender, involving the supersession of the credit facilities available under the bilateral arrangements, would, Cripps stressed, have to be established 'without the participation of the Sterling Area'.[102] To gain the inclusion of the United Kingdom the ECA proposals required modification in three principal areas.

First, it would be necessary to concede the right of the UK to restore quantitative restrictions without prior consultation with the EPU since, Cripps had decided, 'while the application of import restrictions should be restricted to the minimum required on balance of payments grounds, some breach in the liberalisation of trade is a lesser evil than a corresponding breach in the maintenance of full employment'.[103] Secondly, the ECA would have to acknowledge the special position of sterling in the world currency markets and agree to minimise the obligation to make gold settlements with the Continent. Finally, the proposals must leave undisturbed the existing system of neo-bilateralism established under Dalton's Chancellorship.

The British state's attempt to gain a 'privileged position for sterling' and to defuse the more radical implications of the EPU rested upon two familiar arguments, both derived from the problem of reconciling the requirements of the sterling system with that of the closed European trade and payments proposal. The complex, international character of Britain's money markets and the role of sterling precluded any easy harmonisation and the lack of ECA analysis on this point forced the US to major policy concessions.

With over 36 per cent of visible world trade conducted in sterling in 1948, and over 50 per cent of visible and invisible transactions carried out in sterling the maintenance of the neo-bilateral system was adjudged essential by Cripps in his memoranda to the OEEC.[104] Moreover, sterling's role as a world reserve currency led to special difficulties for the UK, since large holdings of sterling by individual nations subjected the pound to wider variations than the generally small holdings of the other currencies of Europe. Given the special role of sterling in world markets, the British state was afraid that the EPU would severely damage the international status of sterling, affecting monetary stability in Europe, and thus precipitate another bout of UK dollar drain. Secondly, Britain's trading pattern differed significantly from that of Western Europe, which by this time had begun to develop more intensive intra-European trade. The largely inflexible capacity of the Sterling Area to supply exports to the United States, including raw materials such as rubber and manufactured goods from the UK – both highly sensitive to fluctuations in US business activity – had the result that sterling was particularly sensitive to adverse movements in world trade. Both these considerations had the effect, the Cabinet decided, that 'changes in conditions in the US and other parts of the world strike the UK hard, and can very rapidly set up pressures upon our reserves – especially when transferability is permitted. The nature, speed and order of magnitude of these pressures are entirely different from those experienced by other participants'.[105] In addition the existence of the large UK sterling balances posed the threat that British liability could be increased if such balances found their way into the clearing mechanism.

To resolve these difficulties Cripps proposed that all sterling claims and debts should continue to be financed under bilateral arrangements, whilst automatic compensations would apply only to intra-Continental countries' surpluses and deficits.[106] Sterling claims would be brought into the compensations only in so far as this would, first, reduce a Continental nation's net indebtedness to the clearing system or, secondly, if such claims exceeded the credit margins granted to the UK, normally entitling the creditor country to demand gold payment from Britain. UK indebtedness to the clearing system would thus theoretically be settled fully in gold, but only after it had been reduced by a similar transfer to the clearing system of all British claims on European nations in excess of the payment agreements credit margins.[107]

The bargaining strength of the British state on this issue, however, was declining, as the first quarter figures for 1950 indicated the substantial accumulation of British foreign currency reserves and the expansion of British production and commodity trade. The strong recovery of Western Europe as a whole led to growing European dissatisfaction with the position adopted by the UK, particularly in France and Belgium. Britain's unilateral decision to devalue, its participation in exclusive US discussions and its attempt to delay and modify France's proposed solution to the German problem (in the shape of the Schuman–Monnet plan) prompted a positive change in French opinion regarding the benefits of a closer multilateralised Europe. The resurrection of the Finebel (Little European Customs Union) proposals in late February exemplified this general Western European dissatisfaction with the development of British policy. The ECA had perceived that British negotiators wished 'to secure for themselves complete freedom to pursue the domestic policies they want on purely national grounds and the complete freedom to exploit all the benefits of their present bilateral trading arrangements'.[108] Under combined European and American scrutiny the British attempt to secure a position in which import controls could be maintained whilst chances of gold accumulation were enhanced and the opportunities of dollar loss were constantly guarded against was seen as increasingly unjust.

Furthermore, Britain's stance was seen as unnecessarily restrictive and even injurious to the expansion of British accumulation itself. Even though the UK had in the previous three years been in current surplus with the nations of Western Europe as a whole, the operation of the neo-bilateral system had resulted in the UK making dollar payments to Continental nations. This situation would not arise under the proposed clearing union since if there were a net surplus with the participants no loss of reserves would occur, and even in deficit conditions the EPU would provide a cushioning credit facility calculated with regard to the UK's £379 million quota. Any debit the UK may incur with the Union up to £76 million (20 per cent of the quota) would involve no loss of gold at all, but be carried as a credit by the EPU. Acceptance of the Union terms therefore meant the UK could exchange a breathing space of approximately £39 million before gold payments began under the neo-bilateral arrangements for a breathing space of £76 million under the EPU. Moreover, unlike the bilateral arrangements whereby debits in excess of £39 million were payable entirely in gold, under the terms of the EPU after the 20 per cent (£76 million) figure was reached, only half of the remaining 80 per cent was payable in gold.[109]

British Acceptance of the Modified EPU Proposals

The weight of these considerations, the replacement of Cripps by Gaitskell in the later stages of the negotiation, and three substantial concessions on the part of the ECA, finally induced the UK to enter the EPU. The US decision to earmark $600 million of ERP funds to support the EPU, regardless of British participation, led the UK to quickly reassess its position and its importance (until this date largely unquestioned) to European viability. Further ECA moves to concede that beyond an agreed point the UK would be allowed to reimpose quantitative restrictions and also that the ECA would reimburse the UK for any gold which it lost to the Union as a result of a Continental claim against sterling balances proved decisive in gaining British participation on 7 July 1950 with the EPU retroactively established from 1 July 1950.

The final EPU agreement was therefore signed to meet three principal objectives. First, it aimed to eliminate all monetary incentives to neo-bilateralism in trade and payments whilst effecting a maximum economy of resources in intra-European settlements.[110] This was to be achieved through a fully automatic multilateral compensation system clearing residual surpluses or deficits amongst the participants as a whole. Secondly, the EPU was designed to induce the participants to accept the risks involved in a regional multilateral scheme (and those inherent in the concomitant trade liberalisation programme) by providing cushioning credits with adequate guarantees against default and exchange risks in circumstances of moderate disequilibria in intra-European payments. Finally, the Union was conceived as a method of stimulating the readjustment policies necessary to check any development of excessive or permanent disequilibria amongst the participants. In addition, the multilateralisation of European payments theoretically carried the commercial implication that there could be no justification for continued trade discrimination amongst EPU members.

However, the oft-quoted figures indicating that by 31 March 1950 Europe's trade had become remarkably liberalised – for instance, showing that Britain had removed 54 per cent of its quotas on private imports (rising to 86 per cent by December 1950) as a result of the liberalisation programme[111] – cannot be taken at face value. Official OEEC reports indicating a high success rate for liberalisation across Europe as a whole failed to emphasise two important aspects of the programme. First, liberalisation only affected private imports (the proportion of private to government varying enormously amongst European nations), and secondly, the liberalisation rules applied only to imports from other OEEC nations.[112] Whilst the British state emphasised its role in promoting trade liberalisation as an example of its multilateralist orientation, the significance of the programme varied widely amongst OEEC members and failed to have the major impact which Hoffman expected in late 1949. The fact that the proportion of imports affected by liberalisation to total imports differed considerably amongst nations meant that whereas by the spring of 1950 compliance with the liberalisation proposals led to the removal of quotas on about 40 per cent of the total imports of Belgium, the figure for Britain was below 10 per cent. Similarly, liberalised imports amounted to 12 per cent of Belgium's gross national product whereas the changed significance of these liberalised private imports in the total British economy meant that in Britain they amounted to approximately only 2 per cent of gross national product.[113] Moreover, the fact that under OEEC statistical procedure the removal of an ineffective quota (a quota large enough initially that is removal made no quantitative difference to imports) was included in the overall count as a greater measure of liberalisation, clearly demonstrates that liberalisation was by no means synonymous with trade expansion.

The Lessons of the EPU Episode

Although the British state's accumulation strategy had undergone a faltering realignment, involving the *de facto* abandonment of Dalton's dual accumulation policy and the acceptance of a regional multilateralist trade and payments arrangement, the final form of this revision remained indeterminate and far from satisfactory in American eyes. Whilst the British state was keen to instance the EPU as a step towards convertibility, the US Treasury stressed that 'the scheme was very different from that originally proposed by the United States'[114] and, apart from the introduction of gold payments, they doubted its contribution towards agreed objectives. The ECA had acknowledged that politically organised schemes for supranationality could not be relied upon and thus they abandoned plans to follow the EPU with a European Monetary Authority. Concessions made to the UK with regard to import restrictions and the sterling balances plus the fact that (in contrast to those accounts which suggest that the EPU was 'a purely Western European creation'[115]) the very existence of the EPU had depended upon US financial injections, all signalled to the American administration that the revised ECA proposals for European integration were to share the fate of their discredited forebears.

The United States had achieved the preservation of a one-world economic system ideally committed in the future to full multilateralism, yet at a price of intensified trade discrimination and an acceptance that Britain and the Sterling Area could not be integrated or forced to harmonise their national policies with those of Western Europe. Nevertheless, from the American viewpoint the events leading up to the signing of the EPU had been significant. The vigorous intra-European trade boom centred around Little Europe (and largely excluding the UK), together with Schuman's proposals for a harmonisation of French and German reconstruction dealing specifically with the vexed issue of coal and steel resources (in which, of course, Britain refused to participate), had indicated that future American policy in Western Europe could viably be developed without reference to the UK, focusing on the definition of a customs union in terms of a common market of strategic commodities (see Milward (1984) chs 7 and 8). Such a direct approach, disregarding the prior establishment of a complex political superstructure, held out a new hope for American capital expansion.

Whilst the EPU episode had forced the United States to a more realistic appraisal of its capacity to restructure the Western European economic system, it had revealed particular strengths and weaknesses in the British state's economic strategy. Cripps's protracted attempt to maintain the neo-bilateral framework, in conditions which clearly merited their abandonment, not only indicated personal limitations but highlighted the intimate way in which British policy in this period was directly related to the level of UK foreign currency reserves. The justifiable fear of national bankruptcy haunted the British Cabinet throughout the negotiations, and it is no exaggeration to suggest that the UK would not have entered the EPU had not its currency reserves significantly increased during the first half of 1950.

Nevertheless, British reticence to endorse the EPU proposals, given the rising level of reserves in 1950, indicated that the UK did not seriously envisage the United States setting up a regional multilateral system which excluded the UK. On this point the UK was seriously misinformed. The strength of the UK lay not (as Attlee and others believed) in the traditional role of Britain as a major world power but more specifically in the maintenance of sterling as the primary international currency, reflecting the efficient and unrivalled development of the City of London. The most valuable asset in the hands of the British negotiators, therefore, remained the UK commitment to worldwide convertibility. The revision of state policy away from the established neo-bilateral framework did not immediately threaten this asset. The reintroduction of full convertibility still depended upon more general equilibrium between the dollar and non-dollar areas, considerably higher foreign currency reserves and the negotiation of complementary policies to be undertaken by the USA which would ensure the security of any steps taken towards full convertibility. Nevertheless, the EPU would assist general Sterling Area viability with the non-dollar world, and, via the supersession of the bilateral trade and payments arrangements, remove an appreciable support to the British postwar system of exchange control and inconvertibility. The Treasury retrospectively cited the importance of the EPU agreement in this sense in early 1952 when it was becoming apparent that Britain had 'reached a point where we must recognise that inconvertibility of sterling in non-resident hands is not a policy which can long be sustained'.[116]

The accumulation strategy pursued by the state within the framework of neo-bilateralism proved to be a highly successful policy in conditions of dollar scarcity immediately following the 1947 sterling crisis. By the end of the first quarter of 1950 industrial production had increased to a level 32 per cent above that achieved in 1947, whilst exports registered an increase of 96 per cent over the same period.[117] The sterling crisis of 1949 had indicated the precarious trading structure of the UK, 52 per cent of whose exports went to the Sterling Area, 16 per cent to dollar markets and 32 per cent to the rest of the world. This pattern left Britain exporting to a variety of markets with very different import requirements and limited and inflexible capacities to take up intensely manufactured goods. The close correlation between business activity in the US and the economic performance of the Sterling Area, particularly its sales of primary products, illustrated the increasing inadequacy of the UK trading position, particularly when the widespread international use of sterling and its role as a reserve currency intensified economic instability. The restoration of sterling viability by 1952 clearly depended upon rising levels of foreign currency reserves. Disregarding the fundamental objectives of the state which remained the maintenance of full employment and the increase of domestic living standards, it is no overestimation to suggest that the state's actions throughout this period were dominated by fluctuations in the level of those reserves. Although it was obvious to many officials that a reconsideration of the sterling/dollar exchange rate would be a necessary aspect in the readjustment of postwar economic relations, Cripps sanctioned such a move only when the declining currency reserves demanded immediate action. Similarly, British acceptance of the EPU proposals was sanctioned by the state only after the level of reserves had recovered to their highest point for two years. Whilst the state had therefore defined the maintenance of full employment and rising living standards as a necessary element – 'essential if fundamental social upheavals were to be avoided'[118] – the development of a strategy to expand accumulation was constrained in this period by the Treasury's holdings of foreign currency.

The measures taken to resolve the 1949 crisis highlight many facets of the state beyond the received accounts which merely indict Cripps for lack of forethought and sluggish decision-making. An analysis particularly of the internal measures employed by the state in this context reveals that in large part its actions were taken for purely political reasons. Official pronouncements of public expenditure and investment cuts were primarily designed as political manoeuvres to regain the confidence of the British electorate in the face of the oncoming General Election and to exert influence over the American administration.

By the beginning of 1950 the major obstacles to expanding accumulation in the postwar era were slowly being overcome. Whilst the imbalance in production and trade between the Eastern and Western hemispheres (of which the dollar famine was a manifestation) remained the primary barrier to accumulation, the United Kingdom's positive adjustment to the changed circumstances of the world economy since 1945 had enabled the state to clarify future economic policy. Devaluation and participation in the Washington talks had dispelled American fears of a British retreat into a soft currency area system. The precise short-term role Britain would adopt, given its long-term commitment to one-world multilateralism, remained unclear, however, until the summer of 1950. Despite growing European dissatisfaction with Britain's intransigence over the terms of the EPU, and the realisation within the UK that regional multilateralism would benefit capital accumulation by reducing dollar loss and stimulating intra-European trade, British acceptance was contingent upon ECA concessions effectively underwriting the financial stability of the UK within the EPU. The revised British accumulation strategy now established on the twin pillars of regional multilateralism in Europe and the maintenance of the Sterling Area system signalled not only Britain's overall multilateralist orientation but also the end of the ECA aim to establish British-led European economic integration. The creation of the EPU could no longer be seen as the first step towards the political and economic integration of Western Europe, although the US acceptance of the 'special position' of the UK and the Sterling Area in the postwar world (and the development of French thought in respect of the German problem) had created an atmosphere conducive to the formation of a Little European Customs Union based on the trading, in a common market, of strategic commodities.

In the short term, however, since neither European integration nor currency realignment had proved adequate steps to secure American objectives (large export surplus, sterling convertibility and worldwide non-discrimination in trade), in the aftermath of the Marshall Plan the US administration faced a major crisis in external economic policy. The resolution of this crisis came with the outbreak of the Korean hostilities, which not only sustained domestic demand to a level which countered the effects of the falling US export surplus, but also enabled the dollar gap to be further closed with military replacing economic aid to Europe, and American political interests safeguarded as the nations of Western

Europe rallied forces against the spectre of 'communist' expansionism. It is thus to the analysis of the British rearmament programme which suddenly became 'the first objective of the government's economic policy'[119] that the penultimate chapter is addressed.

6 The Impact of Rearmament

The last year of Attlee's administration – from mid-1950 until the Election defeat of 26 October 1951 – was dominated by concerns about the impact of rearmament on the strongly recovering British economy. Prior to the outbreak of the major hostilities across the 38th parallel the revised accumulation strategy appeared to be so successful that the usually cautious Economic Survey provisionally claimed that 'by the end of 1950 the immediate task of postwar recovery would be complete'.[1] Yet, contrary to this early optimism (and even before the acceleration of the defence programme), many Treasury officials believed that a large-scale revival of munitions production would 'mean demands on our resources which would render inescapable the abandonment of our efforts at economic recovery under present policies'.[2] According to this view, Britain could not secure viability by early 1952 and at the same time devote substantial resources to rearmament. Even with considerable reductions in production for export and civil use, rearmament was deemed impossible by many analysts without recourse to large American assistance which would once again for an indefinite time-span 'mortgage the future'.[3]

Many theorists have thus claimed that the acceptance of the rearmament programme 'was the end product of the processes of subordination to the global strategy of the United States which Attlee and Bevin had established as the keystone of British policy'.[4] The origins of British postwar economic decline, such writers suggest, can be narrowed down to the critical moment of rearmament when the 'heart of British manufacturing industry and engineering was virtually pulled out of operation' with the result that markets lost during the Korean war were never recovered and a 25-year relative decline of British capitalism was set in train.[5]

Given the wide circulation and importance of these interpretations, it is surprising that a detailed examination of the specific economic impact of rearmament rarely accompanies such claims. This chapter therefore assesses the exact implications of rearmament for the British state's economic strategy. Detailed study reveals that although British

150

rearmament occurred in response to an American request issued to all members of the NATO alliance for 'information concerning the nature and extent of the increased effort both as regards increases in forces and increases in military production',[6] the British defence acceleration cannot be seen as 'evidence of further subordination to the US'. Not only did the UK oppose US policy on many issues, but the overall stance of the British state was in alignment with the newly revised accumulation strategy and the rejection of European integrative proposals. The Cabinet Defence Committee thus viewed British military involvement in the light of the understanding that 'we no longer had to rest content with the knowledge that we were a Great Power, but were becoming able, for the first time since the war, to sustain our worldwide commitments'.[7]

Shouldering a large military burden reinforced opposition to any ECA integrative programme which included the UK and provided the government with an opportunity to indicate to the US that Britain had attained 'independent economic status' in Western Europe and would not be treated as 'just another necessitous European nation'.[8]

A clear appraisal of the impact of rearmament on the progress of British accumulation indicates a far more ambiguous series of effects than the promulgators of the British decline interpretation would lead one to expect. The acceleration of defence revealed many areas of weakness in the state's ability and competence to refashion sections of the economy quickly. However, contrary to popular conception, the limiting factor in the state's reformulation of accumulation was not productive capacity, but turned on problems associated with acute shortages of raw materials and skilled labour. For instance, the Working Party investigating the metal-using industries did not find themselves considering how to make the best use of scarce capacity (by cutting some forms of production to make way for defence) but how to employ capacity which had become spare because of raw material shortages. Deriding the lack of understanding shown on the part of the Ministries of Labour and Supply (and at the Board of Trade), the Working Party concluded: 'what is wrong with productive capacity is not that there are too many claims upon it, but there are not enough claims'.[9] Furthermore, whilst the defence appropriation of supplies of metal-goods increased over the period 1950–2, defence never absorbed more than 12 per cent of the output from this oft-cited group of industries, with exports of metal-goods maintaining a figure of 31 per cent over the same period, and the distribution of supplies of metal-goods used for investment and the home market maintaining their percentage shares.[10]

It cannot, therefore, be stated that the simple effect of British rearmament was to send manufacturing industry into a long-term decline. The precise effects on each of the major candidates for this interpretation – metal-goods industries, textiles and building – reveal ambiguous impacts which are not liable to overall generalisation without analysing the effect of the rise in import prices that resulted from massive US raw material use exacerbating the world raw material shortage.

To approach this more precise specification, and to indicate more generally the state's ability to refashion accumulation, this chapter will first locate the major developments in the British economy that occurred in 1950 before detailing the most significant changes in American domestic and international economic policy from which a close study of the British response can begin.

I   EXPANDED BRITISH ACCUMULATION AND AMERICAN POLICY

Industrial Expansion and De-Stocking

The propitious economic conditions which had facilitated the British state's decision to move away from Dalton's dual accumulation strategy continued throughout 1950. Only with the benefit of hindsight could the Treasury remark in 1952 that the strength of the British economy at this stage had perhaps been overestimated 'because it was not recognised at the time how temporary were so many of the favourable economic circumstances'.[11] Industrial production displayed continued vigour throughout 1950, with the index of industrial production for all industries increasing 11 per cent over the 1949 figure. The principle manufacturing industries outstripped this overall figure by recording a 14 per cent increase on the previous year, with production from the metal, engineering and vehicle industries rising by 16 per cent and textiles achieving a 10 per cent rise.[12] Output from the steel industries similarly exceeded the target given in the Economic Survey for 1950, whilst the total production of motor vehicles increased almost 25 per cent over the 1949 production total.[13]

The continuation of this upward trend in the output of British productive capital could no longer simply be attributed to factors associated with the process of reconversion. Indeed, the objective of the European Recovery Programme, Gaitskell was somewhat prematurely to boast, had already been achieved in the early part of 1950 and the UK economy had completed its basic reconstruction, ceasing to depend on external financial assistance.[14] Increases in productivity were largely the result of the slow and uneven adoption of more intensive productive techniques and the easing of certain international constraints which had up until that point limited British industrial growth. Thus Gaitskell was to claim throughout 1950 that 'technical advance continued unflagging . . . whilst . . . never have greater efforts been made in scientific and industrial research both public and private'.[15] Moreover, full employment and the absence of major selling problems enabled manufacturers to plan for long runs given the temporary easing (experienced towards the end of 1949) in the availability of raw materials and, more cogently for the UK, the ability to purchase freely the precious materials extracted in the USA. This dependence of Western Europe on the supply of US primary products, which accounted for half of US total exports,[16] was to have serious repercussions on British economic performance in 1951 with the imposition of US export controls in late 1950 designed to safeguard supplies for American industry.[17] Nevertheless, the immediate postwar shortages of industrial raw materials had temporarily eased for a six-month period from late 1949 (scarcity becoming a major factor again by mid-1950, resolved only by the decision to run down stocks), reducing a key constraint on British industrial output. The level of gross fixed investment accordingly remained high throughout 1950 achieving a small increase in the physical volume of investment added to an £80 million increase due partly to price changes.[18]

To sustain this industrial output required a degree of coherent forethought which was absent in the British state's policy planning at this time. Robert Hall remarks that the Treasury throughout the first half of 1950 were preoccupied with the outcome of devaluation, the level of gold reserves and the course of US business activity. Consideration of the consequences for British industry of the major destocking programme adopted by the state as part of its dollar economies following devaluation did not occur until mid-September 1950 when, as Hall points out, 'the Treasury finally took the step of pressing the Supply Departments to increase their purchase for stockpiling but . . . it was then too late'.[19]

Gaitskell's diaries similarly reveal the incredulity felt by state officials when it was suggested that shortages of materials would become a problem for British industry in 1951.[20] Nevertheless, as early as October 1949 Hitchman of the Economic Planning staff had pleaded for an increased supply of industrial materials and Hall had even suggested holding vast levels of stocks instead of dollars, thereby postponing the termination of Marshall Aid, since 'the Americans would look less seriously on our assets if these were not too much concentrated on gold'.[21] To the consternation of Hall and Hitchman the Treasury decided to continue destocking as a dollar economy, falling in line with the idea that policies should be as unhampered by financial need as possible.

To a keen observer, substantial destocking in an era characterised by fluctuating raw material supplies would do little to strengthen future prospects for productive capital and in conditions of world rearmament could result in industrial dislocation and a drain of dollar reserves through higher import prices. It is not only in retrospect that the factor of rearmament can be introduced. Hitchman, for instance, had written to Plowden in late 1949 expressing concern about the 'grave dangers in the present situation because of the absence of a policy on industrial supply and rearmament', indicating the 'evil consequences which rearmament would have within the period of recovery'.[22] Neither Cripps nor Gaitskell, however, attended to this advice and so failed to appreciate that the export boom experienced as a result of the industrial growth in 1950 relied upon the expansion of those industries which would be most directly affected by raw material problems and the claims of defence.

The Temporary Trade Surplus in 1950

The impact of devaluation and higher world commodity prices on total UK imports began to be experienced in 1950 when the import bill rose by approximately £400 million over the 1949 figure despite the volume of retained imports showing no appreciable change. Dollar economies adopted to accompany devaluation reduced imports from the Western hemisphere by 3 per cent with the result that the growing scarcity of non-dollar supplies of raw materials (wool, softwood, non-ferrous metals) accelerated a reduction in domestic stocks. Whilst the dramatic rise in import prices experienced through-out 1950 – a 13 per cent increase from January to December – was partially offset by a highly favourable £200 million surplus on invisible account, the British state still relied upon visible exports and re-exports to pay for 93 per cent of the import bill.[23]

The strong export drive received fresh impetus from the upward trend of industrial expansion, increasing over 16 per cent above the 1949 level and achieving an export figure 62 per cent greater than that realised in 1947.[24] Continued expansion of exports of vehicles, metals and engineering goods remained important to the overall growth of export earnings in 1950, comprising over 55 per cent of the total value of UK exports. Moreover, despite the level of export prices remaining fairly constant, the UK achieved a 3 per cent increase in the value of exports to the dollar markets at the slight expense of exports to the Sterling Area.[25] Overall, therefore, the measures taken in late 1949 appeared to have benefited capital accumulation with increased industrial output and expanded exports. A series of favourable international economic circumstances together with the effects of the state's short-term measures adopted to halt the 1949 dollar drain also produced a temporary strengthening of the state's foreign currency reserves.

Thus the balance of payments on current account realised an overall surplus of £244 million (recently upwardly revised to £307 million) to build upon the small £5 million surplus achieved in 1949. The Sterling Area gold and dollar accounts consequently increased reserves from a level of £603 million recorded for 1949, to £1178 million achieved by December 1950. Finally, the UK balance in the EPU, a reflection of the whole Sterling Area balance on current and capital account with EPU nations, recorded a net surplus of £170 million between July and December.[26]

Factors Limiting a Continued Economic Expansion in 1951

British accumulation had been invigorated by the end of 1950 and justified the state's revised economic strategy. In the light of this growth many analysts view the crisis of 1951 solely as the result of the British state's decision to rearm. Close study, however, reveals that the upward pattern could not be expected to continue even in the absence of rearmament. This can be justified on three counts.

First, as mentioned above, the drain in British stocks of raw materials had been accompanied not only by a non-dollar area scarcity in late 1950 but also by the imposition of export controls on the part of the United States designed to retain commodities as part of their large stockpiling programme begun in late 1949. A significant increase in import prices and a slowing down of industrial output were therefore to be expected even before world rearmament became an additional factor. Moreover, the increased demand for Sterling Area primary products experienced in 1950, which greatly contributed to the increase in gold and dollar reserves and EPU surpluses, could only result in larger incomes for the overseas Sterling Area which, when they came to be spent, were bound to effect an increase in expenditure on imports.

Secondly, three additional factors were discernible in 1950 which were to further reduce the strength of the British economy. The termination of Marshall Aid had been arranged for December 1950, whilst the beginning of the UK's obligation to commence repayment under the terms of the loan agreements with America and Canada was to come into operation in 1951. Moreover, a reduction in invisible earnings from Britain's overseas oil industry had been anticipated since 1948[27] and began to look a certainty towards the end of 1950.

Finally, by 1950 the Treasury had expressed anxiety that the British economy was facing increased foreign competition, particularly from the refashioned economies of Germany and Japan. For example, although in the immediate postwar years British cotton textiles dominated world export markets, it had long been anticipated that by 1950 the reconstruction of the Japanese and Pakistani industries (with their relatively plentiful supply of cheap US cotton) would severely limit the expansion of British textile exports. Direct British assistance to the Japanese textile industry in 1948 (agreeing to exchange essential raw materials for over £16 million worth of Japanese cotton textiles[28]) and British dollar economies limiting the importation of technologically advanced textile machinery into Britain both combined to produce a situation whereby in early 1950 Japan had regained full control of its textile production and was suspected of deliberately holding down domestic cloth consumption to facilitate a sustained export drive.

The steady expansion of capital accumulation could not be taken for granted in 1951 simply as a concomitant of the expansion achieved in 1950. Specific factors had arisen which would threaten productive capital growth, limit the expansion of exports and renew pressure on the British balance of payments. The overall structure of British accumulation was therefore far less secure than at first appeared when on 26 July 1950 the US government approached the UK on the subject of rearmament. To understand both the impact of rearmament on the economy and the quick political assent given by

Attlee to the American request (an assent which Gaitskell calmly considered should 'give no cause for alarm' either politically or economically[29]), it is necessary to chart how the American decision to rearm was seen by the State Department as providing a solution to a series of interlocking problems associated with the domestic US economy and the role of the United States in the economic and political reconstruction of Western Europe.

Rearmament as the State Department Solution to Economic and Political Crisis

As the previous chapters have outlined, the strategies adopted by the ECA as steps towards the overall objective of a US-dominated world multilateral system continually ran up against the specific determinations of individual and joint Western European nations. With the termination of Marshall aid to Britain quickly approaching, the US administration now faced a new crisis. Acheson remarked in early 1950 to Truman that 'unless vigorous steps are taken the reduction and eventual termination of extraordinary foreign assistance in accordance with present plans will create economic problems at home and abroad of increasing severity'.[30] Acheson's anxieties focused on conditions for the maintenance of a high export surplus with the most pressing problem: 'how can Europe obtain the dollars necessary to pay for a high level of US exports, which is essential both to their own basic needs and to the well being of the United States economy?'[31] This question, largely insoluble for the ECA and the Treasury Departments, was answered by the State Department in a series of memos which attempted to link the major political crises of the day to the approaching economic difficulties. In the face of Soviet expansionism in Central and Eastern Europe and the establishment of the Chinese People's Republic in October 1949, Acheson and Nitze (who replaced Kennan as head of the Policy Planning staff in 1949) proposed in late 1949 massive American and European rearmament as the solution not only to the deepening Cold War but also to problems of domestic economic policy.

The 'Report to the National Security Council by the Executive Secretary on US Objectives and Programs for National Security' (referred to as NSC–68), prepared in response to a request from Truman and delivered on 7 April 1950, provided a focus for the State Department solution. Arguing in classic Cold War terms, NSC–68 announced: 'the assault on free institutions is worldwide now, and in the context of the present polarisation of power a defeat for free institutions anywhere is a defeat everywhere'.[32] The 'integrity of the capitalist system', it concluded, 'will not be jeopardised by any measures covert or overt, violent or non-violent, which serve the purpose of frustrating the Kremlin design'. NSC–68, however, went further than simply affirming the paranoia of the American Cold War. Drawing on the views of Leon Keyserling from the Council of Economic Advisers, the document suggested that increasing defence expenditure need not result in a drain of government funds or long-term budget deficits.

Whilst at present, the State Department argued, only 5 per cent of the US gross national product was allocated to defence, the US economy was operating well below full capacity. With a higher level of general economic activity, GNP could be raised and the increment used to sustain a significant military build-up without decreasing domestic living standards. In turn, the substantial increase in arma-ment production would stimulate further dynamic growth in the general economy which would again increase the amount available for military-related consumption. In essence NSC–68 provided an interesting variant on Kidron's thesis of the Permanent Arms Economy[33] wherein massive armament production acts to stabilise capital accumulation by stimulating investment, demand for labour, technological 'spin-off' and international trade. In addition to offering a solution to the ailing machine-tool and aircraft production industries it also appeared to secure on a 'politically neutral basis' American economic goals in Western Europe.

The massive export of advanced US military technology and the replacement of Marshall aid by substantial military aid would prevent the development of European regionalism and emphasise the importance of the USA to the reconstruction of Western Europe.[34] Moreover, in support of these proposals the UK Chiefs of Staff had soberly concluded in March 1950 that Western Europe was facing imminent invasion from the Soviet Union. This prompted a major foreign policy reappraisal on the part of the United States, whose military focus on Western Europe had declined since 1947.[35] The revised assumptions for US foreign policy were therefore that the rearmament of the 'free world' was necessary for American security and that large-scale military assistance was necessary for the required scale of rearmament which would have a multiple effect on the rearmament efforts of other nations. The political and security arguments for economic aid in the guise of military assistance, the

Committee on Foreign Economic Policy informed: 'are the same as those long put forward in favour of the containment of communism by economic means'.[36]

After the frustrated efforts of foreign economic policy led by the ECA, the US Administration adopted NSC–68 as official policy in the spring of 1950. In the wake of the outbreak of hostilities across the 38th parallel, Congress immediately broke the $13.5 billion ceiling on defence, increasing this original amount by 257 per cent for the fiscal year 1951.[37] The State Department's advocacy of rearmament had ramifications in three areas. First, despite the rhetorical – almost missionary – tone of documents such as NSC–68, it is clear that domestic and international economic policy considerations were paramount in its construction and important in its final acceptance by Congress. Secondly, the outbreak of hostilities in Korea appeared to verify the political/military sentiments of the State Department's assessment and any interpretation of the hostilities which did not square with this dominant view of global Stalinist expansionism was adjudged incomprehensible. Finally, the Congressional assent to rearm implied that similar policies would be followed by Western European nation states despite the less than stable condition of their economies. Thus the US aide-Mémoire on interim aid communicated to the UK on 3 October 1950 recognised that 'as the size of the defence effort of the UK increases, it will impose progressively greater burdens on the economy',[38] yet such burdens were a necessity since 'if anything happens in Western Europe the whole business goes to pieces'.[39]

Britain's Political Response

The British state's interpretation of the Korean hostilities bore a strong resemblance to that expressed in Washington. Bevin immediately decided that 'Korea was one example of Russian trouble making and there was no telling where or when she might make trouble next'. Therefore, 'the Korean war should not be considered in isolation but as part of a global struggle between the West and Russia'.[40] In fact, recent evidence, supported by Khrushchev's account, suggests that Kim Il Sung acted independently in instigating the hostilities thereby compromising both Stalin and Mao in later support for his North Korean regime.[41]

Attlee's response was immediately to release naval forces from Hong Kong in support of American ground troops. Within one month the British commitment had extended and the UK eventually contributed two infantry brigades, three assorted regiments with supporting ground staff, the Far Eastern Fleet and the Sunderland aircraft of the RAF.[42] Before assessing the impact of the acceleration in defence spending on the UK economy, it is worth reviewing the state's political rationale for such significant involvement in the hostilities.

The popular interpretation of Britain's decision is couched in the familiar framework of 'political subservience to the United States' whereby Attlee and Gaitskell 'felt swayed by the need to back up the Americans at almost all costs'.[43] As with the other capitulation to American hegemony explanations encountered in this book, close study of the British state's actions reveals a rather different and more ambiguous rationale which can easily be lost in generalisation.

To understand the state's decision, attention must initially focus upon the strong economic recovery staged from the second half of 1949 and the adoption of the revised accumulation strategy made possible by that recovery. The British state had proclaimed that Marshall aid would end in December 1950 and had flatly rejected any involvement with American-sponsored European economic integrative schemes. Gaitskell had claimed that the task of postwar recovery was now complete and Britain must preserve its 'economic strength and independence'.[44] This development of economic independence, Bevin and Gaitskell stressed, 'gave us weight in the counsel of nations . . . and allowed us . . . for the first time since the war, to sustain our worldwide commitments'.[45] Moreover, Britain had onerous responsibilities in the Pacific and South East Asia, with military contingents in Hong Kong and Singapore and an active campaign against 'nationalists' being waged in Malaya. Whilst the Cabinet sought to maintain Anglo-American solidarity on issues of foreign affairs this solidarity was perceived by the UK afer 1949 as one of equal partnership. The Western world could not be defended without American military strength but, nevertheless, the outbreak of Korean hostilities would allow 'a useful demonstration of the United Kingdom's capacity to act as a world power with the support of the Commonwealth'.[46] The independent British recognition of the Chinese People's Republic accorded on 2 January 1950 and Britain's refusal throughout the Korean episode to operate political or economic sanctions against the Mao administration (both decisions to the considerable dissatisfaction of Washington[47]) point yet further to the inaccuracy of seeing the British state as involved in a political capitulation.

The state's revised accumulation strategy built upon the twin pillars of regional multilateralism in Europe and the maintenance of the Sterling Area system worldwide could now support, in the Cabinet's opinion, a foreign policy demonstrating Britain's ability to sustain its worldwide commitments in conjunction (whenever convergent) with the interests of the United States. Further support for this interpretation is provided from a study of the finance of British defence which indicates that by October 1950 Bevin and Gaitskell had agreed that Britain's position 'makes it entirely appropriate to find a multilateral examination of what constitutes an equitable distribution of new burdens'.[48] Britain could not submit in isolation a special justification for a direct plea for dollars (despite early moves in that direction) since 'we could not easily reconcile such a presentation with our basic determination to stand on our own feet at the earliest possible moment'.[49] The costs of this determination must be examined.

II ECONOMIC GROWTH AND REARMAMENT

The rearmament programme involved an expansion of defence expenditure over three distinct stages. For a programme which stood in December 1949 at £2340 million for the years 1951–3, an increase to £3400 million was announced in August 1950 (revised to £3600 million in September of that year), and a final planned increment to a level, excluding stockpiling, of £4655 million was unveiled on 19 January 1951.[50] Each increment was announced by Attlee as the most that could physically be achieved without reverting to a war economy, and even with the final rise Gaitskell was resolved that 'the UK's external accounts shall not run into deficit during the rearmament period'.[51] The public blandishments, however, concealed the grave consequences of rearmament outlined by the Treasury.

Meeting Rearmament Costs through Increased Production

As early as October 1948 Treasury officials had assessed that the disruption to productive capital caused by any increased level of rearmament would necessitate severe restrictions in home consumption and social welfare investment. Yet both Attlee and his Parliamentary Private Secretary, Roy Jenkins, were insisting as late as March

1951 that 'the impact of the rearmament programme upon our standard of living is likely to be less dramatic than many people at first believed, since much of the resources would come from increased production'.[52] The idea that the demands of the defence programme could be met from an increase in production was, however, misguided. It was clear that the accelerated defence programme would have a selective impact. Any increase in productivity would not be a flat-rate increase since the various engineering industries would increase production at different rates, with some almost inevitably showing a decline. Attlee's assessment implied free interchangeability of labour and capital within the engineering sector, a suggestion with limited applicability to labour and only marginal accuracy to the transfer of plant capacity. Any increase in overall production would, moreover, derive in part from the installation of new equipment, and to the extent that the defence programme would deprive productive capital of new equipment (and severely limit the importation of new American engineering goods) increased industrial production could in no sense be assumed.

The Ministry of Supply had reached a similar conclusion by August 1950 (that is, before an extra £1075 million had been added to the planned defence expenditure) in noting that 'it would be wrong to imagine that a solution to the main problem can be found in attempting to balance additional defence claims against increases in productivity'.[53] Casual correlations between overall industrial productivity and the selective claims of defence were therefore based upon inaccurate assumptions. To assess the true impact upon productive capital it was necessary to focus on the effects experienced principally by the metal-using industries – that is to say, the industries concerned with engineering, shipbuilding, road and rail vehicles, and electrical manufacture.

The Metal-using Industries and Government Policy

The fundamental difference between the execution of rearmament in 1936–9 (when spare resources typified in unemployment, unoccupied factories and plants, and a surplus of steel from domestic production were available) and that of 1951–3 when the economy was already fully employed, forced the government to adopt the general principle that the industries within the metal-using group engaged in the production of consumer durables should be diverted into defence contract work in order to shield production of essential capital goods for investment and export. To accomplish this task Gaitskell announced: 'we must choose deliberately both on grounds of social policy and to assist the execution of the defence programme, the places where the sacrifices must fall and not leave this to the arbitrary and inefficient operation of inflation'.[54] Yet the state's careful policy objectives did not fully accord with either the domestic or international conditions affecting productive capital at this point and to a large extent it was the decisions of private capital, and the movements in the international supply of raw materials and their effect upon import prices, which determined the outcome of the impact on the metal-using industries. To illustrate these remarks we need to consider the state's proposals for these industries.

The major appraisal of the Service Departments anticipated that the defence work carried out by the metal-using industries (excluding vehicles) would increase by over two-and-a-half times the level preceding the Korean war. The production of military aircraft would substantially exceed the manufacture of all aircraft carried out in 1950, whilst at least one-third of the capacity of the vehicle industry would be devoted to defence, and the volume of work for the navy undertaken by shipyards and marine engineering establishments would exceed by 40 per cent their current output.[55] To achieve this programme the government decided the following policy objectives.

A substantial transfer and reallocation of labour would be required in four related areas. First, at least 250 000 additional workers were likely to be needed in the aircraft and Royal Ordnance factories alone over the period 1951–3 since the specialised capacity of these groups was not fully utilised under peacetime conditions. Secondly, some of the defence load would fall upon industries that were in any case experiencing a decline in size. The new orders would therefore 'assist in avoiding trouble' in such industries as shipbuilding where the additional naval orders would limit the rate of decline of the labour force.[56] Thirdly, the Board of Trade, in conjunction with the Ministry of Local Government and Planning, decided that reallocation of labour would be made as part of an overall strategy to relieve pressure on congested areas, diversify industry in specific localities and bring work to 'development areas'.[57] Finally, with regard to the transfer of labour, the key overall objective was stated to be the transfer within firms and industries of workers from civil to military types of work. In addition to the efforts to be made in 'squeezing labour out of non-manufacturing employment' (such as the distributive trades) and the concentration on plant capacity in undeveloped areas, together with the transfer from consumer durable goods to defence contract work, the government decided to create substantial new capacity in certain sections of the metal-using groups, in particular for aircraft and tank production.[58]

The discussion on the restriction of civil consumption also explored more drastic measures of discriminatory allocation of scarce resources, the prohibitions of end-use of scarce materials, the limitation of supply orders and the specific direction of firms to make particular products.[59] Whilst the prohibition of end-use was employed for certain inessential articles made of nickel, copper, zinc and brass, the other measures failed to be widely adopted due to administrative difficulties and 'the likelihood of arousing strong opposition in peacetime'.[60]

Overall, the policy measures were taken to meet the government's main objectives in the metal-using industries which were, first, to ensure that the defence impact fell upon consumption goods for the home market rather than upon exports or essential domestic investment, and secondly, to ensure that the demand for productive resources (in particular labour) did not outstrip supply in some areas whilst in others resources were left unused.

Constraints on Industrial Restructuring

The ability of the state to restructure sections of productive capital in this manner was severely constrained by both the nature of productive capital at this time and the international scarcity of raw materials. Gaitskell discovered to his dismay in 1951 that almost 80 per cent of the resources of the metal-using industries were employed on civil work. There was no question, he decided, of detailed government control either over the size of their output or its destination. 'There is neither the staff nor the knowledge to work such a system', he concluded.[61] This situation contrasted sharply with that in 1943 when over 80 per cent of the labour in the metal-using industries was working directly or indirectly for the Supply Departments. Moreover, as the Economic Planning staff soon discovered in 1951, there was a fallacy in the widespread assumption that defence work would be available to absorb the capacity which would become free as a result of the reduction in output of consumer durables. The 'essential fact', they discovered, was that 'material supplies are limited – this would compel some firms to curtail their activities; it would not help to maintain employment merely to give defence work to these firms at the expense of others'.[62] The Working

Party under the Productive Capacity Committee concluded that the state's policy objectives were based on major errors of judgement. Productive capacity, they decided, was not a bottleneck in the defence programme and, short of full-scale war, may never be a bottleneck: 'the real bottlenecks are raw materials and skilled labour, with productive capacity a very poor third'.[63]

The state's aim, to make the best use of scarce capacity by cutting down some forms of production to enable others to develop, was misconceived since the real difficulty was to employ capacity which had or was likely to become spare because of raw material shortages. On financial grounds, moreover, it was clear to the Working Party that, contrary to the ambition of finding employment for capacity which became spare, 'it would be better to let it go (or cause it to go) out of operation and let such materials and skilled labour as are available to go to those firms who are getting defence contracts naturally because they are the best fitted to undertake them'.[64] This view is verified by the fact that even at the height of rearmament, the government could not fulfil its planned level of expenditure with defence spending 30 per cent below the level envisaged in January 1951. Moreover, evidence from Treasury memoranda suggests that the state was not able to assist firms making consumer durables to secure defence work.

In February 1951 the government already had more firms on its trade lists than it could employ and was receiving offers of capacity at the rate of 400 a week.[65] Alfred Robens (Bevan's successor) complained that a number of firms with outstanding vacancies for work on the defence programme were employing labour within the same institution on more profitable civilian work. In addition, there were numerous other examples of main contractors who would need to sub-contract part of their orders, tending to place sub-contracts with their regular suppliers instead of expanding contacts and trying other firms since they were viewed as inexperienced and possibly more expensive even if labour and facilities were available.[66]

The state's inability to refashion sections of productive capital due to the nature of that capital and the limitations imposed by international raw material supply has thus been demonstrated particularly with regard to the transfer of labour and the transfer of industrial capacity to meet the new defence requirements. Insight into the nature of the relations between the state and productive capital can be further gained from an analysis of the state's efforts to create new productive capacity, particularly its efforts to establish new tank production facilities.

The Leyland Tank Lesson

In view of the serious deficiency in tank production capacity the Ministry of Supply invited the Leyland Motor Company in March 1951 to erect and manage two new tank production lines in Lancashire. The selection of Leyland was based upon their similar work in 1939, their retention of the same managerial and technical staff who had completed the earlier work and their large research and development facilities.[67] In view of the state's official policy concerning the relief of pressure on congested areas (particularly where labour was fully employed), the diversification of industry in each locality, the transfer of work to development areas and the creation of work in areas not already dominated by essential export industries, the government was particularly anxious that Leyland set up a new factory away from their present location and start production in an area where the labour situation was comparatively easy. Unless this principle was firmly applied, R. F. Bretherton informed the Economic Planning Committee, 'most of our efforts to speed up the defence programme will defeat themselves; and the grounds for abandoning it in this – the first important test case – seems inadequate'.[68] Leyland however refused such directives and proposed that they should undertake the new work, provided the new tank factory was erected on vacant land adjacent to their existing plant at Leyland. The company estimated that for an output of 500 tanks a year it would require a new workforce of at least 2500 operatives.

The implications of accepting Leyland's decision were at total variance with the state's policy objectives. Whilst the town of Leyland itself supported a working population of 15 500, it had a maximum unemployment figure during 1949 of 40. The surrounding areas (Preston, Chorley, Wigan and Blackburn) had a total number of job vacancies in December 1950 standing at 3625 with a maximum unemployed total of 1673.[69] Moreover, the principal manufacturers in the region were directly involved in export-related production (chemical, engineering, aircraft and textile industries) with further requirements for labour already existing in key defence production areas at English Electric in Accrington and Preston (for Canberra aircraft production), Royal Ordnance factories at Chorley and Blackburn, and De Havillands in Bolton. In an area whose contribution to direct exports was second only to the Midlands, and where there was absolutely no prospect of additional accommodation being provided for incoming operatives, the decision to comply with

Leyland's ultimatum would reduce the government's policy objectives to a series of worthless statements. Nevertheless, despite opposition from Harold Wilson and Bevan, the Cabinet approved Leyland's offer on 21 March 1951 with no regard to the requirements of the existing defence and export industries in the area and no restrictions or guidance to be placed upon or given to the Leyland management. The Leyland episode is not an isolated case. A review of new buildings sanctioned in connection with the defence programme reveals a similar account of private productive capital exploiting the state's commitment to the defence programme. In the case of new buildings, the Board of Trade suspected that 'firms may be tempted to use this opportunity to obtain authorisation for extensions which they desire, but cannot obtain, for the normal development of their business'.[70] In this respect can be cited the Rootes Ltd extension of 227 400 sq. feet; the GEC Ltd extension of 52 000 sq. feet; the Austin Motors Ltd extension of 965 660 sq. feet; and the Rover Company Ltd extension of 300 000 sq. feet – all in the West Midlands region and all producing similar commodities, despite the Cabinet's policy objectives of diversifying industry and limiting industrial expansion in congested areas.[71]

In spite of official policy objectives, it is clear that by 1951 the state was unable to refashion those sections of productive capital upon which its programme was based. The benefits accruing to the more astute sections of productive capital were considerable in this period and enabled in particular the vehicle industries to secure expansion in buildings and equipment (Leyland, moreover, received 'financial assistance over and above what we paid in the Government contract'[72]) far beyond that which would have been secured under normal conditions. Contrary to those claims which depict rearmament 'pulling the heart out of British manufacturing', the above episode suggests that the state (rather unwittingly) gave great assistance to the more astute sections of productive capital, laying the foundations for the industrial expansion experienced in the following years.

Furthermore, an analysis of the distribution of supplies of metal-goods over the 1950–2 period shows that even at its peak defence did not absorb more than 12 per cent of the output from this industrial group. Whilst defence appropriated the 8 per cent increase in the production of metal-goods over the two years, the supplies allocated to exports, investment and consumer goods for the home market remained constant.[73] Those interpretations which claim that the metal-using industries were decimated in the rearmament drive are guilty, first, of according the state a degree of direction and control over productive capital which it clearly did not possess in 1951; secondly, underestimating the precise obstacles to the simple transfer of production from civil to military output; and thirdly, of understating the regulatory effects of the raw material shortage to which this account must shortly turn as part of the consideration of the effect of rearmament on British trade and balance of payments.

The state had long anticipated that a major effect of rearmament would be the retardation of the government's social policies which had already been launched. Towards the end of 1948 it had been assessed that 'from the economic point of view we should (in the wake of rearmament) aim at diverting resources away from consumption and social welfare investment leaving unscathed as far as possible exports and productive investment'.[74] Considerable hardship for the lower income groups was seen as unavoidable since, as Gaitskell announced, 'the redistribution of real income which is the consequence of rising prices followed by rising wages etc., . . . is mainly to the disadvantage of the lower fixed income groups and may confront us before long with difficult political problems'.[75] Such political problems were, however, deemed secondary in the face of the government's overall economic resolve that 'the UK's external accounts shall not run into deficit during the rearmament period, except to the extent of strategic stockpiling'.[76]

Priority Guidance for Exports

To meet this objective attention focused on the priority guidance to be given to firms in the event of conflicts arising between the demands of dollar export and those of the defence programme. Although the state's ability to intervene directly in the export effort was severely hampered by the government's policy to leave the conduct of the export trade almost entirely in the hands of private industry and commerce, proposals were drawn up to guide the export industry through this uncertain period.

First, as a general principle it was decided that defence and export orders should rank as an equal first priority over all other supplies but with a tendency for defence orders to take precedence in the last resort.[77] The principle was established and implemented, to the chagrin of the Minister of Supply who argued that 'if a decision is taken on political or defence grounds to prefer defence supplies to dollar exports, it should be taken with the full recognition that the promising Canadian market for engineering goods will be lost permanently'.[78] The inability of the UK to compete with US deliveries would justify, he argued, the deeply rooted suspicion that in time of emergency the UK will be an unreliable source of supply. The implications of this view are worth assessing and its accuracy will be analysed shortly. Secondly, the state reinforced the existing obligation of the export industry to maintain exports to the dollar areas as a basic axiom of policy. An expansion of total earnings at the expense of exports to these vital markets would not bring compensatory benefits. Thirdly, the state implored that exports to the Commonwealth should be maintained and rank in priority immediately after defence supplies and dollar exports. The supply to Commonwealth nations was essential since they were viewed as dollar savers, some exports would contribute directly to Commonwealth defence programmes, and in the view of the Treasury, 'the Commonwealth is our best long-term market'.[79] Finally, the state advised that firms receiving enquiries from Western Europe should refuse orders where they are willing to do so, and in other cases give orders from all other sources precedence over orders from Eastern Europe.

Although the UK prevented the export to Eastern Europe, China and North Korea of strategic items capable of contributing directly to the production of arms, the British state throughout the Korean hostilities refused the American demand of preventing the export of UK goods which would serve to 'increase a country's basic industrial strength'.[80] The reasoning behind this rather curious line of policy was economic. The Export Credit Guarantee Department (ECGD) had assessed that if delivery of goods to these nations were stopped, the state would be liable for 90 per cent of the value of goods for which payment had not yet been made. The disposal of such goods elsewhere would be difficult and 'public funds would no doubt also have to bear the cost of compensating firms [including those not covered by the ECGD] who were involved in the loss of their exports'.[81]

The priority guidance system had an overall effect of consolidating the view that British interests would best be safeguarded by directing exports to the dollar areas and the Commonwealth. Whilst the state recognised that it must allow for large reductions in the volume of exports of raw materials, coal and steel if the output of productive capital was to be sustained, it decided that it would be unreasonable to expect to secure any increase in the total volume of exports of engineering goods (which had contributed 50 per cent of total UK exports in 1950) due to the claims of defence and the raw material shortages. It was therefore to the consumer goods industries (which roughly accounted for 45 per cent of exports in 1950) that the government looked for an increase in the total volume of exports in the wake of rearmament. However, the threat of direct foreign competition in Western European markets from the rise of Germany and Japan prompted the government to exhort industry to export to the more well-established British export destinations. The perception that in Europe, German competition was to be most severe and that the raw material shortages would give impetus to the Japanese to develop consumer goods products specifically for European markets which did not involve heavy use of scarce metals, led the British state to the conclusion that 'we expect once again to be in a much stronger position in dealing with foreign competition in the sterling Commonwealth markets than in most others notably Europe'.[82]

Japanese competition in textiles and miscellaneous consumer goods was likely to be at its keenest in Europe rather than in the independent Commonwealth nations, whilst the Germans 'are a little reluctant to challenge our commanding position in the Commonwealth'.[83] Priority guidance reinforced the tendency for British exports to sell in the largely uncompetitive and undemanding Commonwealth nations, excluding Britain from the expanding European high-value export destinations and continuing to leave the UK foreign trade sector largely subject to movements in the American economy and to perceptions in the Western hemisphere of the reliability of British delivery. The pressures which the rearmament programme were thought to entail for British exports consolidated the conservatism of the state with regard to export destination – a conservatism which in no small part was significant in the subsequent decline in the economic growth of the UK in relation to other Western European nations, whose concentration on intra-European trade at this time was at the expense of many traditional export markets. However, before drawing any overall conclusions, the precise impact of the defence programme on the export trade must be examined.

Raw Materials and Trade Balance in 1951

As late as 12 September 1950 Attlee was convinced that 'as to raw materials, it is not considered that there should be any serious shortage'.[84] By October, however, the international scramble for all major raw materials (sulphur, sulphuric acid, zinc and copper in particular) was well under way and this position did not ease until the summer of 1951. The raw material shortage, due principally to the increases in industrial production in Western Europe (accentuated by the dramatic rise of West German industry) and, from late 1949 onwards, the recovery of the USA from its mild recession, had been exacerbated by the massive American stockpiling policy begun prior to June 1950 and fed by the speculative demand for commodities engendered by expectations of rising prices and limited supplies.[85] World rearmament intensified this shortage with predictable results for the UK. The price of raw materials rose from an index which stood at 100 in December 1949 to 215 points by June 1951. This increased overall UK import prices by 60 per cent over the same period.[86] The total import bill for 1951, therefore, showed an increase of £1100 million over 1950 with two-thirds of the rise due to higher prices resulting mainly from the raw material shortage and a 16 per cent increase in the volume of imports made principally to counteract the reckless run-down of strategic stock carried out in 1950.[87]

In attempting to anticipate the likely effects of the raw materials situation on the output of exports, the government decided the following points: first, over the period 1950–2 the export of metal-goods would, in view of defence, only be maintained at the 1950 level on the most optimistic reading; secondly, the high level of world commodity prices and the inflationary pressures generated by these prices and by defence programmes should definitely support a level of world demand for many other classes of manufactures substantially higher than that recorded in 1950;[88] thirdly, the government decided to advise export industries to increase their prices (by as much as 36 per cent), where this could be done without damaging either long-term commercial prospects or the chances of substantially increasing the volume of foreign sales.[89] Overall, however, the government was convinced that the expected reduction in the volume of metal-goods and raw material exports would fail to meet the required export objective, which for 1952 was £3200 million.[90]

In this assessment they were broadly accurate, despite underestimating the size of the import bill in 1951 and overstating the impact of defence on the metal-using industries in both years. In spite of the shortage of steel and other raw materials for industry the volume of engineering exports increased by 4 per cent in 1951, contrary to government expectations. This, however, must be seen against the background of an export increase of 16 per cent experienced in the year 1949–50. Overall the volume of exports increased by 1 per cent in 1951 compared with a 16 per cent rise in the previous year.[91] With the peak of rearmament expenditure occurring in 1952, the metal-using industries failed to increase overall production, and exports from this group fell slightly in volume. The fact, however, that defence took nearly one-eighth of the total supplies of metal products in 1952 compared with less than one-twelfth the year before should be borne in mind together with the greatly increased foreign competition in metal-goods in overseas markets experienced in 1952, when assessing the effect of defence on exports.[92]

The impact of rearmament on the export trade over these years was important in that it acted to check the substantial export drive at a time when the rise in import prices precipitated yet another balance of payments crisis. Important sectors of the engineering industries were engaged on defence work when their output would otherwise have contributed to substantial export gains. Moreover, the retention of manpower within the armed services at a time of acute civilian labour shortage only created fresh difficulties for firms primarily engaged on production for export. Indeed, the total level of British exports declined in early 1952 and did not regain the level achieved in 1951 until the second half of 1953.[93] A number of economic circumstances, however, contributed to this decline (circumstances whose analysis transgresses the boundaries of this study) and it would be grossly inaccurate to claim that rearmament alone caused the reductions. It must be concluded that the pressures generated by rearmament, first, reinforced the conservatism of the state with regard to export destination and, secondly, acted to check the UK's essential export drive at a time of acute balance of payments difficulties. Analysis of the state's abrupt foreign currency drain will further elucidate these conclusions and enable the study to clarify the precise impact of rearmament upon accumulation.

Labour's Last Crisis

The massive increase in UK import prices for 1951 dislocated the British balance of payments which had been strengthened in 1950. A large surplus on the balance of payments was reversed by almost £680 million, producing a deficit of £369 million for 1951.[94] As noted earlier it should have been possible to foresee that many costs would be incurred in 1951 even without intensive world inflationary pressure.

The interest and amortisation on the US and Canadian loans would cost the UK over £75 million annually, seriously depleting invisible earnings, especially with the termination of Marshall aid. In addition increased foreign competition was assured from the end of 1950 reducing the hitherto 'sellers market', and the strategic materials that had been run down over 1950 would also need replacement. An exceptional conjunction of unfavourable developments in the second half of 1951 intensified the pressure on sterling. Thus the 60 per cent increase in UK import prices over an eighteen-month period (the result, it should be stressed, of raw material shortages which began before rearmament could have an impact) was accompanied by a sharp fluctuation in world demand for textiles and the Persian seizure of the Abadan oil refineries which incurred a new cost of over £100 million a year for replacement dollar oil.[95]

This unfavourable situation had an immediate effect on the UK's gold and dollar reserves which began to decline substantially in June 1951 from a level of £1381 million to end the year at £834 million. UK imports from the Western hemisphere by value increased over $840 million during 1951 and the gold and dollar drain was not halted until the second quarter of 1952 when world commodity prices had stabilised, raw material shortages had eased and Butler had imposed sharp import cuts.[96] In addition, the UK balance in the EPU showed signs of increasing speculative movements against sterling after the first quarter of 1951, with an accumulated deficit of £300 million by October of that year and the very real prospect of the gold free credit available to the UK running dry by the beginning of 1952.

To assess the precise impact of rearmament on these unfavourable developments we need to clarify the level of defence expenditure throughout this period and relate this to the changing fortunes of sterling. Despite the government's intention of raising defence expenditure from just under £800 million in 1950 to £1694 million in 1953 (1950 prices), it appears that rearmament reached its peak in 1952 at a level of £1250 million, some 30 per cent below the level planned in January 1951.[97] Expansion from the pre-Korean position was therefore no more than two-thirds, with defence, which absorbed 7 per cent of GNP in 1950, not rising above an absorption level of 10.5 per cent in 1952.[98] The principal impact of rearmament was felt in 1952; yet by the end of that year the balance of payments was showing a surplus of £163 million and the gold and dollar reserves had recovered from a low of £602 million at the end of the second quarter to a figure of £659 million by December 1952.[99]

This change in the fortunes of sterling was achieved because import prices were well past their peak (Gaitskell had forecast an import burden of £3600 million for 1952 whereas the actual figure was below £2950 million[100]. The terms of trade had improved for the UK, and Butler's policies of further reducing the social programme and imposing import cuts whilst reducing the amount of trade Britain had liberalised within the EPU from 90 per cent to 60 per cent, renewed international confidence in the stability of sterling.

The conclusion with regard to rearmament and the crisis in the state's currency holdings is that the phenomenal rise in import prices fuelled by the shortage of raw materials (which in turn was a result of the substantial increases in Western European and American industrial activity in 1950 together with the massive US stockpiling policies all intensified by the later *world* rearmament process) was the principal precipitating factor in the 1951 balance of payments crisis (see Cairncross's authoritative work which also emphasises the effects of world rearmament, Cairncross (1985) ch. 8). Although defence expenditure absorbed approximately 1.5 per cent more of available resources in that year than previous years its effect on the deteriorating balance of payments was minimal compared to the rise in import prices. When the world commodity prices stabilised in 1952 the balance of payments recovered sharply, despite the fact that this was the peak year for defence expenditure. The foregoing analysis cannot, therefore, support the simplistic view that the British rearmament programme 'caused a severe balance of payments crisis'.[101]

Nevertheless, there can be little doubt that in the conditions of an overloaded economy any diversion of resources would increase the burden experienced in all spheres of accumulation. The balance of payments crisis was exacerbated by the increased imports of defence supplies and the increased proportion of supplies of metal-goods used for defence. Although this increased proportion remained below 12 per cent even at the peak time of rearmament demand, it none the less absorbed resources which otherwise might have been employed in the export drive, whilst also checking the rise in industrial investment at a time when the engineering industry was at full capacity.

Realising this position the incoming Conservative government reassessed the demands of rearmament. Butler scrapped Gaitskell's 'priority guidance' system by reaffirming the need of the government to put 'full weight behind the export drive'.[102] In addition, he reduced the planned impact of defence requirements on the metal-using industries and attempted to realign the scaled-down defence programme to the requirements for the expansion of total social capital.

The conclusions of the impact of rearmament upon overall capital accumulation can now be clarified. First, it is clear that the state's quick political assent to accelerate the defence programme cannot be adequately seen as political subservience to the USA. The state's determined resistance to American attempts to impose economic hegemony on the UK throughout the postwar period had partially succeeded by early 1950 inasmuch as the revised accumulation strategy signalled the end of the ECA's attempt to subordinate the UK within a US-dominated world multilateral system, the first step of which was premissed upon British-led European economic and political unification. The apparent economic success of Britain's new accumulation strategy enabled the state to attempt a political consolidation of its new position by demonstrating that for the first time since the war it could, with the aid of the Commonwealth, meet its worldwide commitments. The response of the British state to the outbreak of Korean hostilities must be seen in terms of the economic expansion of 1950 and the political determination which this expansion enabled.

Secondly, the effects of rearmament on various aspects of capital were ambiguous, uneven and often indirect. The analysis cannot lend credence to the simplistic view that rearmament caused Britain's relative economic postwar decline. When assessment is made of the impact on productive capital it is clear that the effect on the metal-using industries (the industrial group most directly affected) was less severe than would be imagined. At the peak of rearmament, defence absorbed one-eighth of the supplies from this industrial group, whilst supplies to investment and exports remained constant over the entire 1950–2 period. The more perceptive and astute sectors of productive capital were able throughout this period to increase their industrial infrastructure at the direct expense of the state in a manner which would not have been possible under more normal circumstances. In particular (although by no means exclusively), the motor industry can be seen to have benefited immensely via subsidised construction of new plant and buildings.

The effect of rearmament on trade was rather less ambiguous inasmuch as the new defence requirements clearly absorbed resources which otherwise would have increased the export drive. Exports of metal-goods increased only slightly in 1951. Overall exports managed only a 1 per cent increase in 1951 compared with a 16 per cent increment previously. The check to exports was made more severe by the unexpectedly large increase in the 1951 import bill. Moreover, the difficulties which the state believed defence would bring to the export drive (difficulties largely overemphasised) reinforced the 'safe' geographical distribution for British exports which had been decided in late 1949. The state's resolve, consolidated in the Korean period, to maintain the traditional structure of UK trade left Britain in future years supplying a wide variety of markets with very different absorption rates for higher productivity manufactured exports. This was in contrast to most other European nations whose turn to higher levels of intra-European trade both precipitated the development of competitive high productivity exports and largely sheltered these nations from the more severe manifestations of periodic US recession.[103]

Finally, it has been suggested that the state's management of sterling was affected not so much by the overall level of defence expenditure, which even at its peak remained some 30 per cent below the planned level, but by the impact on the balance of payments of increased imports of defence supplies and increases in the supply of the raw materials necessary to increase general industrial output. In conditions of astronomical raw material price increases, which would have seriously affected the UK even in the absence of British rearmament, the impact of increasing the defence appropriation of the GNP by almost 4 per cent over three years was to add an unnecessary burden to an already overloaded economy. In this sense, rearmament had a contrary impact to that experienced in the United States, where a long period of strategic stockpiling and under-utilised capacity enabled rearmament to temporarily expand general economic growth.

In the UK, rearmament came at a time when a number of economic factors combined to slow economic growth. Its particular contribution to this interruption in British economic development was the check it caused to the export industry. But this selective impact was temporary and easily reversed. Labour left office in October 1951 under somewhat of a political and economic cloud. Nevertheless, the serious barriers to accumulation had been overcome in the postwar years and conditions had been lain for a decade of unrivalled capitalist prosperity.

7 Conclusion

The most pressing task facing the incoming Attlee government in 1945 had been to reconstruct Britain's international payments system to sustain economic development in conditions of production and trade imbalance. By the time of Attlee's electoral defeat in 1951 Britain had overcome the primary barriers to accumulation which had constrained the economy in 1945, and despite recurrent balance of payments crises had established a payments system which facilitated high rates of economic growth.

In retrospect it may be argued that the very success of Britain's resistance to American pressure proved her later undoing. Although Britain reluctantly gave up the dual accumulation strategy and accepted a partial multilateral payments system in 1949, the Treasury was insistent that Britain's best interest lay in a withdrawal from Europe a concentration on trade with the Sterling Area and a 'special relationship' with the United States. As a consequence the UK continued its traditional geographical distribution of exports and was largely excluded from the expanding intra-Western European trade markets where increased demand for advanced consumer goods stimulated manufacturing productivity and increased exports.

To infer, however, that the British state was mistaken in resisting American pressure to lead European integration is to introduce a long-term perspective which is clearly absent in capitalist economic policy-making. Short-term considerations are paramount in the management of contemporary economies. The postwar state treated each specific barrier to accumulation as an end in itself and was unconcerned with long-term implications. From this perspective the costs of taking the European route would have been very heavy in the short term. Fluctuations in the balance of payments largely determined at what pace the state would adopt multilateral trade and payments arrangements. European integration (and the US wish for immediate full convertibility) and the scrapping of Commonwealth relationships were inconceivable for the postwar state since it would have entailed a radical restructuring of production and trade and the abandonment of the privileged world role for sterling. Having gained hard-won advances in economic growth since 1945 the Treasury was justifiably resistant to risking future economic performance for the benefit of dubious American political objectives.

Seen from this perspective (and in many ways it is the only valid perspective which can be used to assess capitalist economic development), the state's postwar accumulation strategy was highly successful. The following decade saw a generalised European economic boom which was not the result of the United States imposing its model of development on the UK and the rest of Europe. The boom was rather the result of individual nations pursuing specific accumulation strategies in an unevenly reconstituted European trade and payments system characterised by inter-imperialist rivalry. This conclusion has important implications for some dominant schools of international relations theory.

The traditional realist–mercantilist accounts of postwar reconstruction – so uncritically adopted by the majority of neo-Marxist writers – do not stand close scrutiny. The basic force version of the cycle of *pax hegemonica* is empirically inaccurate and theoretically misleading. The more subtle neo-realist writers, such as Keohane, recognise this point and agree that 'simplistic notions of hegemony as either complete dominance or selfless dedicated leadership hinder rather than promote historical understanding' (Keohane (1984) p. 138). However, the realist theoretical framework is premissed on the view that power – often viewed in a behavioural sense – is the ultimate arbiter in the political system and that the distribution of nation-state power determines the relations of dominance in the international order.[1] Since for the realist this international order is determined by the power of nation-states based on the relative success of 'national economies', some notion of hegemony remains central to the perspective. Despite the considerable conceptual problem of retaining the notion of 'national capital',[2] the realist position is plagued by controversy over the nature of hegemony. Keohane, for instance, acknowledges Diebold's point that the postwar American administration has no memoirs called 'my days as a happy hegemon'.[3] He attempts therefore to develop a notion of 'qualified hegemony' or 'non-hegemonic co-operation' by arguing that the United States rejected a policy of all-out domination in favour of extensive co-operation and mutual policy adjustment exemplified by the Marshall Plan and the EPU. A more blatant example of modifying the theory to fit the revised history would be difficult to find! The earlier argument of this book clarifies that the American policy-makers did not 'banish force' and reject 'dictating terms to the world' (Keohane (1984) p. 177) in favour of mutual co-operation. Rather, the reverse is true. Only in the face of the combined resistance of Western European nations, in particular Britain, to repeated direct assertions of American dominance did a pattern of postwar reconstruction emerge far different from that envisaged by the State Department. To claim, therefore, as does Keohane, that the United States followed a 'strategy of hegemonic leadership' which consisted of non-hegemonic co-operation is somewhat contradictory and shows the difficulties encountered in retaining the realist view of hegemony in principle.

A potentially more promising approach to understanding inter-state relations is found in the work of the so-called 'transnational historical materialists' who nevertheless retain a notion of hegemony deriving from Gramsci.[4] A particular strength of this approach is its consideration of structural and relational power alongside behavioural power.[5] However, this aspect is as yet undeveloped and the perspective is better known for its elaboration of the concept of hegemonic rule. As understood by Cox and Gill, Gramscian analysis highlights the role of ideas and culture at national and international levels of the political economy. Moreover, hegemony is not simply that of one nation relative to others but rather of one class or class fraction relative to others.[6] Applying this approach, therefore, to the pattern of postwar reconstruction leaves Gill with an explanation of Anglo-American relations which states that the UK gave priority to the USA and the Commonwealth rather than to Western Europe because of 'the worldview of the British ruling classes' (Gill and Law (1988) p. 79). The 'nature of the consciousness' of the British leadership explains 'this apparently irrational choice of policy' (Ibid., p. 79). As with the retention of the realist concept of hegemony, there are specific theoretical and historical problems with the use of its Gramscian cousin. The preceding chapters have sought to demonstrate the essential rationality of Britain's commitment to traditional trade routes. The refashioning of the special relationship and the maintenance of the Sterling Area can only be viewed as irrational, given long-term retrospection. Moreover, the Gramscian position entails an unacceptable reductionism in its recourse to notions of 'the nature of consciousness' and its reiteration of fractionalist analyses of economic policy.

Gill and Law's attempt to explain economic policy in terms of the tension between the strategies espoused by a 'military–industrial bloc' and a 'liberal internationalist' fraction is simply another example of up-dated pluralism.[7] The pluralist approach to economic policy suggests that the state's actions are the result of pressures applied from both 'polyarchy' (free elections, free political and media debate) and organised interests.[8] A series of pressure groups or capital fractions compete and state policy reflects the ascendency of a particularly well articulated or most powerful interest. With the state seen as a neutral institution, aberrations in state policy can be laid at the door of numerous external pressure groups.

The basic weakness of the pluralist framework is its overt empiricism. The attempt to explain state policy by reference to the supposed ascendency of the group in whose interest the policy is said to lie, introduces a pattern of circular reasoning. Analysis is reduced to the tautology that powerful interests are those that prevail and they prevail because they are powerful. This approach cannot generate productive explanations of the role of the state in the capitalist economy or assess the constraints within which the state attempts to overcome barriers to accumulation.

The fractionalist account suggests an image of the state as an institution awaiting instructions from a particular fraction of capital. In reality, the state's task is at one level removed from such a passive role. The objective of the postwar state, for instance, was to secure the conditions for general accumulation regardless of the direct wishes of particular capital fractions. Securing the conditions for successful domestic accumulation, of course, means securing the conditions for global production, distribution and exchange. This is the fundamental role of the state apparatus which must seek to maintain the rule of the market, the rule of money and the sanctity of private property. It is a role which cannot be reduced to the play of capital fractions.

Rather, therefore, than seeking to remedy the 'social or cultural deficiency' of political economy,[9] the first step in building a viable non-reductionist (non-hegemonic) analysis of the international state system lies in clarifying the state's relation to the accumulation process.

I STATE, CAPITAL AND THE 'GENERAL INTEREST'

In the total productive circuit of accumulation, capital takes three basic forms.[10] In the course of its reproduction cycle we can distinguish between productive capital, producing profit in the sphere of production, and the two forms belonging to the sphere of circulation:

commodity capital and money capital. These functional forms can be further identified in the form in which they operate at the surface of society, in terms of industrial capital, commodity-dealing and merchant capital, and money-dealing and bank capital respectively. It is, of course, on the basis of this differentiation that fractionalists explain state policy by reference to successful political representation of particular interests. This is an error easily committed when the notion of 'capital-in-general' is omitted from analysis.

The concept of capital-in-general is a fundamental one analytically prior to a specification of particular capitals and the state.[11] Its particular value is that it enables us to conceptualise the social limits to the relations between particular capitals and the activity of the state. Capital-in-general only exists in the form of particular capitals, which likewise can only be seen as differentiated parts of a social whole. Ultimately the limits within which capital-in-general are bound, and which press upon particular capitals, are limits on the ability to produce and realise profit. These limits are therefore social but are perceived as natural barriers limiting a particular aspect of economic development.

Bearing in mind that each functional form of capital is simply a particular form of the total social capital, we can suggest two important points for an assessment of the relation between interests and the state. First, no particular form of capital can have an adequate understanding of its own interest in the reproduction of total social capital since it will only have a partial view of the circuit in which its own fate depends. Secondly, whilst particular capitals have an interest in common with others in preserving the overall rule of capital, different capitals will have slightly different emphases in relation to this common interest.

Competition between capitals and ignorance of their interdependence means that no fraction of capital (or pressure group interest) can constitute the general capitalist interest. Economic policy, which concerns general accumulation, cannot therefore be determined by the interplay of particular interests. The task of realising particular interests within the framework of general accumulation falls to the capitalist state. Identifying the 'general interest' is the precondition for the realisation of particular interests, regardless of whether the general interest is described as 'economic growth', 'capital-in-general' or 'capital accumulation'.

Thus the state can only realise the interests of particular groups to the extent that it can secure the sustained accumulation of capital, which in turn is constrained by material, social and financial factors. The earlier chapters of this book have shown that these constraints were primary in determining the pattern of accumulation and the form of postwar state intervention and so limited the extent to which particular interests could be realised. In devising an overall strategy not only does the state not express a general interest determined outside it, but it cannot do so – only the state can define the general interest of capital, since interests of particular capitals necessarily conflict.

This is not, however, to argue that everything the state does is 'functional' for capital. Whilst each individual capitalist seeks to overcome the barrier of the market by selling commodities at their highest possible price, the reproduction of capital-in-general depends on the subordination of all individual capitals to the discipline of the market. The interest of capital-in-general, therefore, is not equivalent to the combined interests of the individual capitals that are its component parts. Rather, the interest of total social capital is opposed to the specific interests of particular capitals and confronts them as a barrier in the form of competition in the market. The state, therefore, is not simply functional for capital. It does not act to directly secure the interests of particular capitals. Rather, the state meets the interest of capital-in-general by enforcing the discipline of the market through the rule of law and the rule of money which are the mediated forms in which the rule of the capitalist market is imposed on the working class and all particular capitals.

Within the capitalist system there is no other basis for the formation of the general interest than the state. In this sense, the state has an autonomy which is not political but which rests on its role of expressing the general conditions of accumulation and determining overall economic strategy. The key point to note is that, although this general strategy may favour particular capitals/interests rather than others, this is an unintended consequence of policy and there is no necessary relation to their political representation. In the postwar period, for instance, the restoration of sterling was essential to restore productive capital. It was also a policy favouring City interests, but this was a consequence of a strategy directed towards the reconstruction of general profitable accumulation. In fact, far from the City being the fifth columnist forcing the Labour government to capitulate, it was the City and the Treasury with an interest in the restoration of sterling that offered the most resistance to American multilateral objectives.

The role of the state in the capitalist economy, therefore, is essentially negative, removing barriers to accumulation. Whilst the state can act as an employer and intervene directly in some sectors of the economy, it cannot displace the market without destroying the capitalist mode of production. At best it can intervene to remove barriers to economic growth. The barriers to the accumulation of capital, however, do not directly confront the state, but appear as fiscal, financial and monetary crises. If the state is to overcome these barriers it must develop an accumulation strategy that will enable capital to successfully expand accumulation. The limits of state action, however, are determined by the fact that such a strategy is constrained in the short term by the existing pattern of economic development. Economic policy in 1945 was not decided on the basis of state rulers working out their own interests or theorising on the best economic strategy for the next twenty years. The task of the state was to find a strategy which would provide for general economic growth, given the uneven world development of capitalism.

In conditions of serious imbalance in production and trade between the Eastern and Western hemispheres, the British state's primary objective was to construct an international payments system which would sustain the economy until the 'dollar gap' could be overcome. Other Western European nations had a similar objective, whilst the United States sought to exploit its powerful position and impose international political and economic domination. The reconstruction of the world financial system was thus the critical issue in the postwar era. Having clarified some basic categories, it is now possible to develop an understanding of the nature of the international state system and its relation to global accumulation. A review of the progress made by Mandel in this direction is a useful introduction.[12]

II INTER-IMPERIALIST RIVALRY AND GLOBAL CIRCUITS OF ACCUMULATION

In an attempt to clarify the long-term developmental tendencies of the international centralisation of capital and its relationship to the late capitalist state, Mandel makes strict distinctions between the internationalisation of the realisation of surplus value (the sale of commodities), the internationalisation of the production of surplus value (the production of commodities), the internationalisation of the purchase of the commodity labour power, and the internationalisation of the power of command over capital which is ultimately based on the internationalisation of capital ownership.[13] While the sale of commodities reached its international zenith on the eve of the First World War, with exports accounting for an increasing share of industrial output in the advanced capitalist economies, this process entered a relative decline before overtaking its previous level in the 1960s. The internationalisation of the production of commodities, by contrast, constitutes a new and specific late capitalist development beginning after the Second World War and provides an international framework for the competition of capital. Concomitantly, the internationalisation of the purchase of labour power has accompanied the previous development although in a fundamentally uneven fashion (since production abroad can proceed without much foreign labour power), and the material infrastructure enabling capital to exercise a real international power of command has only arisen in the wake of the third technological communications revolution. Building on this work, Mandel cites three variant types of state strategy which may accompany these developments.

First, the international centralisation of capital may be accompanied by the international extension of the power of one single state with foreign capitalists participating as junior partners. Alternatively, the international development of capital may see a gradual dismantling of the power of various nation states and the rise of a new federal supranational bourgeois state power. A third variant is that of the relative indifference of internationalised capital to the late capitalist state. Each theorisation posits a possible model for the international structure of the metropolitan political system.

Thus the first state variant is linked to the model of super-imperialism in which a single imperialist power possesses such hegemony that other nations lose real independence of it and sink to the status of semi-colonial small powers. Ultra-imperialism, by contrast, incorporates elements of the relative indifference variant plus the supranational interpretation by suggesting that the fusion of capital has advanced so far that all critical differences of economic interest between the capital owners of the different nationalities disappear. The state is thereby no longer an imperialist nation state but a supranational world state. Finally, as a counter to this updated Kautskian thesis, Mandel cites a variant of Lenin's model of inter-imperialist competition wherein, although the international fusion of capital has proceeded far enough to replace a larger number of independent imperialist powers with a smaller number of imperialist superpowers, the counteracting force of the uneven development of capital prevents the formation of an actual global community of interest for capital.[14] Capital fusion is thus achieved on a continental level but thereby intercontinental imperialist competition is all the more intensified. Mandel, of course, subscribes to this latter position, given his observation that 'the main tendency of the intensifying international competitive struggle today is not for big capital to merge on a world scale, but for several imperialist formations to harden in their mutual antagonism'.[15]

Mandel's contribution lies less in his rather mechanical attempt to account for the internationalisation of capital than in his effort to relate developments in state form to a model of the global accumulation system. To make his observations on inter-imperialist competition more productive we need to explain the hierarchy of dominance between nation-states and develop a more sophisticated treatment of the internationalisation of capital.

Earlier it was stressed that capital can only exist as many capitals and it is through the interaction between particular capitals that the principles of capital-in-general are realised.[16] Competition between capitals, however, is not confined within a domestic economy. The accumulation of capital within the domestic economy depends on the accumulation of capital on a world scale. The role of the capitalist state is to express the 'general interest' of capital. However, the national form of the state implies that the state can only constitute this 'general interest' on a national basis. Nation-states therefore have a similar relation of conflict and collaboration as individual capitals. Whilst there is little love lost amongst the capitalist class in their mutual competition, they are nevertheless 'united by a real freemasonry *vis-à-vis* the working class as a whole'.[17] Similarly, whilst each nation-state is involved in a competitive struggle to secure individual economic growth, the overall interests of nation-states are not directly opposed, and the relation of antagonism and collaboration is reproduced on the world stage.

The concept of inter-imperialist competition is, therefore, a useful one helping us to understand the international state system in the postwar world. It is in marked contrast to the simplistic neo-mercantilist view wherein nation-states are seen as directly opposed and international state strategy is viewed in terms of a zero sum power game. Modifying the notion of inter-imperialist competition enables us to develop a more advanced study of the relations of dominance between postwar international states.

The preceding chapters have indicated that although the nations of Western Europe competed fiercely to gain advantage in the postwar scramble for dollars, they were nevertheless united in their resistance to the American aim of world domination. Struggles in determining the pattern of European trade and payments agreements illustrates the degree of conflict which existed in Western Europe, as each nation sought a competitive advantage in the solution to the dollar gap. Yet Western European nation-states were opposed to America adopting a super-imperialist position, as resistance exemplified in the CEEC and the OEEC amply demonstrates. Whilst the British state was the supreme advocate of Western European resistance to the hegemonic aims of the US, this attitude of collaboration coexisted with one of conflict towards Western Europe which found its expression in Britain's withdrawal from intra-European trade in 1949, in favour of consolidating Commonwealth trading links. For its part, the United States clearly wished to impose itself as the super-imperialist state and prevent Britain establishing a privileged position in Western Europe. However, as immediate postwar scarcities receded in 1950, British and American interests were partially reconciled in Atlantic partnership as both nations modified earlier strategies and moved towards a limited form of economic multilateralism. In the context of the encroaching Cold War, this economic partnership was reinforced by political unity in 1950 as Britain joined the US in large-scale rearmament.

Developing a notion of inter-imperialist competition in this fashion allows us to construct a hierarchical command structure of nation-states at particular historical moments without recourse to abstract concepts of hegemony. Reopening efficient channels for global accumulation was a prerequisite for Western Europe and the United States in the course of postwar reconstruction. A productive framework for clarifying relations of dominance between nation-states, therefore, should begin by analysing changes in the international circuits of accumulation. This has been the guiding principle of the present study which initially focused on the major developments in the international commodity markets up until 1945 and then related the maldistribution in world trade to the underlying imbalance in the structure of world production, relating both these factors to the ambiguous position of the United States in respect of transatlantic money markets. This approach highlighted the dilemma facing the US that, whereas America was in a clear position of dominance in terms of production and trade (hence the world dollar shortage), it could not convert this dominance into international hegemony since specific factors existed within the US preventing New York financial markets displacing London as the world financial centre and sterling as the world's premier currency.

By way of developing a framework for future research on inter-state relations this study offers three observations. First, since the international system is still primarily one of politically constructed nation-states providing the domestic underpinning for the mobility of capital, analysis should not reduce state policy to the interplay of the interests of capital fractions. The state's primary accumulation strategy is necessarily at a higher level of operation. A review of the relation between 'interests' and the state shows that since the interests of particular capitals are in conflict, as manifest in competition, there is no other basis for the formation of a 'general interest' other than the state. This is not, however, to argue that the state simply represents the general interests of capital against the particular interests of specific capitals. The 'general interest' of capital, as of the 'nation', is a pure abstraction. All that exists is the particular resolution of conflicting interests, with the 'general interest' being the precondition for the realisation of particular interests, whether this is called 'economic growth' or 'capital accumulation'.

Secondly, a view of the state politically constituting the 'general interest' and economically securing a framework for economic growth does not imply that the state must firstly advance a 'hegemonic project' in order to provide an 'accumulation strategy'. This mechanistic approach to state action is conceptually untenable in dividing political and economic levels, and unrealistic since historical study shows that the state attempts to restructure accumulation in general with the success of any political strategy largely dependent on economic performance.

Finally, it has been stressed that since accumulation of capital within the 'domestic economy' depends upon the accumulation of capital on a world scale, nation-states have a similar relation of conflict and collaboration as individual capitals. To understand this tension and to chart the hierarchy of dominance between international states, a modified notion of inter-imperialist competition is valuable. It offers a framework from which a nation-state's articulation with the world accumulation process can be assessed and relations of dominance analysed in a non-reductionist manner which avoids the use of vague assertions of hegemony and understands a nation's position in terms of international production, and commodity and money markets. The efficient operation of the global political economy does not depend upon 'hegemonic power'. World capitalism is, however, premissed on the construction and maintenance of global circuits of accumulation. Individual nation-states secure these circuits domestically and through international agreement on a world level by upholding the rule of the market, law and money. The prosperity of specific nation-states does not depend on their working within a sphere of 'hegemonic stability'. Rather, it relies primarily on their relative adoption of production regimes and their position in global commodity and money markets. This is now recognised by some international relations theorists who are beginning to clear some of the confusion in the debate on the 'decline of the United States' by distinguishing between a state's relational and structural power and capacities.[18]

For Britain the pattern of postwar reconstruction yielded the legacy of a twenty-year economic boom. On this boom rode the unlikely partners of social democracy and relative capitalist prosperity. Yet the boom housed a central contradiction: that the short-term success of the state's reconstruction of international trade and payments carried with it the long-term drawback of a Sterling Area trade policy with diminishing economic returns. Despite Britain's (untimely) entry into the European Economic Community and the approach of a single European market, the consequences of this contradiction are still to be seen in irrational British outbursts of indignation at the loss of 'national industries' and the spread of 'international capital'. The difficulty many theorists have, including unfortunately many socialists, in abandoning the concept of 'Little England' and its 'national capital' is an unacknowledged legacy of the pattern of postwar economic reconstruction. It is a fine and topical example of the Marxist truth that 'Men make their own history, but they do not make it just as they please; they do not make it under circumstances chosen by themselves, but under circumstances directly encountered, given, and transmitted from the past.'[19]

Appendix: The Changing Structure of Monetary Account Areas in 1947

JULY 1947

Sterling Area (Scheduled Territories)

United Kingdom, Ireland, Australia, New Zealand, South Africa, Southern Rhodesia, India, Pakistan, Ceylon, Burma, British Colonies, Iceland, Iraq, Palestine, Jordan, Greenland, the Faroe Islands.

American Account Area

United States, Philippines, Bolivia, Columbia, Costa Rica, Cuba, Dominica, Ecuador, Guatemala, Haiti, Honduras, Mexico, Nicaragua, Panama, Salvador, Venezuela, Chile, Peru.

Transferable Account Area

Argentina, Belgium, Brazil, Canada, Czechoslovakia, Egypt and Sudan, Ethiopia, Finland, Iran, Italy, Netherlands, Norway, Portugal, Spain, Sweden, Uruguay.

Nations Involved in Specific Negotiation

Germany (occupation authorities), France, Japan (occupation authorities), Switzerland.

Nations with whom Agreement had not been Signed by 15 July 1947

Austria, Bulgaria, China, Denmark, Greece, Hungary, Paraguay, Poland, Romania, Siam, Turkey, USSR, Yugoslavia.

Miscellaneous Area Unaffected by Convertibility Episode

Afghanistan, Albania, Korea, Liberia, Nepal, Saudi Arabia, Tangier.

STRUCTURE OF MONETARY AREAS FOLLOWING THE SUSPENSION OF CONVERTIBILITY ON 20 AUGUST 1947

Sterling Area

Unchanged except for the removal of the Faroe Islands and Greenland.

American Account Area

As before except for the removal of Chile and Peru.

Transferable Account Area

Chile, Czechoslovakia, Faroe, Egypt and Sudan, Ethiopia, Finland, Italy, Netherlands, Norway, Poland, Spain, Sweden, USSR, West Germany.

Bilateral Accounts

Argentina, Belgium, France, Brazil, Bulgaria, Canada, China, Hungary, Japan, Paraguay, Peru, Portugal, Romania, Switzerland, Tangier, Turkey, Uruguay, Yugoslavia (the Exchange Control Act of 1 October 1947 also placed Denmark, Austria and Greece in this category).

Miscellaneous Group

Unchanged.

SOURCES: H. C. Debates, 26 November 1946; Shannon (1949) p. 223; Zupnick (1954) Tables 46, 48; PRO T236/1667, various documents.

Notes

Notes to the Preface

1. The original reads 'What is his object in doing this?' (Marcus Aurelius, *Meditations*, Book 10:37, p. 165 [Harmondsworth, Middx.: Penguin, 1964; trans. M. Staniforth]). Although my paraphrase slightly alters the implication of the original it carries over the same essential meaning and is more acceptable without the gender bias.
2. The work of Morgan (1984), Pelling (1984), Eatwell (1979), Hinton (1983), Tomlinson (1986), Gilliat (1983) and Bullock (1983) has been written with this purpose in mind.
3. T. Benn quoted in Freeman (1982) p. 167.
4. S. Clarke (1982) provides a rigorous analysis of this theme.
5. Weber (1968) vol. 1, p. 4.
6. Tenbruck makes this suggestion: see Kalberg (1979).
7. S. Clarke (1982) in this respect interestingly observes the development of Weber's methodology within the context of marginalist economics, citing Menger as particularly influential.
8. Weber, 'Politics as a Vocation', in Gerth and Mills (1964) p. 77.
9. Weber in Giddens and Held (1982) pp. 60–86; see also Held (1983) p. 38.
10. Weber in Gerth and Mills (1964) p. 181; see also Crompton and Gubbay (1977).
11. Mann (1984); Urry also makes a claim that 'a separation of Marxist and Weberian theory is now not theoretically profitable . . . an adequate theory may well seem eclectic incorporating elements of both approaches' (Abercrombie and Urry, 1983, p. 152); see also Urry (1981, 1982, 1983). For an account of the 'post-Marxism' of Urry (1981, 1982, 1983) and Cohen (1983), see Pierson (1984). Far from this approach offering anything productive, it is simply another form of pluralism which attempts to broaden analysis by including interests found in 'civil society'. Urry, for instance, displaces the 'class struggle' with an emphasis on consumerist categories based on divisions such as 'house purchasers', 'old-age pensioners' and 'car-owners' (Urry, 1981, p. 143).
12. Marx (1976) p. 92.
13. Marx (1981) p. 152.
14. Althusser is renowned for this suggestion (1965, 1972). For an appropriate critique see S. Clarke (1979, 1980); and for a general review see Callinicos (1976). A broader discussion of Marxism and positivism can be found in Colletti (1972) (esp. ch. 1), McLennan (1981) and Rose (1978).
15. The clearest account of commodity fetishism is still that given by Marx (1976) ch. 1. See also Rubin (1973).
16. Marx (1981) p. 368.

17. Marx, 'Wage Labour and Capital', in Marx and Engels, *Selected Works*, vol. 1 p. 90. (Moscow, 1962).
18. Draper's translation of Marx, in Draper (1977) vol. 1, pp. 570–1.
19. Marx (1964) pp. 45–6.

Notes to Chapter 1: International State System

1. Marx (1981) p. 353.
2. Marx (1976) p. 742.
3. See Van der Pijl (1988) p. 32.
4. Chase-Dunn (1981) p. 32; see also Picciotto (1988).
5. See Picciotto (1988) on how the internationalisation of capital has not acted against the nation-state.
6. Robert Keohane (1980) popularised the term 'hegemonic stability theory' in relation to the work of Kindleberger, Gilpin and Krasner. For accounts of hegemonic stability see Keohane (1980, 1984, ch. 3); Stein (1984); Russett (1985); Snidal (1985); Strange (1987, 1988); and Gill and Law (1988). The following account of hegemonic stability is influenced in particular by Stein (1984) and Strange (1987).
7. Kindleberger (1973, 1976); Gilpin (1975, 1977); and Krasner (1976, 1978).
8. For a discussion of these themes see Stein (1984); Lake (1984); and Snidal (1985). On American decline and economic crisis see Russett (1985); Rosecrance (1976); Oye (1979); Calleo (1987). For a critique see Strange (1987, 1988).
9. Arrighi (1982) provides one of the more sophisticated arguments for a 'crisis of hegemony'.
10. Altvater (1987).
11. See the work of Aglietta (1979, 1982); Lipietz (1982, 1984); De Vroey (1984); Elbaum and Lazonick (1986); Noel (1987); and Jessop (1988).
12. Keohane (1984) pp. 31–46; Hirsch and Doyle (1977); Cox (1981, 1983); Gill (1985, 1986); and Gill and Law (1988).
13. A point realised by Keohane (1984) p. 39, but this does not prevent him ultimately advancing a 'qualified hegemony' argument. See my conclusion for details.
14. Also see Strange (1988) pp. 235–40; Russett (1985).
15. For a summary of recent criticism see Guerrieri and Padoan (1988).
16. Milward (1984) is the only major study to challenge this conventional view. The argument of this book draws on Milward's study and lends support to this overall thesis. However Milward's analysis begins from 1947 and focuses on Western Europe rather than Britain in detail.
17. See for instance Keohane (1984) pp. 37–9.
18. Hogan (1987); Wexler (1983); Milward (1984). Also see Kindleberger (1987, ch. 14) for his assessment of Milward.
19. Strange (1987) p. 552; also see Gill (1986) on realism and its influence on the views of the Trilateral Commission. It should be pointed out that realism in this international relations sense bears no relation to the term

'realism' as it is employed in debates on the philosophy of science and social science. For an example of the latter usage see Keat and Urry (1975).

20. Brett *et al.* (1982); Brett (1985); Gilliat (1983) and Pople (1980) are in a similar vein. Van der Pijl (1984) and Overbeek (1988) work within a much more productive theoretical framework than Brett yet still offer a version of the capitulation thesis. Much of the more narrative work on the postwar Labour governments sanction the capitulation view, including Eatwell (1979); Pelling (1984); Morgan (1984); Hinton (1983); and Coates (1975). Cairncross (1985) on which I draw, is an accurate view.
21. Brett *et al.* (1982) p. 132, and below p. 138.
22. Radice (1984) p. 125.
23. Brett (1985) p. 139, and below ibid.
24. Ibid., p. 140.
25. Ibid., p. 140.
26. Gott (1987).
27. Ibid.
28. Brett (1985) p. 141, and below pp. 142–3.
29. Brett *et al.* (1982) pp. 137–8, see in particular his isolated quote of Cripps's *worry* on this point.
30. Van der Pijl (1984) pp. 35 and 167.
31. Ibid., pp. 161, 138.
32. Brett *et al.* (1982) pp. 137–8.
33. Ibid., and Saville (1983) p. 159.
34. Morgan (1983) p. 434.
35. Aaronovitch and Smith (1981) pp. 70, 77.
36. Lipietz (1987) p. 40; a collection of Lipietz's essays.
37. Truman as reported in LaFeber (1972) p. 53; see also Keohane (1984).
38. See the classic studies by Miliband (1972); Pelling (1965, 1972); Coates (1975); and more recently Hinton (1983).
39. J. Morgan (1981) p. 342; see also Saville (1983).
40. Telegram, Playfair to Christelow, 20 September 1947 in PRO T236/1667.
41. See Rubin (1987) ch. 3.
42. Gaitskell's and Bevin's assessment in PRO CAB 129/42.

Notes to Chapter 2: Towards the Washington Negotiations

1. *Financial Agreement*, Cmd 6708 (HMSO, 1945), Treasury publication.
2. Reprinted in Keynes (1979) p. 256.
3. Stage III had been designated by government economists as the period after the defeat of Japan.
4. These and the immediately following statistics are drawn from *Statistical Material* Cmd 6707 (HMSO, 1945), and *Economist*, 15 December 1945.
5. See Lidbury (1947) p. 168, in Modern Records Centre, University of Warwick archive MSS 200/F/3/D3/3/2.
6. See Robinson's reflections (1986), p. 166.
7. Robinson (1986) confirms this point, p. 170.

8. Robinson, Plowden, Sinclair and others agreed; ibid., p. 168.
9. *The Banker*, September 1946, p. 131.
10. Sayers (1956) p. 198; Cairncross (1985) p. 7; *Economist*, 15 December 1945.
11. *Economist*, 15 December 1945, p. 874; Cairncross (1985).
12. H. C. *Debates*, 12 December 1945, col. 441.
13. Public Records Office (PRO hereafter) Treasury paper, 'Britain's Bargaining Power', T230/136.
14. Ministry of Food, *How Britain was Fed in Wartime* (HMSO, 1946) Tables 1 and 2.
15. United Nations, *A Survey of the Economic Situation* (1948).
16. 'Imports of Manufactured Goods', *Monthly Digest of Statistics* (1938).
17. United Nations (1948).
18. Ibid., and *Board of Trade Journal*, 12 June 1948.
19. See Robinson (1986) p. 166; Allen (1946).
20. See Mikesell (1949).
21. See Balogh (1948) p. 458, Table 2.
22. Milward (1984) p. 28.
23. *Board of Trade Journal*, 10 December 1946.
24. *Board of Trade Journal*, Janaury–June 1939, p. 288, Table 4.
25. United Nations (1948) p. 55.
26. League of Nations (1945) p. 13.
27. Van der Pijl (1984) p. 78.
28. Ibid., p. 19.
29. Gramsci (1971) p. 303.
30. *United Nations, Economic Survey of Europe* (1953).
31. Ibid., p. 10.
32. This term is associated with the 'Regulation school' approach to political economy. See Aglietta (1979, 1982); Lipietz (1982, 1984); De Vroey (1984).
33. Williams (1968).
34. See Morgan and Thomas (1962) pp. 88 and 94.
35. Williams (1968) p. 270.
36. Joslin (1963) p. 110.
37. Imlah (1958) pp. 70–5.
38. Block (1977) p. 14.
39. Van der Pijl (1984) p. 42, and Block (1977) p. 16.
40. Ingham (1984) p. 203; Aglietta (1982) p. 13.
41. Sargent, in Worswick and Ady (1952) p. 532; Strange (1971) p. 545; Block (1977) pp. 29–30.
42. R. Clarke (1982) p. 71 (posthumous: edited by A. Cairncross).
43. Keynes (1933) p. 37.
44. Radice (mimeo, 1986) argues that Keynes's interwar views on national self-sufficiency were not a protectionist aberration but a main aspect of his thought up until his death in 1946. He suggests that Keynes mapped out a path for the postwar government between protectionism and *laissez-faire* – a path that 'vanished into thin air' – which 'in essence was the same programme of practical protectionism that he had followed since 1924' (p. 26). Radice has no documentation to support this claim.

In fact, Keynes thoroughly dismissed protectionism as a postwar policy and saw his goal as 'setting up a postwar international economic community of the character sought by the USA' (Keynes's 1945 memo). Richard Clarke recalls that 'nobody could have persuaded Keynes to abandon his multilateral orientation' in autumn 1945 (Clarke (1982) p. 57), and Keynes's government papers 'Comments on Plan II – a reply to Clarke', Minute on 'What happens if we do not get the US loan', and 'If Congress rejects the loan' (reprinted in Clarke, ibid.) all confirm Keynes's rejection of protectionism. As in his earlier writing (1984), Radice simply concludes that *laissez-faire* was established by a capitulation to American hegemony.

45. For general expositions of multilateralism see Block (1977); Gardner (1969).
46. Keynes (1979) pp. 256–93.
47. Keynes to Brand, 24 April 1945, reprinted in Keynes (1979) pp. 310–7; also see Keynes to Brand, 5 June 1945, ibid., pp. 343–5.
48. Ibid., p. 312.
49. See Cairncross (1985) p. 95 on this point.
50. USA/UK Financial arrangements in Stage III – Notes of Treasury meeting, 23 July 1945, PRO T236/450.
51. Keynes (1979) p. 292.
52. Keynes in *H. L. Debates*, 18 December 1945, vol. 138, col. 793.
53. See R. Clarke (1982) p. 55.
54. On this relationship see Pimlott (1985) p. 428.
55. See the text of the Charter in the *New York Times*, 15 August 1941.
56. Welles (1947) p. 8.
57. Ibid., p. 176.
58. *H. C. Debates*, 12 December 1945, cols 480–1.
59. *The Times*, 25 February 1942.
60. These were published as part of a more substantial document, 'Proposals for the Expansion of World Trade and Employment' (Washington, 1945); see Gardner (1969) p. 146.
61. *Banker*, August 1946, p. 74; Lidbury (1947) p. 170.
62. C. Baillieu, 'The Basis of Britain's Future Foreign Economic Policy', in Modern Records Centre, University of Warwick, MSS 200/F/3/D3/3.
63. PRO CAB 128/4 CM(45)50, 6 November 1945.
64. *Board of Trade Journal*, 15 December 1945, p. 719.
65. Brett *et al.* (1982), and Brett (1985) p. 140.
66. See Block (1977) ch. 3.
67. Bernstein (1944), and Block (1977).
68. Meade (1948) pp. 9–10.
69. Kipping's papers, in Modern Records Centre, University of Warwick, MMS 200/F/3/D3/3/3.
70. Reply by W. L. Clayton, 5 June 1945, PRO T236/450.
71. Block (1977) ch. 3, and Milward (1984) ch. 6.
72. Block (1977) p. 56.
73. J. Williams (1944), and Mikesell (1945).
74. Mikesell (1945) p. 569.
75. Van der Pijl (1984) p. 144.

76. Balogh (1948) p. 456.

Notes to Chapter 3: The Washington Loan Agreement

1. *H.C. Debates*, 13 December 1945, col. 676.
2. *H.C. Debates*, 12 December 1945, col. 443.
3. Dow (1964) p. 17; Morgan (1984) p. 144.
4. *H.C. Debates*, 13 December 1945, col. 720.
5. Boothby, *H.C. Debates*, 13 December 1945, col. 455; Amery (1946).
6. See Letters to the Editor, *The Times*, 12 December 1945.
7. *H.C. Debates*, 12 December 1945, cols 468–9.
8. See Empire Industries Association Parliamentary Minutes, 25 April 1945, 19 November 1945, in Modern Records Centre, University of Warwick MMS 221/1/2/2.
9. Both reprinted in R. Clarke (1982).
10. R. Clarke's figure (1982) p. 58.
11. Ministry of Food, *How Britain was Fed in Wartime* (HMSO, 1946).
12. Keynes's minute to D. Waley, February 1946, reprinted in R. Clarke (1982) p. 151.
13. R. Clarke (1982) p. 70.
14. Cairncross (1985) p. 98.
15. Keynes (1979) p. 366; Keynes addressing House of Lords, 18 December 1945, vol. 138, col. 790.
16. Pimlott (1985) p. 439.
17. Chester (1951) p. 5.
18. Roseveare (1969) p. 273.
19. Middlemas (1979) p. 271.
20. Dow (1964) p. 13; Chester (1952) p. 337.
21. PRO CAB 129/21.
22. Ibid., Morrison in *H.C. Debates*, 28 February 1946, cols. 2128–31.
23. Robinson (1986) p. 183.
24. Robbins (1971) p. 207.
25. Jay (1980) p. 137.
26. PRO CAB 128/4 CM(45)50; T236/450.
27. *Financial Agreement*, Cmd 6708 (HMSO, 1945).
28. *The Times*, 12 December 1945.
29. *UK Balance of Payments 1946–53*, Cmd 8976 (HMSO, 1953).
30. Dalton (1962) p. 81.
31. *Economist*, 8 December 1945, p. 821.
32. Gardner (1969); Brett *et al.* (1982).
33. See *Banker*, September 1946, Table 1.
34. See Mr Spence's address to House of Representatives, 14 June 1946, in Kress (1949).
35. See *Banker*, August 1946.
36. Letter to Clayton from R. Wood (Chairman of Sears Roebuck and Co.) 26 November 1945, see Gardner (1969) p. 197.
37. See Spence's report in Kress (1949) document 5, p. 9.

38. Memo to E. Bridges, PRO T 236/1667.
39. See Sargent (1952); Wright (1954); Shannon (1949); *Economist*, 14 January 1950.
40. Sargent (1952) p. 532.
41. Shannon (1949) p. 218.
42. Wright (1954) p. 560.
43. Ibid., p. 575.
44. *H.C. Debates*, 12 December 1945, col. 425.
45. Milward (1984) Table 13.
46. Brett (1985) p. 140; Brett *et al.* (1982) pp. 130–42.
47. Van der Pijl (1984) Introduction and ch. 6, p. 167; Coates (1975) ch. 3.
48. Attlee (1961) pp. 8–9.
49. Dalton (1962) p. 3.
50. Milward (1984) p. 51.
51. Miliband (1972) p. 193.
52. Cole (1931).
53. Tawney (1932) pp. 323–45.
54. See Durbin (1985) ch. 4; Eatwell and Wright (1978).
55. *The Times*, 27 July 1945, p. 4.
56. Pimlott (1985) ch. 27 on Dalton's view.
57. Jay (1980) p. 139.
58. PRO CAB 128/4 CM(45)57 Minute 3.
59. Treasury Archive Memorandum 1961, H. Ellis-Rees, PRO T 267/3.
60. *H.C. Debates*, 6 August 1947, col. 1488.
61. Milward (1984) Tables 3 and 5.
62. Statistics drawn from *Board of Trade Journal*, 31 January 1948.
63. Calculated from 'Economic Report', Table 9, CAB 129/30.
64. *Board of Trade Journal*, 29 January 1949.
65. Dow (1964) p. 22.
66. As recently expressed by Milward (1984).
67. See Bareau in *Banker*, February 1948, p. 79.
68. *The Economist*, 9 June 1945, p. 783; Patterson and Polk (1947) Table I and II.
69. League of Nations, *International Trade Statistics* (1938).
70. Mikesell (1947–8); Patterson and Polk (1947).
71. See the accounts in PRO T 267/3 and related Treasury documents.
72. *Monetary Agreement between the UK and Belgium*, Cmd 6557 (HMSO, 1944).
73. PRO T267/3, p. 11; Zupnick (1954) p. 163.
74. PRO T267/3, p. 10.
75. R. Clarke (1982) p. 185; Zupnick (1954) p. 165.
76. See the various accounts of PRO T267/3; Zupnick (1954); Bareau (1948); Shannon (1949); Cairncross (1985).
77. Bareau (1948) p. 81.
78. PRO T267/3, p. 33.
79. Zupnick (1954) p. 169, Bareau (1948) p. 82.
80. See Bareau (1948); Patterson and Polk (1947).
81. Clayton's term in PRO T236/1667 – the three enshrined principles, of

course, being convertibility, non-discrimination and preference elimination.

82. PRO T267/3, p. 17.
83. Jay (1985) p. 121.
84. PRO T267/3, pp. 29–32; Balogh (1949) p. 41; Zupnick (1954) p. 166.
85. PRO T267/3, p. 31.
86. 'Convertibility', memo by Playfair, 17 September 1947, PRO T236/1667.
87. 'Tariff Concessions at Geneva and the $400m, memo to Eady, PRO T236/1667.
88. *H.C. Debates*, 6 August 1947, col. 1494.
89. See Henderson (1947) p. 279.
90. Telegram from Foreign Office to Washington, 18 April 1947, PRO T236/686.
91. 'Text of US Statement on Relaxation of Loan Agreement Provisions', PRO T236/686; memo to Bridges, T236/1667.
92. 'Dollar Drain Committee Papers', US Treasury Meeting, 8 June 1949, PRO 230/177.
93. *H.C. Debates*, 7 August 1947, col. 1663.
94. Telegram from Playfair to Christelow, 20 September 1947, PRO T236/1667.
95. Memo to Bridges, PRO T236/1667.
96. C. Baillieu Presidential Address, March 1946, Modern Records Centre, University of Warwick, MSS 200/F/4/61/4.
97. Meade's paper 'The Balance of Gain and Loss', PRO T230/136.
98. Glickman (1946–7) pp. 439–70.
99. 'The Future of Multilateral International Economic Co-operation', 12 September 1949, PRO CAB 129/36.
100. Ellis-Rees in PRO T267/3.
101. 'Summary of Fundamentals', PRO T232/199.
102. Ellis-Rees, PRO T267/3.
103. 'Convertibility', memo by Playfair, 18 September 1947, PRO T236/1667.

Notes to Chapter 4: The Marshall Offensive

1. Manderson-Jones (1972) p. 7.
2. W. Clayton, 'The European Crisis', 27 May 1947, reprinted in Clayton (1963) p. 496.
3. Franks (1978) p. 3.
4. Acheson's speech of May 1947, reprinted in Bundy (1952) pp. 48–9; see also Arkes (1972) ch. 2.
5. Dalton (1962) p. 187.
6. Morgan (1984) p. 331.
7. Ibid., p. 277.
8. Gamble (1981) p. 108.
9. Van der Pijl (1984) p. 138.
10. Ibid., p. 167.

11. Mayne (1970) p. 107.
12. Clayton (1947), reprinted in Clayton (1963) p. 496.
13. Chancellor's Economic Report, 4 November 1948, Table 1, PRO CAB 129/30 CP(48)255.
14. Chancellors Economic Report, 12 June 1950, PRO CAB 129/40 CP(50)122.
15. PRO CAB 129/30 CP(48)255, Table 2.
16. Ibid., Table 6.
17. PRO CAB 129/30; Cmd 7268 *Capital Investment in 1948*, (HMSO, 1948) p. 8.
18. *Capital Investment in 1948*, Cmd 7268 (HMSO, 1948) p. 8.
19. Clayton (1963) p. 496.
20. PRO CAB 129/30, Tables 12, 13; Milward (1984) p. 14, Table 2.
21. *Board of Trade Journal*, 24 January 1948, pp. 161–71.
22. Ibid., p. 162.
23. PRO CAB 129/30 CP(48)255.
24. 'Fundamentals', by H. Gaitskell, PRO T232/199.
25. PRO CAB 129/30 CM(47)30; 'The Exhaustion of the Dollar Credit', 27 March 1947, CAB 129/17; 'Import Programme 1947/48', 28 May 1947, CAB 129/19.
26. Block (1977) p. 79.
27. *Board of Trade Journal*, 24 January 1948, p. 171.
28. Ibid.
29. PRO CAB 129/30, Table 9.
30. Brett *et al.* (1982); Brett (1985); Radice (1984) and Evans (1985).
31. Brett (1985) p. 143.
32. Ibid., p. 142.
33. 'Brief for US Negotiations', PRO T236/782.
34. 'How the Credit was Used', Annex of Pt 2, PRO T267/3.
35. Ibid.
36. 'US Balance of Payments 1946–1953', Annex, in Commission on Foreign Economic Policy (1954) p. 15.
37. 'Brief for US Negotiations', PRO T236/782.
38. PRO T267/3.
39. Maier (1981) p. 342.
40. Morgan (1984) p. 277.
41. 'Dollar Crisis (European Reconstruction)', telegram Washington to Foreign Office, PRO T236/782.
42. Commission on Foreign Economic Policy (1954) p. 23.
43. 'Fundamental discussions with the US', telegram Washington to Foreign Office, 23 June 1950, PRO T232/199.
44. Block (1977) p. 82.
45. 'US Balance of Payments 1946–53', in Commission on Foreign Economic Policy (1954) p. 15.
46. Jackson (1978–9) p. 1053.
47. Ibid., p. 1053.
48. Hogan (1977).
49. Rappaport (1981) p. 122.
50. Ibid., p. 123.

51. US Department of State, Bulletin 16, 18 May 1947 pp. 991–4.
52. Telegram, Washington to Foreign Office, 3 June 1947, PRO T236/782.
53. Ibid.
54. Hogan (1982) p. 282; Jackson (1978–9) p. 1060.
55. Milward (1984) ch. 2; Block (1977) p. 89.
56. Bevin's account of the incident recalled in a speech to the National Press Club of Washington, 1 April 1949, reprinted in Bullock (1983) p. 405.
57. Pritt (1963) chs 10 and 15; Pelling (1984) p. 188; Van der Pijl (1984) p. 177.
58. Lovett to US Embassies in London and Paris, quoted in Bullock (1983) p. 535.
59. 'Fundamental discussions with the US', 9 March 1950, PRO T232/199.
60. 'Dollar Crisis', ERP note by UK Delegation, June 1947, PRO T236/782.
61. 'Attitude of UK towards European Integration', note on consequence of European integration, PRO T232/194.
62. 'European Reconstruction', May/June 1948, PRO T236/811.
63. 'The UK and Marshall Aid', 4 October 1947, PRO CAB 129/21.
64. Ibid.
65. 'Summary of Fundamentals of External Financial Policy', PRO T232/199.
66. PRO CAB 129/21.
67. 'Raising the Wind', memo by W. Eady, 29 August 1947, PRO T236/1667.
68. Ibid.
69. Ibid.
70. Morgan (1984) p. 270.
71. Memo by Balfour, 29 May 1947, PRO T236/1887.
72. Telegram Washington to Eady, 2 June 1947, PRO T236/782.
73. 'Consequences of Contemporary Movements in Western Europe', PRO T232/194.
74. Secretary of State G.C. Marshall's address, Harvard, 5 June 1947, reprinted in OECD (1978) Annex, pp. 227–9.
75. Franks (1978) pp. 19–20.
76. 'Programme of European Reconstruction', 6 June 1947, PRO T236/782.
77. Telegrams, 2 and 3 July 1947, PRO T236/1890.
78. *New York Times*, 7 January 1949, reprinted in Milward (1984) p. 61.
79. 'Programme of European Reconstruction', PRO T236/782.
80. 'Draft Invitation to European Governments', 2 July 1947, PRO T236/1890.
81. Van der Beugel (1966) p. 68.
82. Milward (1984) p. 66.
83. *Convention for European Economic Co-operation*, Cmd 7388 (HMSO, 1948).
84. Vandenberg (1954) p. 377.
85. Lovett, quoted in Milward (1984) p. 81.
86. Van der Beugel (1966) p. 80.
87. *The Times*, 17 April 1948, p. 4.
88. Marshall's Harvard address, in OECD (1978) pp. 227–9.

89. Franks (1978) p. 20.
90. *Economic Co-operation Agreement*, Cmd 7446 (HMSO, 1948).
91. 'General Outline of the Draft Agreement', PRO T236/811.
92. 'Draft Economic Agreement', 2 June 1948, PRO CAB 134/218 EPC(48)48.
93. PRO T236/811.
94. Ibid.
95. Ibid.; Milward (1984) p. 117.
96. PRO T236/812 CM(48)43, 25 June 1948.
97. Milward (1984) pp. 120–1.
98. Gordon (1956) p. 4.
99. MacBride to Bevin, 14 December 1948, PRO T232/113.
100. Cripps to UK Delegation, 22 October 1948, PRO T232/18.
101. UK Delegation on OEEC Structure, 20 December 1948, PRO T232/113.
102. Hall-Patch to London, 11 September 1948, see Milward (1984) p. 184.
103. Hall-Patch, 'Re-Organisation of OEEC', 16 November 1948, PRO T232/113.
104. Ibid.
105. 'Economic Reconstruction', telegram UK Delegation to London, 19 October 1948, PRO T232/18.
106. 'Note of informal meeting on OEEC', 22 December 1948, PRO T232/113.
107. For an assessment of these issues which go beyond the scope of this book, see Milward (1984).
108. *Interim Report* OEEC (1948) p. 177.
109. *The Economist*, 22 January 1949, p. 130.
110. R.W. Gifford, 'How the Marshall Plan Can be Made to Work Effectively', 26 January 1948, Modern Records Centre, University of Warwick, MSS 200/F/3/D3/5/41.
111. Ibid.
112. Van der Pijl (1984) pp. 148–9.
113. Maier (1977) pp. 607–33.
114. Ibid., p. 615.
115. Senate Foreign Relations Committee Hearings on Extension of ERP, reprinted in Arkes (1972) pp. 309–10.
116. 'Report of Hoffman's speech on British Industrial Productivity', 19 July 1948, PRO T232/101.
117. 'Anglo-US Council on Productivity Report', PRO T232/101.
118. 'National Production Advisory Council on Industry – TUC Section', 23 July 1948, PRO T232/101.
119. 'American Assistance', 22 July 1948, PRO T232/101.
120. PRO T232/101, ibid.
121. Ray Gifford correspondence, Modern Records Centre, University of Warwick, MSS 200/F/3/D3/5/41.
122. Cable to F. Bain, 28 February 1948, ibid.; Gifford's speech, 26 January 1948, ibid.
123. M. MacKenzie letter to W. Stephenson, 16 November 1948, ibid.
124. Notes of Discussion at Board of Trade, 3 June 1948, ibid.

125. Diebold (1952) p. 45, Table 3; Milward (1984) p. 102, Table 18, pp. 103–4, Table 19.
126. 'Treasury Note on Intra-European Payments', 2 December 1947, PRO T236/800.
127. Bean (1948); Diebold (1952) p. 24.
128. 'Summary of Fundamentals of External Financial Policy', PRO T232/199; 'Treasury Note', PRO T232/800.
129. Bean (1948) p. 408.
130. Diebold (1952) p. 27.
131. 'Extract from US Government Document on ERP', 3 January 1948, PRO T236/800.
132. 'Treasury note', PRO T236/800.
133. Diebold (1952) p. 38.
134. Ibid., p. 45, Table 3.
135. Bank for International Settlements, 19th *Annual Report* (1949) p. 205.
136. Diebold (1952) p. 42.
137. Triffin (1957) pp. 148–9.
138. 'Treasury note', PRO T236/800.
139. Triffin (1957) pp. 153–4.
140. Ibid., p. 158.
141. Ibid., p. 160.
142. H. Callender in *New York Times*, 1 July 1949.
143. Milward (1984) p. 279.
144. 'Import Licencing Restrictions', 28 May 1949, PRO CAB 129/35 CP(45)124.
145. PRO CAB 129/35 CP(49)137, 18 June 1949.
146. Morgan (1984) p. 272.
147. 'Exhaustion of Dollar Credit', 21 March 1947, PRO CAB 129/17; 'Import Programme 1947/48', 28 May 1947, PRO CAB 129/19.
148. *European Co-operation*, Cmd 7572 (HMSO, 1948).
149. *Capital Investment in 1948*, Cmd 7268 (HMSO, 1948).
150. Ibid.
151. Cripps, quoted in Cooke (1957) p. 373.
152. Corina (1961) chs 1 and 2.
153. *Statement on Personal Incomes, Costs and Prices*, Cmd 7321 (HMSO, 1948).
154. 'Economic Consequences of Receiving No Marshall Aid', Cripps' memo, 23 June 1948, PRO CAB 129/28 CP(48)161.
155. Morgan (1984) p. 277.
156. Pritt (1963) p. 173.
157. Morgan (1984) p. 492 has a similar argument.
158. Dow (1964) pp. 31–2.
159. 'Review of the Investment Programme'; 'Investment and Inflation – note by Economic Section', PRO T229/66.
160. *H.C. Debates*, 6 April 1949, col. 2075; Dow (1964) p. 38.
161. Morgan (1984) p. 493; Cairncross (1985) ch. 17 provides an accurate account, as does Maier (1977) pp. 629–30.
162. 'Review of the Investment Programme', PRO T229/66.
163. Maier (1981) Table, p. 342; PRO CAB 128, Cabinet Conclusions, 11

December 1950; *H.C. Debates*, 13 December 1950, col. 1162.
164. Hoffman, February 1950, quoted in Van der Pijl (1984) p. 149.
165. Maier (1981) p. 342.
166. Bank for International Settlements, 19th *Annual Report* (1949) p. 20; Milward (1984) pp. 96, 100.
167. Calculated from *Board of Trade Journals*, 1946–50; *UN Yearbook of International Trade Statistics* (various); Milward (1984) Table 19, pp. 103–4.
168. 'UK Revised 1949/50 Programme', 17 May 1949, PRO T232/78 EPC(49)52.
169. Milward (1984) p. 105.

Notes to Chapter 5: The Revision in State Strategy

1. Although Cripps did not officially resign until 19 October 1950 his position as Chancellor had effectively passed to Gaitskell – acting as Minister for Economic Affairs since 23 February – following Cripps's final budget in April of that year.
2. This chapter draws on Cairncross's various accounts (1983, 1985) but attempts to place the discussion of devaluation within the wider context of the strains experienced by the state in regard to such issues as European/British/American co-operation, trade and payments negotiations, and the fundamentals of British policy on multilateralism.
3. *Board of Trade Journal*, 22 January 1949, p. 131.
4. Cripps, 'Address to Commonwealth High Commissioners', 23 February 1949, Cripps Papers, Nuffield College, Oxford.
5. 'Economic Report', 12 June 1950, PRO CAB129/40; *Board of Trade Journal*, 22 January 1949.
6. Cripps, 'Address to Commonwealth High Commissioners'.
7. Ibid.
8. Calculated from Table 6 of Nurkse (1956) p. 129.
9. Gamble (1981) p. 122.
10. Eatwell (1982) p. 129.
11. The following statistics are drawn from Cripps, 'Address to Commonwealth High Commissioners'; PRO CAB 129/40; *Board of Trade Journal*, 22 January 1949.
12. 'The Gold Drain', *Banker*, July/August 1949.
13. Cripps, 'Speech to Imperial Defence College', 22 November 1948, Cripps Papers, Nuffield College, Oxford.
14. Calculated from OEEC, *Statistical Bulletins of Foreign Trade* (various).
15. Cripps, 'Speech to IDC'.
16. 'The Future of Sterling', memo by R. Clarke, 25 February 1948, PRO T236/2398.
17. Ibid.
18. Ibid.
19. G. Bolton, 'The Devaluation of Sterling', 30 March 1948, PRO T236/2398.

20. Ibid.
21. Cripps, 'Notes on Address to Labour Party Conference', Blackpool, 7 June 1949, Cripps Papers, Nuffield College, Oxford.
22. Ibid.
23. Memo by H. Morrison on the Economic Situation, 21 July 1949, PRO CAB 129/36.
24. Cairncross (1985) pp. 196–7.
25. 'Summary of main points covered in Ministerial Discussions since 12 July 1949', PRO PREM 8/1178.
26. 'Economic Report', 12 June 1950, Table 1, PRO CAB 129/40.
27. *Board of Trade Journal*, 21 January 1950; PRO CAB 129/40, Tables 9 and 10.
28. Ibid.
29. ECA (1951) Table 36.
30. Calculated from PRO CAB 129/40, Table 11.
31. H. Ellis-Rees, 'The Convertibility Crisis', PRO T267/3.
32. 'Statement by Chancellor to US and Canadian Ministers', 7 September 1949, PRO CAB 129/36.
33. 'Crisis Continued', *The Economist*, 16 July 1949.
34. Calculated from Polak (1952–2) Table 4 and p. 10.
35. Detailed accounts of the US recession can be found in Hall (1950); Milward (1984); Polak (1951–2); *Banker*, August 1949.
36. Milward (1984) Table 39, pp. 344 and 349; Cairncross (1985) p. 276.
37. *Banker*, July/August 1949; MacDougall (1957) p. 49.
38. 'The Dollar Crisis 1949', 11 January 1950, PRO CAB 134/225.
39. Leffingwell (1949–50); 'Defeat or Opportunity', *The Economist*, 24 September 1949.
40. 'Summary of Main Points', PRO PREM 8/1178.
41. 'Fundamentals – Some Comments', 13 April 1950, PRO T232/199.
42. Cripps, 'Notes on Speech to Empire Parliamentary Association', 25 October 1948, Cripps Papers, Nuffield College, Oxford.
43. Cripps, 'Speech to IDC'.
44. Williams (1983) p. 130.
45. H. Wilson's letter to Attlee, 8 August 1948, PRO PREM 8/1178.
46. 'Statement to US and Canadian Ministers', 7 September 1949, PRO CAB 129/36.
47. 'The Economic Situation', PRO CAB 128/16 CM53(49).
48. 'Statement to US and Canadian Ministers', PRO CAB 129/36.
49. 'The Economic Situation', memo by Morrison, 21 July 1949, PRO CAB 129/36.
50. 'Summary of Main Points', PRO PREM 8/1178.
51. 'The Economic Situation', PRO CAB 129/36.
52. 'Summary of Main Points', PRO PREM 8/1178.
53. PRO CAB 129/36 CP(49)159, 21 July 1949.
54. Ibid.
55. 'The Washington Talks', PRO CAB 128/16 CM52(49) Minute 2.
56. See Conference of Socialist Economists (1979) Introduction and ch. 1, for an account of 1976.
57. See Smith (1984, 1985) for an analysis of 'decline' theories.

58. Eatwell (1982) p. 129; Gamble (1981) and Morgan (1984) also subscribe to such a theory.
59. 'The Investment Programme', memo by H. Wilson, 24 August 1949 PRO PREM 8/1178 CP(49)178; and 'Interim Report of Investment Programme Committee', ibid.
60. *H.C. Debates* 18 April 1950, col. 51; Cairncross (1985) p. 195; Nurkse (1956) Table 6, p. 129.
61. *H.C. Debates*, 26 October 1949 vol. 468, cols 1358, 1392; Dow (1964) p. 46.
62. Dow (1964) p. 46; Cairncross (1985) p. 195.
63. 'Meeting of Commonwealth Finance Ministers', July 1949, Annex to CP49(159), PRO CAB 129/36.
64. See Hemming, Miles and Ray (1958) Table 6.
65. Gaitskell memo on Washington talks, 23 August 1949, PRO CAB 129/36 CP(49)175.
66. 'Statement by Cripps to Tripartite Meeting', 7 September 1949, PRO CAB 129/36.
67. H. Wilson's letter to Attlee, 8 August 1949, PRO PREM 8/1178.
68. Gaitskell's memo, 23 August 1949, PRO CAB 129/36.
69. Memo by Hall-Patch, 10 March 1950 PRO CAB 134/225; PRO CAB 128/16, CM53(49), August 1949.
70. PRO CAB 129/36, CP(49)175.
71. 'The Future of Multilateral International Economic Co-operation', 12 September 1949, PRO CAB 129/36, CP(49)198.
72. Memo by H. Wilson, 12 September 1949, PRO CAB 129/36.
73. 'The Future of Multilateral International Economic Co-operation', PRO CAB 129/36.
74. 'Fundamentals – Some Comments', PRO T232/199.
75. Ibid. (both quotes).
76. 'Joint Communiqué, issued at the end of the tripartite discussions in Washington', 12 September 1949, PRO CAB 129/36.
77. H. Wilson's letter to Attlee, 8 August 1949, PRO PREM 8/1178.
78. 'Fundamental Discussion with the USA', 9 March 1950, PRO T232/199.
79. Gaitskell memo, 'The Washington Talks', 23 August 1949, PRO CAB 129/36.
80. 'Council of Europe', August 1949, PRO CAB 128/16 CM(49)41, Minute 5.
81. 'The Washington Talks', 23 August 1949, PRO CAB 129/36, CP(49)175.
82. 'Economic Report', 12 June 1950, PRO CAB 129/40 CP(50)122.
83. Polak (1951–2) pp. 2–5.
84. PRO CAB 129/40; Hall (1950) p. 868.
85. 'Fundamentals: Gold and European Payments', Gaitskell's memo, PRO T232/199.
86. 'Fundamentals – Some Comments', 13 August 1950, PRO T232/199.
87. 'Summary of Fundamentals', Draft Annex, April 1950, PRO T232/199.
88. 'Fundamentals – Some Comments', PRO T232/199.
89. Telegram, Washington to Foreign Office, 23 June 1950, PRO T232/199; W.M. Martin's quote is also taken from this telegram.
90. 'Note of a Meeting in H.W. Smith's Room', 27 June 1950, PRO

T232/199; 'Fundamental Discussions with USA', memo by H. Smith, 18 April 1950.

91. ECA document, 'The Problem of W. Europe's Competitive Position', 19 July 1949, reprinted in Colebrook (1971) Appendix 3(A).
92. Hinshaw (1951); Block (1977) ch. 4.
93. ECA cable, 'European Clearing Union', 26 November 1949, reprinted in Colebrook (1971), Appendix 3(d); Hoffman's speech reprinted in Van der Beugel (1966).
94. ECA document, 'European Monetary Authority', 5 December 1949, reprinted in Colebrook (1971) Appendix 3(e).
95. Hinshaw (1951) p. 56; Manderson-Jones (1972) p. 72.
96. Hall-Patch, 10 March 1950, PRO CAB 134/225.
97. 'EPU', memo by Cripps, 27 January 1950, PRO CAB 134/225; *Banker*, January 1950; Milward (1984) p. 304; Triffin (1957) ch. 5.
98. Hoffman, in *New York Times*, 14 January 1950.
99. PRO CAB 128/16 CM(49)41, August 1949.
100. Milward (1984) p. 310.
101. 'EPU', memo by Cripps, PRO CAB 134/225.
102. Report by Cripps, 10 February 1950, PRO CAB 134/225 EPC(50)28.
103. 'European Payments Scheme', February/March 1950, PRO CAB 134/225.
104. Ibid.
105. Ibid.
106. See Triffin (the ECA architect of the EPU) (1957) p. 165.
107. Ibid.
108. 'ECA Views on British EPU Proposals', 8 April 1950, reprinted in Colebrook (1971) p. 145.
109. Sargent (1952) p. 527.
110. 'Mechanics of the EPU', *The Economist*, 15 July 1950; Triffin (1957) p. 168.
111. Diebold (1952) Table 7, p. 164.
112. Mikesell (1954) ch. 6; Diebold (1952) p. 183.
113. Diebold (1952) pp. 182–3.
114. Telegram, 23 June 1950, PRO T232/199.
115. Kenwood and Lougheed (1983) p. 278.
116. 'Inconvertible Sterling', 15 February 1952, PRO T236/3245.
117. Calculated from 'Economic Report', 12 June 1950, Tables 1 and 9, PRO CAB 129/40.
118. 'The Future of Multilateralism', memo by H. Wilson, 12 September 1949, PRO CAB 129/36.
119. *Economic Survey for 1951*, Cmd 8195 (HMSO, 1951).

Notes to Chapter 6: The Impact of Rearmament

1. *Economic Survey for 1951*, Cmd 8195 (HMSO, 1951) p. 3.
2. Draft memo, 'The Progress and Likely Impact of Defence Orders on the Economy', PRO T229/704.

3. Attlee's phrase taken up by Gaitskell, see Cmd 8195, p. 4.
4. Saville (1983) p. 159.
5. Aaronovitch (1981) p. 70; Smith (1981) p. 77.
6. 'The Finance of Defence', 23 October 1950, PRO CAB 129/42.
7. Ibid.
8. Gaitskell's and Bevin's assessment in ibid.
9. 'Limitations of Civil Output in the Metal Using Industries', 19 March 1951, PRO T229/383.
10. *Economic Survey for 1954*, Cmd 9108 (HMSO, 1954) p. 27, Table 15.
11. 'Defence and the Balance of Payments', PRO T229/585, 30 April 1952.
12. 'Economic Report', 22 June 1951, Table 3, PRO CAB 129/46.
13. Ibid., Tables 5 and 7.
14. See Gaitskell, in Cmd 8195, p. 27.
15. Ibid.
16. 'Dollar Drain Committee Papers', PRO T230/177.
17. The United States, for example, extracted 95 per cent of the world's total sulphur supplies.
18. Cmd 8195, p. 23, Table 8.
19. 'Fall in Stocks', 29 March 1951, PRO T230/177.
20. See P. Williams (1983) p. 223.
21. PRO T230/177; T229/704.
22. Hitchman to Plowden, 22 October 1949, PRO T229/704.
23. PRO CAB 129/46, Table 10; PRO T229/376.
24. PRO T229/376; PRO CAB 129/46, Table 9.
25. PRO CAB 129/46, Table 10.
26. *Economic Survey for 1952*, Cmd 8509 (HMSO, 1952) p. 10, Table 2; PRO CAB 129/46, Table 11; 'The Economic Position' PRO CAB 129/48; *Economic Trends Annual Supplement* (HMSO, 1981).
27. See Gaitskell's diaries, P. Williams (1983) p. 54.
28. Singleton (1986) p. 95.
29. Cmd 8195, p. 37.
30. Quoted in Kolko (1972) pp. 471–2.
31. Ibid., p. 472.
32. Quoted in Gaddis (1982) pp. 91 and 95.
33. Kidron (1970).
34. Block (1977) p. 107.
35. See CFEP (1954) pp. 33–6; Lowe (1986) p. 144.
36. Commission on Foreign Economic Policy (1954) p. 35.
37. Gaddis (1982) p. 113.
38. PRO CAB 129/42, Annex 1.
39. Acheson to Senate Foreign Relations Committee, quoted in Gaddis (1982) p. 114.
40. PRO CAB 129/47, CP(51)266.
41. See Cumings (1981 and 1983); Lowe (1986); Khrushchev (1971).
42. O'Neill (1981) p. 462.
43. Among the numerous examples see Saville (1983) p. 159; Morgan (1984) p. 434.
44. Cmd 8195, p. 45.
45. PRO CAB 129/42, 23 October 1950.

46. PRO CAB 128/19, Cm3(51); FO371/81655.
47. Lowe (1986) p. 112; PRO CAB 129/45, CP(51)127.
48. 'The Finance of Defence', PRO CAB 129/42.
49. Ibid.
50. Cmd 8195; PRO CAB 129/44 CP(51)20.
51. *H.C. Debates*, 29 January 1951, col. 590; Cmd 8195, p. 9.
52. Hitchman to Plowden, PRO T229/704; Jenkins in *The Tribune*, 9 March 1951.
53. 'The Impact of the Defence Programme on Exports of Engineering Goods', 16 August 1950, PRO T229/846.
54. 'Economic Implications of the Defence Proposals', 19 January 1951, PRO CAB 129/44.
55. 'The Progress and Likely Impact of the Defence Orders', PRO T299/704; 'The Economic Implications of the Defence Proposals', PRO CAB 129/44.
56. 'Defence Priorities', PRO T229/846.
57. Economic Policy Committee memo March 1951, PRO T229/846, EPC(51)26.
58. 'The Economic Implications of the Defence Proposals'. PRO CAB 129/44.
59. 'Limitations of Civil Output', 20 April 1951, PRO T229/383.
60. Ibid.
61. PRO CAB 129/44, CP(51)20.
62. 'Limitations on the Production of Goods', PRO T229/383.
63. A. Jenkins to Shillito, 19 March 1951, PRO T229/383.
64. Ibid.
65. Notes of a meeting, 14 February 1951, PRO T229/383.
66. Memo to Robens, 27 June 1951, PRO T229/383.
67. 'Tank Production: Leyland Factory', 14 March 1951, PRO T229/846.
68. Memo, 19 March 1951, PRO T229/846, EPC(51)56.
69. 'Tank Production', PRO T229/846.
70. 'New Building in Connection with the Defence Programme', 22 May 1951, PRO T229/846.
71. Ibid., Appendix B.
72. Memo to Humphreys-Davies, 20 March 1951, PRO T229/846.
73. *Economic Survey for 1953*, Cmd 8800 (HMSO, 1953) Table 24; Cairncross (1985) pp. 228–9.
74. 'Impact on the Economy of the Defence Programme', PRO T229/704.
75. PRO CAB 129/44, CP(51)20.
76. Cmd 8195, p. 9.
77. 'Defence Priorities', various documents, PRO T229/846.
78. 'The Impact of Defence on the Exports of Engineering Goods', 16 August 1950, PRO T229/846.
79. 'Arrangements for Minimising the Impact of the Defence Programme on Export Markets', PRO T229/846.
80. 'The Impact of Defence on the Exports of Engineering Goods', PRO T229/846.
81. Ibid.

82. 'The Export Programme in Relation to the Accelerated Defence Programme', PRO T229/376.
83. Ibid.
84. Attlee to House of Commons, 12 September 1950, vol. 478, cols 953–71; Mitchell (1963) p. 56.
85. Dow (1964) p. 55.
86. Ibid., p. 56, footnote 1.
87. Cmd 8509, p. 809.
88. 'Background Material on Export Targets', PRO T229/376.
89. 'Export Targets – Memo by E. Wright to Mr. Allen', PRO T229/376.
90. Ibid.
91. Cmd 8509; *Economic Survey for 1953*, Cmd 8800 (HMSO, 1953).
92. Cmd 8800, p. 34; Cmd 9108, p. 50.
93. *Economic Survey for 1954*, Cmd 9105, HMSO, 1954.
94. *Economic Trends Annual Supplement* (HMSO, 1981).
95. 'Economic Position' 31 October 1951, PRO CAB 129/48; Cmd 8509; Cmd 8800.
96. 'Defence and the Balance of Payments', 30 August 1952, PRO T229/585.
97. PRO CAB 129/44, CP(51)20; Cairncross (1985) pp. 215, 228; PRO CAB 134/225/6.
98. Ibids.
99. Cmd 8509, p. 9; Cmd 8800, p. 7.
100. 'Export Targets', PRO T229/376 Cmd 9108, p. 9.
101. The direct implication of Aaronovitch's account (1981) p. 70.
102. Butler's memo, 31 October 1951, PRO CAB 129/48; 'Defence and the Balance of Payments', PRO T229/585.
103. See Milward (1984) and Cairncross (1985) for an elaboration of these conclusions.

Notes to Chapter 7: Conclusion

1. See Gill and Law (1988) p. 25 for an outline of the theoretical premises of realism.
2. See Radice (1984) on the 'myth of the national economy'.
3. Diebold, as quoted in Keohane (1984) p. 138.
4. See the work of Cox (1981 and 1983) and Gill (1986).
5. Also see Strange (1988) Parts I and II.
6. Gill and Law (1988) p. 78.
7. Ibid., p. 344; other examples include Aaronovitch (1961) and Longstreth (1979). For an interesting variant of fractionalism see Van der Pijl (1984) and Overbeek (1988; unpublished).
8. For an account of the constraints on the state from a pluralist viewpoint see Lindblom (1977).
9. The suggestion of Gill and Law (1988) p. 348.
10. See Marx (1978) for an analysis of the functional differentiation of the total productive circuit of capital:

$$M - C\frac{LP}{MP} \ldots P \ldots C' - M'$$

11. I am indebted to Simon Clarke (1977, 1978, 1988) for many ideas in this discussion of the state and the general interest.
12. Mandel (1968, 1975, 1978); see also Holloway (1983).
13. Mandel (1978) ch. 10.
14. Kautsky (1970) translation; Lenin (1917); Mandel (1978) p. 372; Holloway (1983).
15. Mandel (1978) p. 338.
16. See Barker (1978).
17. Marx (1981) p. 300.
18. See in particular Strange (1987) pp. 564–74, and (1988) p. 235.
19. Karl Marx, 'The Eighteenth Brumaire of Louis Bonaparte' (1869), in Feuer (1969) p. 360.

Bibliography

MANUSCRIPT COLLECTIONS

Public Records

Cabinet

CAB 124 – Lord President of the Council
          Files
CAB 128 – Cabinet Conclusions
CAB 129 – Cabinet Papers
CAB 130 – Cabinet Committees
CAB 134 – Cabinet Committees

Foreign Office

FO 371

Prime Minister's Office

PREM 8 – PM Office Files, 1945–51

Treasury

T229 – Central Economic Planning
       Staff Files
T230 – Economic Section Papers
T232 – European Economic Co-
       operation Committee Files
T233 – Home Finance Division Files
T236 – Overseas Finance Division Files
T267 – Treasury Historical Memoranda

Private Papers

Cripps Papers (Nuffield College, Oxford)
Kippings Papers – CBI Predecessor Archive
    (Modern Records Centre, University of
    Warwick)
Empire Industry Association Parliamentary
    Minutes (Modern Records Centre,
    University of Warwick)

OFFICIAL RECORDS AND PAPERS

United Kingdom (HMSO)

Central Statistical Office

Annual Abstract of Statistics

	Economic Trends
	Economic Trends Annual Supplement
	Monthly Digest of Statistics
Foreign Office	*European Co-operation* (Cmd 7545)
	European Co-operation (Cmd 7572)
	Economic Co-operation Agreement (Cmd 7446)
	Convention for European Economic Co-operation (Cmd 7388)
House of Commons	*Parliamentary Debates* (Hansard)
House of Lords	*Parliamentary Debates* (Hansard)
Ministry of Food	*How Britain was Fed in Wartime*
Political and Economic Planning	*Britain and World Trade* (1947)
Prime Minister	*Statement on Personal Incomes, Costs, and Prices* (Cmd 7321)
Treasury	*Capital Investment in 1948* (Cmd 7268)
	Economic Survey (Annual, 1947–55)
	Financial Agreement Between the Governments of the United States and the United Kingdom (Cmd 6708)
	National Income and Expenditure of the UK (Annual, 1946–51)
	Monetary Agreement between the UK and Belgium (Cmd 6557)
	Statistical Material Presented During the Washington Negotiations (Cmd 6707)
	United Kingdom Balance of Payments (from 1948)

International and United States

Bank for International Settlements	*Annual Reports*
	The Sterling Area (1953)
Commission on Foreign Economic Policy (US)	*Staff Papers* (1954)
Committee of European Economic Co-operation	vol. 1: *General Report* (1947)

Department of State	*Foreign Relations of the United States*
Economic Co-operation Administration	*The Sterling Area: An American Analysis* (1951)
League of Nations	*Industrialisation and Foreign Trade* (1945)
Organisation for Economic Co-operation and Development	*From Marshall Plan to Global Interdependence* (1978)
Organisation for European Economic Co-operation	*European Recovery Programme*, vols 1 and 2 (1950) *Interim Report on the ERP* (1948) *Statistical Bulletin of Foreign Trade*
US Senate 85th Congress	*Foreign Aid Programme*, 1st Session (1957)
United Nations	*A Survey of the Economic Situation and Prospects of Europe* (1948) *Economic Survey of Europe* (annual from 1949) *Economic Survey of Europe since the War* (1953) *The European Steel Industry and the Wide Strip Mill* (1953) *Monthly Bulletin of Statistics* *Statistical Yearbooks*

NEWSPAPERS AND PERIODICALS

The Banker
The Board of Trade Journal
The Economist
The Guardian
Lloyds Bank Review
The New York Times
The Times

UNPUBLISHED WORKS

Colebrook, M.J. (1971), 'Franco-British Relations and European Integration 1945–50' (PhD, University of Geneva).

Corina, J. (1961), 'The British Experiment in Wage-Restraint' (DPhil, Oxford University).

Gilliat, S. (1983), 'The Management of Reconstruction' (DPhil, University of Sussex).

Overbeek, H. (1988), 'Global Capital and Britain's Decline' (PhD, University of Amsterdam).

Pople, A. (1980), 'The External Economic Constraints on the British State in the Immediate Postwar Years' (MA, University of Sussex).

Rees, H. (1962), *The Convertibility Crisis* (in PRO T267/3).

Smith, B. (1984), *Alternative Theories about Economic and Social Development* (ESRC Working Paper 14, University of Birmingham).

Smith, B. (1985), *Alternative Explanations for Economic Change* (ESRC Working Paper 18, University of Birmingham).

Tomlinson, J. (1986), *The Macroeconomic Objectives of the Labour Government 1945–51* (ESRC End of Grant Report, September).

PUBLISHED WORKS

Aaronovitch, S. (1961), *The Ruling Class* (London: Lawrence Wishart).

Aaronovitch, S. (ed.) (1981), *The Political Economy of British Capitalism* (London: McGraw-Hill).

Aaronovitch, S. (ed.) (1981), 'The Relative Decline of the UK', in Aaronovitch (ed.) (1981).

Abercrombie, N. and Urry, J. (1983), *Capital, Labour and the Middle Classes* (London: Allen and Unwin).

Aglietta, M. (1979), *A Theory of Capitalist Regulation* (London: NLB).

Aglietta, M. (1982), 'World Capitalism in the Eighties', *New Left Review*.

Allen, R. (1946), 'Mutual Aid between the US and the British Empire, 1941–45', *Journal of the Royal Statistical Society*, vol. 109, no. 3.

Almond, G. (1983), 'Corporatism, Pluralism and Professional Memory', *World Politics*, no. 135.

Althusser, L. (1965), *For Marx* (Harmondsworth, Middx: Penguin).

Althusser, L. (1972), *Politics and History* (London: New Left Books).

Altvater, E. (1987), 'The Crisis of the World Financial System', *Annals of the American Academy of Political and Social Science*, July.

Amery, L. S. (1946), *The Washington Loan Agreements* (London: Macdonald).

Arkes, H. (1972), *Bureaucracy, the Marshall Plan and the National Interest* (Princeton, N.J.: Princeton University Press).

Arrighi, G. (1982), 'A Crisis of Hegemony', in S. Amin (ed.), *Dynamics of Global Crisis* (London: Macmillan).

Attlee, C. (1961), *A Prime Minister Remembers* (London: Heinemann).

Bacon, R. and Eltis, W. (1976), *Britain's Economic Problem* (London: Macmillan).

Balogh, T. (1948), 'The United States and International Economic Equilibrium', in S. Harris (ed.), *Foreign Economic Policy of the US* (Cambridge, Mass.: Harvard University Press).

Balogh, T. (1949), 'Britain's Economic Problem', *Quarterly Journal of Economics*, pp. 32–67.

Balogh, T. (1950), 'The Crisis of the Marshall Plan', *Finanzarchiv*, N.F.12.

Bareau, P. (1948), 'The New Bilateralism', *Banker*, February, pp. 79–84.

Barker, C. (1978), 'A Note on the Theory of Capitalist States', *Capital and Class*, no. 4.

Barry-Jones, R. (1982), 'International Political Economy', *Review of International studies*, vol. 8.

Bean, R. (1948), 'European Multilateral Clearing', *Journal of Political Economy*, vol. 56.

Benjamin, R. and Elkin S. (eds) (1985), *The Democratic State* (Lawrence, KS: Kansas University Press).

Berger, S. (1981), *Organising Interests in Western Europe* (Cambridge: Cambridge University Press).

Bernstein, E. M. (1944), 'A Practical International Monetary Policy', *American Economic Review*, vol. 34.

Block, F. (1977), 'The Ruling Class does not Rule', *Socialist Revolution*, vol. 33.

Block, F. (1977), *The Origins of International Economic Disorder*, (Berkeley, Calif.: University of California Press).

Block, F. (1980), 'Beyond Relative Autonomy', *Socialist Register*.

Bosanquet, N. (1983), *After the New Right* (London: Heinemann).

Brett, T. *et al.* (1982) 'Planned Trade, Labour Party Policy, and US Intervention', *History Workshop*, vol. 13.

Brett, T. (1985), *The World Economy Since the War* (London: Macmillan).

Brookings Institution (1952), *Re-armament and Anglo-American Economic Relations* (Washington, D.C.: Brookings Institution).

Browning, P. (1986), *The Treasury and Economic Policy, 1964–1985* (London: Longman).

Bullock, A. (1983), *Ernest Bevin, Foreign Secretary, 1945–51* (London: Heinemann).

Bundy, M. (1952), *The Pattern of Responsibility* (Boston, Mass.: Houghton Mifflin).

Cairncross, A. and Eichengreen, B. (1983), *Sterling in Decline* (Oxford: Blackwell).

Cairncross, A. (1985) *Years of Recovery* (London: Methuen).

Calleo, D. (1987), *Beyond American Hegemony* (Brighton: Wheatsheaf).

Callinicos, A. (1976), *Althusser's Marxism* (London: Pluto).

Carnoy, M. (1984), *The State and Political Theory* (Princeton, N.J.: Princeton University Press).

Chase-Dunn, C. (1981), 'Interstate System and Capitalist 'World Economy', *International Studies Quarterly*, vol. 25, no. 1.

Chester, D. N. (1951), *Lessons of the British War Economy* (Cambridge: Cambridge University Press).

Chester, D. N. (1952), 'Machinery of the Government and Planning', in Worswick and Ady (eds) (1952).

Clarke, R. (1982), *Anglo-American Economic Collaboration in War and Peace 1942–49* (Oxford: Oxford University Press).

Clarke, S. (1977), 'Marxism, Sociology and Poulantzas' Theory of the State', *Capital and Class*, vol. 2.

Clarke, S. (1978), 'Capital, Fractions of Capital and the State', *Capital and Class*, vol. 5.

Clarke, S. (1979), 'Socialist Humanism and the Critique of Economism', *History Workshop*, vol. 8.

Clarke, S. (1980), 'Althusserian Marxism', in S. Clarke (ed.) *One-Dimensional Marxism* (London: Allison Busby).

Clarke, S. (1982) *Marx, Marginalism and Modern Sociology* (London: Macmillan).

Clarke, S. (1983) 'State, Class Struggle and Capital Reproduction', *Kapitalistate*, nos 10/11.

Clarke, S. (1988), *Keynesianism, Monetarism and the Crisis of the State* (Aldershot, Hants.: Edward Elgar).

Clayton, W. (1963), 'GATT, the Marshall Plan, and OECD', *Political Science Quarterly*, vol. 78, no. 4.

Coates, D. (1975), *The Labour Party and the Struggle for Socialism* (Cambridge: Cambridge University Press).

Coates, D. and Hillard, J. (eds) (1986), *The Economic Decline of Modern Britain* (Brighton: Wheatsheaf).

Cohen, J. (1983), *Class and Civil Society* (Cambridge, Mass.: University of Massachussetts Press).

Cole, G. D. H. (1931), 'The Old Labour Party and the New', *New Statesman*, 14 November.

Colletti, L. (1972), *From Rousseau to Lenin* (New York: MRP).

Conference of Socialist Economists (1979), *Struggle Over the State* (London: CSE Books).

Conference of Socialist Economists (1980), *The Alternative Economic Strategy* (London: CSE Books).

Cooke, C. (1957), *The Life of R. S. Cripps* (London: Hodder and Stoughton).

Cox, R. (1981), 'Social Forces, States and World Orders', *Millennium*, vol. 10, no. 2.

Cox, R. (1983), 'Gramsci, Hegemony and International Relations', *Millennium*, vol. 12, no. 2.

Crompton, R. and Gubbay, J. (1977), *Economy and Class Structure* (London: Macmillan).

Cumings, B. (1981), *The Origins of the Korean War* (Princeton, NJ: Princeton University Press).

Cumings, B. (ed.) (1983), *Child of Conflict* (London: University of Washington Press).

Dahl, R. (1961), *Who Governs?* (New Haven, Conn.: Yale University Press).

Dahl, R. (1978), 'Pluralism Revisited', *Comparative Politics*, vol. 10.

Dalton, H. (1962), *High Tide and After* (London: Muller).

De Vroey, M. (1984), 'A Regulation Approach Interpretation of Contemporary Crisis', *Capital and Class*, vol. 23.

Diebold, W. (Jr) (1952), *Trade and Payments in Western Europe* (New York: Harper and Row).

Dow, J. C. R. (1964), *The Management of the British Economy, 1945–60* (Cambridge: Cambridge University Press).

Draper, H. (1977), *Karl Marx's Theory of Revolution, vol. 1* (London: MRP).
Durbin, E. (1985), *New Jerusalems* (London: Routledge and Kegan Paul).
Eatwell, J. (1982), *Whatever Happened to Britain?* (London: BBC Publications).
Eatwell, R. (1979), *The 1945–51 Labour Governments* (London: Batsford).
Eatwell, R. and Wright, A. (1978) 'Labour and the Lessons of 1931', *History*, vol. 63.
Elbaum, B. and Lazonick, W. (eds) (1986), *The Decline of the British Economy* (Oxford: Clarendon Press).
Evans, P. *et al.* (1985), *Bringing the State Back In* (Cambridge: Cambridge University Press).
Evans, T. (1985), 'Money Makes the World Go Round', *Capital and Class*, no. 24.
Feuer, L. (ed.) (1969), *Marx and Engels: Basic Writings* (London: Fontana).
Fine, B. and Harris, L. (1986), *The Peculiarities of the British Economy* (London: Lawrence and Wishart).
Flamant, M. and Singer-Kerel, J. (1968), *Modern Economic Crises* (London: Barrie and Jenkins).
Foot, M. (1984), *Another Heart and Other Pulses* (London: Collins).
Frankel, B. (1983), *Beyond the State?* (London: Macmillan).
Franks, O. (1978), 'Lessons of the Marshall Plan Experience', in OECD (1978).
Freeman, A. (1982), *The Benn Heresy* (London: Pluto).
Friedman, M. and Friedman, R. (1980), *Free to Choose* (Harmondsworth, Middx.: Penguin).
Gaddis, J. L. (1982), *Strategies of Containment* (Oxford: Oxford University Press).
Gamble, A. (1979), 'The Free Economy and the Strong State', *Socialist Register*.
Gamble, A. (1981), *Britain in Decline* (London: Macmillan).
Gardner, R. (1969), *Sterling–Dollar Diplomacy* (Oxford: Oxford University Press).
Georgiou, G. (1983), 'The Political Economy of Military Expenditure', *Capital and Class*, vol. 19.
Gerth, H. and Mills, C. (eds) (1964), *From Max Weber* (London: Routledge and Kegan Paul).
Giddens, A. and Held, D. (eds) (1982), *Classes, Power and Conflict* (London: Macmillan).
Gilbert, F. (ed.) (1975), *The Historical Essays of Otto Hintze* (Oxford: Oxford University Press).
Gill, S. (1985), 'From Atlanticism to Trilateralism', in S. Smith (ed.), *International Relations* (Oxford: Blackwell).
Gill, S. (1986), 'Hegemony, Consensus and Trilateralism', *Review of International Studies*, vol. 12.
Gill, S. and Law, D. (1988), *The Global Political Economy* (Brighton: Harvester).
Gilpin, R. (1975), *US Power and the Multinational Corporation* (London: Macmillan).

Gilpin, R. (1977), 'Economic Interdependence and National Security in Historical Perspective', in K. Knorr (ed.), *Economic Issues and National Security* (Kansas: Regents Press).

Gilpin, R. (1987), *The Political Economy of International Relations* (Princeton, NJ.: Princeton University Press).

Glickman, D. (1946–7), 'The British Imperial Preference System', *Quarterly Journal of Economics*, vol. 61.

Glyn, A. and Sutcliffe, B. (1972), *British Capitalism, Workers and the Profits Squeeze* (Harmondsworth, Middx.: Penguin).

Gordon, L. (1956), 'The OECD', *Inernational Organisation*, vol. 10.

Gott, R. (1987), 'Sentimental Island Story', *The Guardian*, 30 January.

Gramsci, A. (1971), *Selections from Prison Notebooks* (London: Lawrence and Wishart).

Guerrieri, P. and Padoan, P. (1988), 'International Co-operation and the Role of Macroeconomic Regimes', in P. Guerrieri and P. Padoan (eds), *The Political Economy of International Co-operation* (London: Croom Helm).

Haines, J. (1977), *The Politics of Power* (London: Cape).

Hall, M. (1950), 'The UK after Devaluation', *American Economic Review*, vol. 40.

Hall, P. (1986), *Governing the Economy* (Cambridge: Polity).

Ham, A. (1981), *Treasury Rules* (London: Quartet Books).

Hayek, F. (1984), *1980s Unemployment and the Unions* (London: Institute of Economic Affairs).

Held, D. (ed.) (1983), *States and Societies* (Oxford: Martin Robertson).

Hemming, F., Miles, C. and Ray, G. (1958), 'A Statistical Summary of the Extent of Import Control in the UK Since the War', *Review of Economic Studies*, vol. 26.

Henderson, H. (1946), 'The Anglo-American Financial Agreement', *Bulletin of the Oxford University Institute of Statistics*, vol. 8.

Henderson, H. (1947), 'The Implications of the Marshall Speech', *Bulletin of the Oxford University Institute of Statistics*, vol. 9.

Hinshaw, R. (1951), 'Consideration of Some Criticisms', *Review of Economics and Statistics*, vol. 33.

Hinton, J. (1983), *Labour and Socialism* (Brighton: Wheatsheaf).

Hirsch, F. and Doyle, M. (1977), 'Politicization in the World Economy', in F. Hirsch and M. Doyle (eds), *Alternatives to Monetary Disorder* (New York: McGraw-Hill).

Hirschman, A. (1951), 'The EPU', *Review of Economics and Statistics*, vol. 33.

Hogan, M. J. (1977), *Informal Entente: The Private Structure of Co-operation in Anglo-American Economic Diplomacy, 1918–1929* (Columbia, Mo.).

Hogan, M. J. (1982), 'The Search for a Creative Peace', *Diplomatic History*, vol. 6.

Hogan, M. J. (1987), *The Marshall Plan* (Cambridge: Cambridge University Press).

Holloway, S. (1983), 'Relations among Core Capitalist States', *Canadian Journal of Political Science*, June.

Hyman, R. (1986), 'British Industrial Relations: the Limits of Corporatism', in O. Jacobi (ed.), *Economic Crisis, Trade Unions and the State* (London: Croom Helm).

Imlah, A. (1958), *Economic Elements in the Pax Britannica* (Oxford: Oxford University Press).

Ingham, G. (1984), *Capitalism Divided?* (London: Macmillan).

Jackson, S. (1978–9) 'Prologue to the Marshall Plan', *Journal of American History*, vol. 65.

Jay, D. (1980), *Change and Fortune* (London: Hutchinson).

Jay, D. (1985), *Sterling* (London: Sidgwick and Jackson).

Jessop, B. (1982), *The Capitalist State* (Oxford: Martin Robertson).

Jessop, B. (1983), 'Accumulation, State, and Hegemonic Projects', *Kapitalistate*, nos 10/11.

Jessop, B. (1988), 'Regulation Theory, Post-Fordism and the State', *Capital and Class*, no. 34.

Joseph, K. (1979), *Solving the Union Problem* (Centre for Policy Studies pamphlet).

Joslin, D. (1963), *A Century of Banking in Latin America* (Oxford: Oxford University Press).

Kalberg, S. (1979), 'The Search for Thematic Orientations', *Sociology*, vol. 13.

Kautsky, K. (1970), 'Ultra-Imperialism', *New Left Review*, vol. 59.

Keat, R. (1981), *The Politics of Social Theory* (Oxford: Blackwell).

Keat, R. and Urry, J. (1975), *Social Theory as Science* (London: Routledge and Kegan Paul).

Keith, Lord (1977), 'Industry, the City of London and Our Economic Future', in Coates and Hillard (eds) (1986).

Kenwood, A. and Lougheed, A. (1983), *The Growth of the International Economy 1820–1980* (London: Allen and Unwin).

Keohane, R. (1980), 'The Theory of Hegemonic Stability and Changes in International Regimes', in O. Holsti (ed.), *Change in the International System* (Boulder, Col.: Westview).

Keohane, R. (1984), *After Hegemony* (Princeton, NJ: Princeton University Press).

Keynes, J. (1933), 'National Self-Sufficiency', *New Statesman and Nation*, July.

Keynes, J. (1979), *The Collected Writings of J.M. Keynes*, vol. 24 (Cambridge: Cambridge University Press).

Khrushchev, N. S. (1971), *Khrushchev Remembers* (London: Deutsch).

Kidron, M. (1970), *Western Capitalism Since the War* (Harmondsworth, Middx.: Penguin).

Kindleberger, C. (1973), *The World in Depression, 1929–1939* (Harmondsworth, Middx.: Penguin).

Kindleberger, C. (1976), 'Systems of International Economic Organisation', in D. Calleo (ed.), *Money and the Coming World Order* (New York: New York University Press).

Kindleberger, C. (1987), *Marshall Plan Days* (London: Allen and Unwin).

King, R. (1986), *The State in Modern Society* (London: Macmillan).

Kolko, J. and Kolko, G. (1972), *The Limits of Power* (New York: Harper and Row).

Krasner, S. (1976), 'State Power and the Structure of International Trade', *World Politics*, vol. 28, no. 3.

Krasner, S. (1978), *Defending the National Interest* (Princeton, NJ: Princeton University Press).

Kress, A. (ed.) (1949), *The Documents of Economic Diplomacy* (Washington, D.C.: Georgetown University, Foreign Service).

Labour Party (1982), *The City: A Socialist Approach* (London: Labour Party).

LaFeber, W. (1972), *America, Russia and the Cold War 1945–71* (New York: Wiley).

Lake, D. (1984), 'Beneath the Commerce of Nations', *International Studies Quarterly*, vol. 28.

Lash, S. and Urry, J. (1984), 'The New Marxism of Collective Action', *Sociology*, vol. 18, no. 1.

Lawson, N. (1978), 'The Moral Dimension', in A. Seldon (ed.), *The Coming Confrontation* (London: Institute of Economic Affairs).

Leffingwell, R. C. (1949–50), 'Devaluation and European Recovery', *Foreign Affairs*, vol. 28.

Lenin, V. (1917), *Imperialism, the Highest Stage of Capitalism* (Moscow: Progress).

Levitt, M. S. (1985), 'The Economics of Defence Spending', mimeo.

Lidbury, C. (1947), 'G. B. in Relation to the World's Trade Situation', *Journal of the Royal Society of Arts*, January.

Lindblom, C. (1977), *Politics and Markets* (New York: Basic Books).

Lipietz, A. (1982), 'Towards Global Fordism?', *New Left Review*, vol. 132.

Lipietz, A. (1984), 'Imperialism or the Beast of the Apocalypse', *Capital and Class*, no. 22.

Lipietz, A. (1987), *Mirages and Miracles* (London: Verso).

Longstreth, F. (1979), 'The City, Industry and the State', in C. Crouch (ed.), *State and Economy in Contemporary Capitalism* (London: Croom Helm).

Lowe, P. (1986) *The Origins of the Korean War* (London: Longman).

MacDougall, D. (1957), *The World Dollar Problem* (London: Macmillan).

McLennan, G. (1981), *Marxism and the Methodologies of History* (London: Verso).

Maier, C. S. (1977), 'The Politics of Productivity', *International Organisation*, vol. 31.

Maier, C. S. (1981), 'The Two Postwar Eras', *American Historical Review*, vol. 86.

Mandel, E. (1968), *Europe versus America?* (London: New Left Books).

Mandel, E. (1975), 'International Capitalism and Supranationality', in H. Radice (ed.), *International Firms and Modern Imperialism* (Harmondsworth, Middx.: Penguin).

Mandel, E. (1978), *Late Capitalism* (London: Verso).

Manderson-Jones, R. B. (1972), *The Special Relationship* (London: Weidenfeld and Nicolson).

Mann, M. (1984) 'The Autonomous Power of the State', *European Journal of Sociology*, vol. XXV.

Maravall, J. (1979), 'The Limits of Reformism', *British Journal of Sociology*, vol. 30.

Martin, R. (1983), 'Pluralism and the New Corporatism', *Political Studies*, vol. 31.

Marx, K. (1962a), 'Wage Labour and Capital' in Marx (1962b).

Marx, K. (1962b), *Selected Works*, vol. 1 (Moscow: Progress Books).

Marx, K. (1964), *The German Ideology* (Moscow: Progress Books).

Marx, K. (1976), *Capital*, vol. 1 (Harmondsworth, Middx.: Penguin).

Marx, K. (1978) *Capital*, vol. 2 (Harmondsworth, Middx.: Penguin).

Marx, K. (1981), *Capital*, vol. 3 (Harmondsworth, Middx.: Penguin).

Mayne, R. (1970), *The Recovery of Europe* (London: Weidenfeld and Nicolson).

Meade, J. (1948), 'Bretton Woods, Havana and the UK Balance of Payments', *Lloyds Bank Review*, no. 7.

Middlemas, K. (1979), *Politics in Industrial Society* (London: André Deutsch).

Mikesell, R. (1945), 'The Key Currency Proposal', *Quarterly Journal of Economics*, vol. 59.

Mikesell, R. (1947–8), 'Regional Multilateral Payments Arrangements', *Quarterly Journal of Economics*, vol. 62.

Mikesell, R. (1949), 'International Disequilibrium and the Postwar World', *American Economic Review*, vol. 39.

Mikesell, R. (1954), *Foreign Exchange in the Postwar World* (New York: Twentieth-Century Fund).

Miliband, R. (1964), *The State in Capitalist Society* (London: Quartet Books).

Miliband, R. (1972), *Parliamentary Socialism* (London: Merlin).

Miliband, R. (1983), 'State Power and Class Interests', *New Left Review*, vol. 138.

Mills, C. W. (1959), *The Sociological Imagination* (Harmondsworth, Middx.: Penguin).

Milward, A. (1984), *The Reconstruction of Western Europe, 1945–51* (London: Methuen).

Minns, R. (1982), *Take Over the City* (London: Pluto).

Mitchell, J. (1963), *Crisis in Britain 1951* (London: Secker and Warburg).

Morgan, E. and Thomas, W. (1962), *The Stock Exchange: Its History and Functions* (London: Elek).

Morgan, J. (ed.) (1981), *The Backbench Diaries of Richard Crossman* (London: Cape).

Morgan, K. (1984), *Labour in Power, 1945–51* (Oxford: Oxford University Press).

Noël, A. (1987), 'Accumulation, Regulation and Social Change', *International Organisation*, vol. 41, no. 2.

Nordlinger, E. (1981) *On the Autonomy of the Democratic State* (Cambridge, Mass.: Harvard University Press).

Nurkse, R. (1956), 'The Relation between Home Investment and External Balance, Britain 1945–55', *Review of Economics and Statistics*, vol. 38, no. 2.

O'Neill, R. (1981), *Australia in the Korean War*, vol. 1 (Canberra: Australian Government Publications).

Overbeek, H. (1980), 'Finance Capital and the Crisis in Britain', *Capital and Class*, no. 11.

Oye, K. (1979), 'The Domain of Choice', in K. Oye (ed.), *Eagle Entangled: US Foreign Policy in a Complex World* (London: Longman).
Patterson, G. and Polk, J. (1947), 'The Emerging Pattern of Bilateralism', *Quarterly Journal of Economics*, vol. 62.
Pelling, H. (1965), *The Origins of The Labour Party, 1880–1900* (Oxford: Oxford University Press).
Pelling, H. (1972), *A Short History of the Labour Party* (London: Macmillan).
Pelling, H. (1984), *The Labour Governments, 1945–51* (London: Macmillan).
Picciotto, S. (1988), 'The Control of Transnational Capital and the Democratisation of the International State', *Journal of Law and Society*, vol. 15, no. 1.
Pierson, C. (1984), 'New Theories of State and Civil Society', *Sociology*, vol. 18.
Pimlott, B. (1985), *Hugh Dalton* (London: Cape).
Pliatzky, L. (1982), *Getting and Spending* (Oxford: Blackwell).
Polak, J. J. (1951–2), 'Contributions of the September 1949 Devaluations to the Solution of Europe's Dollar Problem', in *IMF Staff Papers*, vol. 2.
Pollard, S. (1982), *The Wasting of the British Economy* (London: Croom Helm).
Poulantzas, N. (1973), *Political Power and Social Classes* (London: New Left Books).
Poulantzas, N. (1976), 'The Capitalist State', *New Left Review*, vol. 95.
Poulantzas, N. (1978), *State, Power, Socalism* (London: Verso).
Poulantzas, N. (1979), Interview, *Marxism Today*, July.
Pritt, D. N. (1963), *The Labour Government, 1945–51* (London: Lawrence and Wishart).
Radice, H. (1984), 'The National Economy: a Keynesian Myth?', *Capital and Class*, no. 22.
Radice, H. (1986), 'Keynes and the Policy of Practical Protectionism', mimeo.
Rappaport, A. (1981), 'The United States and European Integration', *Diplomatic History*, vol. 5.
Robbins, Lord (1971), *Autobiography of an Economist* (London: Macmillan).
Robinson, A. (1986), 'The Economic Problems of the Transition', *Cambridge Journal of Economics*, vol. 10.
Rose, G. (1978), *The Melancholy Science* (London: Macmillan).
Rosecrance, R. (ed.) (1976), *America as an Ordinary Country* (Ithaca, NY: Cornell University Press).
Roseveare, H. (1969), *The Treasury: The Evolution of a British Institution* (London: Allen and Unwin).
Rubin, B. (1987), *Secrets of State* (Oxford: Oxford University Press).
Rubin, I. (1973), *Essays on Marx's Labour Theory of Value* (Montreal: Black Rose).
Russett, B. (1985), 'The Mysterious Case of Vanishing Hegemony; or, Is Mark Twain Really Dead?', *International Organisation*, vol. 39, no. 2.
Sargent, J. (1952), 'Britain and Europe', in Worswick and Ady (eds) (1952).
Sargent, J. (1952), 'Britain and the Sterling area', in Worswick and Ady (eds) (1952).
Saville, J. (1983), 'C. R. Attlee: an Assessment', *Socialist Register*.

Sayers, R. S. (1956), *Financial Policy, 1939–45* (London: Longman).

Schmitter, P. (1985), 'Neo-corporatism and the State', in W. Grant (ed.), *The Political Economy of Corporatism* (London: Macmillan).

Shannon, H. (1949), 'The British Payments and Exchange Control System' *Quarterly Journal of Economics*, vol. 63.

Singleton, J. (1986), 'Lancashire's Last Stand', *Economic History Review*, vol. 39, no. 1.

Skocpol, T. (1979), *States and Social Revolutions* (Cambridge: Cambridge University Press).

Skocpol, T. (1981), 'Political Response to Capitalist Crisis', *Politics and Society*, vol. 10.

Skocpol, T. (1985), 'Bringing the State Back In', in Evans *et al.* (1985).

Smith, R. (1981), 'The Historical Decline of the UK', in Aaronovitch (ed.) (1981).

Snidal, D. (1985), 'The Limits of Hegemonic Stability Theory', *International Organisation*, vol. 39, no. 4.

Stein, A. (1984), 'The Hegemon's Dilemma: Great Britain, the United States, and the International Economic Order', *International Organisation*, vol. 38, no. 2.

Stepan, A. (1978), *The State and Society* (Princeton, NJ: Princeton University Press).

Strange, S. (1971), *Sterling and British Policy* (Oxford: Oxford University Press).

Strange, S. (1985), 'Protectionism and World Politics', *International Organisation*, vol. 39, no. 2.

Strange, S. (1987), 'The Persistent Myth of Lost Hegemony', *International Organisation*, vol. 41, no. 4.

Strange, S. (1988), *States and Markets* (London: Frances Pinter).

Sylvan, D. (1981), 'The Newest Mercantilism', *International Organisation*, vol. 35, no. 2.

Tawney, R. (1932), 'The Choice Before the Labour Party', *Political Quarterly*, vol. 3.

Thain, C. (1984), 'The Treasury and Britain's Decline', *Political Studies*, vol. 32.

Therborn, G. (1986), 'Karl Marx Returning', *International Political Science Review*, vol. 7, no. 2.

Treud, M. and Mikesell, R. (1955), *Postwar Bilateral Payments Agreements* (Ann Arbor Mich.).

Triffin, R. (1957), *Europe and the Money Muddle* (New Haven, Conn.: Yale University Press).

Trimberger, E. (1977), *Revolution from Above* (New Brunswick: Transaction).

Urry, J. and Wakeford, J. (eds) (1973), *Power in Britain* (London: Heinemann).

Urry, J. (1981), *The Anatomy of Capitalist Societies* (London: Macmillan).

Urry, J. (1982), 'Some Themes in the Analysis', *Acta Sociologica*, vol. 25, no. 4.

Urry, J. (1983), 'De-industrialisation, Classes and Politics', in R. King (ed.), *Capital and Politics* (London: Routledge and Kegan Paul).

Vandenberg A. H. (Jr) (1954), *The Private Papers of Senator Vandenberg* (London: Gollancz).

Van der Beugel, E. (1966), *From Marshall Aid to Atlantic Partnership* (London: Elsevier).

Van der Pijl, K. (1984), *The Making of an Atlantic Ruling Class* (London: Verso).

Van der Pijl, K. (1988), 'Capitalist Internationalism and Revolutionary Internationalism', in P. Waterman (ed.), *The Old Internationalism and the New* (The Hague: International Labour Education).

Wallerstein, I. (1980), *The Modern World System, 2* (New York: Academic Press).

Weber, M. (1919), 'Politics as a Vocation', in Gerth and Mills (eds) (1964).

Weber, M. (1968), *Economy and Society*, vol. 1 (New York: Bedminster).

Welles, S. (1947), *Where Are We Heading?* (New York: Harper and Row).

Wexler, I. (1983), *The Marshall Plan Revisited* (London: Greenwood).

Williams, D. (1968), 'The Evolution of the Sterling System', in C. Whittlesey and J. S. Wilson (eds), *Essays in Money and Banking* (Oxford: Clarendon).

Williams, J. (1944), 'International Monetary Plans: After Bretton Woods', *Foreign Affairs*, October.

Williams, P. (ed.) (1983), *The Diary of Hugh Gaitskell, 1945–1956* (London: Cape).

Worswick, G. and Ady, P. (eds) (1952), *The British Economy, 1945–50* (Oxford: Oxford University Press).

Wright, K. (1954), 'Dollar Pooling in the Sterling Area, 1939–1952', *American Economic Review*, September.

Zupnick, E. (1954), *Britain's Postwar Dollar Problem* (New York: Columbia University Press).

Index

Acheson, Dean, 36, 71, 82, 87, 157
administrative transferability, 62, 64, 102
Aldrich, Winthrop, 40
Altvater, Elmer, 4
American Council of Aid to European Industry, 100–1
Amery, L. S., 44
Anglo-American Financial Agreement, 9, 16, 43–70, 85–6, 126, 173
Anglo-American Productivity Council, 97–100
Anglo-American 'special relationship', 84, 131, 133, 177, 179
Anglo-Belgian Financial Agreement, 61–2
Argentina, 63
Atlantic Charter, 32–3, 49
Attlee, Clement, 9, 55, 66, 127, 161–2, 171
Austin Motors, 167
automatic transferability, 63–4, 102–3, 137

Baillieu, Clive, 35
Balogh, Thomas, 42
Bareau, Paul, 60
barriers to accumulation, 9, 12, 14, 21, 148, 177, 182–3
Belgium, 45, 61, 65, 102–3, 111, 142, 144
Benn, Tony, vii
Bevin, Ernest, 46, 48, 83, 88, 126, 131, 159
Block, Fred, 39
Bolton, George, 120–1
Boothby, Robert, 44
Brand, Lord, 31
Bretherton, Russell, 166
Brett, Edward, 5–7, 54
Bretton Woods, 31, 36–7, 42, 51, 70, 80, 137

Britain, economic decline of, 108, 118, 124, 150, 177
Butler, Rab, 72, 173, 175

Cairncross, Alec, 121, 174, 193n, 203n
capital
  forms of, 180–1, 209–10n
  capital-in-general, 180–3
  global circuits of, 183–8
capitulation thesis, 5, 43, 54, 57, 65, 73, 90, 92, 160
Chester, Norman, 47
China, 12, 160–1
Churchill, Winston, 33, 44
city of London 9, 25–6, 40, 77, 182
Clarke, Richard, 35, 44–5, 94, 120–1, 195n
class, ix, xi
Clayton, William, 36, 39, 51, 71, 75, 80
Coates, David, 54
Cobbold, C. F., 63
Committee of European Economic Co-operation (CEEC), 10, 72, 87–90, 113, 186
Commonwealth Finance Meeting, 130
convertibility, 50, 63, 69–70, 77, 103–5, 146
convertibility crisis, 10, 73–80, 122–3
Cox, Robert, 4, 179
Cripps, R. Stafford, 96, 106–9, 116–19, 125–7, 131, 142, 146–7, 203n

Dalton, Hugh, 18, 32, 43, 47, 49, 55, 67, 107
Davis, Charles, 100
devaluation, 11, 116, 120–30, 135
development areas, 166
Diebold, William, 178
disinflation, 107–8

dollar pooling mechanism, 28, 49–50, 52–3
domestic reconstruction priorities, 14, 18, 45, 55–7, 76, 80, 108–11, 118, 147, 178
Dow, J. C. R., 47
dual accumulation strategy, 59–62, 65, 140

Eady, Wilfrid, 44
Eatwell, John, 128–9
Eccles, David, 43
Economic Co-operation Administration (ECA), 88, 93, 98, 106, 125, 137, 140–1
Economic Co-operation Agreement, 91–2
economic policy-making, 15, 46–8, 177
Eden, Anthony, 129
Egypt, 18, 60
Ellis-Rees, Hugh, 57, 63
European integration, 12–13, 67, 84–5, 94–5, 125, 133, 137, 140, 179
European Monetary Authority, 138, 145
European Payments Union (EPU), 11, 106, 133, 137, 139–48
   American objectives for, 139–43
   lessons of, 145–9
European Recovery Programme (ERP), *see* Marshall Aid

Federation of British Industries (FBI), 67, 100
First Agreement on Multilateral Monetary Compensation, 102–4
Fordism, 22–3, 97, 99–101, 113–14
foreign currency and gold reserves, 14, 21, 26, 62–3, 69, 76–9, 85–6, 107, 112, 119, 122, 126, 134–5, 140–3, 146, 155, 173–4
fractionalism, 180, 187, 209n
Franks, Oliver, 71, 88
Fraser, Leon, 40
full employment, 14, 57, 76, 118, 131, 147, 153, 172

Gaitskell, Hugh, 126, 133, 135, 153, 160–1, 163–4, 168, 175, 203n
General Agreement on Tariffs and Trade, 91
Germany, 22, 83, 91, 95, 123, 171
   economic competition from, 170
Gifford, Ray, 96, 100
Gill, Stephen, 4, 179
Gramsci, Antonio, 179

Hall, Robert, 153–4
Hall-Patch, Edmund, 93–4, 131, 139
Healey, Dennis, 128
hegemonic stability theory of, 2, 5, 8, 188
hegemony, 5, 12, 54–5, 175, 178–9, 187–8
Henderson, Hubert, 44
Hitchman, Alan, 154
Hoffman, Paul, 88, 97–8, 138–9
Hull, Cordell, 36

Imperial Preference, 38, 44, 65, 68
India, 18, 21, 53, 68
inter-imperialist rivalry, 183–6
internationalisation of capital, 1–2, 183–5
International Monetary Fund, 34, 37, 48, 86, 92
International Trade Organisation Charter, 34, 91–2

Japan, 16, 91–2
   economic competition from, 156, 170
Jay, Douglas, 48, 65, 126
Jenkins, Roy, 128, 161–2

Kautsky, Karl, 184
Keohane, Robert, 3–4, 178–9
Key Currency Proposals, 39–40, 66, 80–3
Keynes, John Maynard, 16–7, 29–31, 45–9, 61, 194–5n
Khrushchev, Nikata, 159
Kidron, Michael, 158
Kim Il Sung, 159
Kindleberger, Charles, 2, 72, 82, 88
Kipping, Norman, 38, 100

Korea, 7, 12, 91, 129, 148, 150–76
Krasner, Stephen, 3

Labour Party, 9, 35, 55, 86, 112
    1930s theoretical revision, 56–8
Lamont, Thomas, 27
lend-lease, 20, 33, 48
Lenin, Vladimir Illich, 184
Leyland tank production, 166–8
Lidbury, Charles, 35
Lovett, Robert, 84, 89

MacBride, Sean, 93
Mandel, Ernst, 183–5
Marshall Aid, 10, 71–115, 133, 135,
    156
    American objectives for, 81, 95
    economic lifeline, 108–11
    industrial restructuring and, 96–
    101
    trade and payments and, 101–6
Martin, McChesney William, 136
Marx, Karl, x xiii, 1, 188
metal-using industries and
    rearmament, 152, 162–4
Middlemas, Keith, 46
Miliband, Ralph, 55
Milward, Alan, 5, 55, 72, 76, 145,
    192n
Morgan, J. P., 26
Morgan, Kenneth, 109
Morgenthau, Henry, 36
Morrison, Herbert, 47, 121, 127
most-favoured nation clause, 38, 50,
    91
multilateralism, 29–30, 51, 58, 68,
    113, 116, 122, 125–6, 132, 135–
    40, 177
Mutual Aid Agreement, 33, 49

National Security Council (NSC–
    68), 157–9
neo-bilateralism, 54, 59–62, 68, 104–
    5, 135–6, 140, 143, 146
New Deal, 27, 36
New York, 27, 31, 40, 86, 117
non-committal co-ordination, 11,
    83–5, 94, 113

non-discrimination in trade, 50, 63,
    65, 91, 113, 132

Organisation for European Economic
    Co-operation (OEEC), 10, 72,
    90–6, 104, 113, 133, 186

'pax hegemonica', 4, 71, 178
permanent arms economy, 158
Playfair, E., 67
Plowden, Edwin, 154
pluralism, 180
Pimlott, Ben, 46
Pijl, Kees van der, 7, 54, 193n
Polak, J. J., 134
priority guidance system, 168–71
public expenditure cuts, 127–9

realism–mercantilism, 2–5, 178–9,
    192n
rearmament, 11–12, 129, 150–76
Revised Payments Agreements,
    103–4
Robens, Alfred, 165
Robbins, Lionel, 48
Robinson, Austin, 17, 47
Rockefeller nexus, 22
Roosevelt, Franklin, 27, 36–7
Rowan, Leslie, 91

Sadd, Clarence, 86
scarce currency clause, 37
Soviet Union, 38, 87–8, 157–8
state, xii, xiii, 181–3, 187–8
steel mill construction, 23
Sterling, 25–8, 39, 126, 134–5, 140–
    2, 147, 176
Sterling Area system, 38, 44–6, 49–
    54, 63, 117, 123–4, 130, 140–1,
    155, 169–70, 179, 189–9
Sterling balances, 18, 50, 104, 141–2
Sterling bloc system, 28, 52
stockpiling, 132, 155–6, 171–2
Strange, Susan, 4

trade liberalisation, 67, 106–7, 115,
    138, 143–4
'transnational historical
    materialism', 179

Tripartite talks, 130–4
Trades Union Congress, 98, 108
two-world trading structure, 126, 145

United States
  State Department, 37–8, 41–2, 69,
    73, 76, 82, 89, 137, 157–9
  Treasury Department, 36, 42, 73,
    137
  see also European Payments
    Union, Marshall Aid

Vinson, Fred, 36

Waley, David, 62
Washington Loan Agreement *see*
  Anglo-American Financial
  Agreement
Weber, Max, viii–x
welfare and social services, 14, 131,
  163, 168, 175
White, Harry Dexter, 34–6
Williams, John, 40
Wilson, Harold, 126, 129
World War I, 26, 68, 184
World War II, 14, 16, 69